VIDEO-BASED INFORMATION SYSTEMS

A GUIDE FOR EDUCATIONAL, BUSINESS, LIBRARY, AND HOME USE

WILLIAM SAFFADY

CHICAGO • **AMERICAN LIBRARY ASSOCIATION** • 1985

Copublished, and distributed exclusively in all parts
of the world except the United States of America, Canada,
the United Kingdom, and Japan, by:
Elsevier Science Publishers BV
P.O. Box 1991
1000 BZ Amsterdam
The Netherlands

Designed by Ellen Pettengell

Composed by Modern Typographers,
Inc., in Linotron Garamond ITC
and Helvetica

Printed on 50-pound Glatfelter,
a pH-neutral stock,
and bound in 10-point
Carolina cover stock by
Malloy Lithographing, Inc.

Library of Congress Cataloging in Publication Data

Saffady, William, 1944–
Video-based information systems.

1. Information display systems. 2. Television display systems. 3. Video tape recorders and recording—Library applications. 4. Television display systems—Library applications. 5. Information display systems—Library applications. 6. Library science—Technological innovations. 7. Information storage and retrieval systems.
I. Title.
TK7882.I6S23 1985 621.388'36 84-21567
ISBN 0-8389-0425-4

Printed in the United States of America.

CONTENTS

FIGURES

INTRODUCTION

This book is intended for information specialists, business systems analysts, librarians, and others who want a comprehensive survey of major developments in video technology and their impact on information storage, retrieval, and dissemination in offices, libraries, and homes. For purposes of this discussion, video-based information systems are defined as those which maintain and convey information in the raster scanning format defined more fully in chapter 1 and/or which display information on a video screen. Except for a brief discussion of consumer-oriented video cameras included for the sake of completeness in chapter 2, the book does not deal with video production equipment or techniques.

The book is divided into eight chapters; each of which surveys an important group of video-based information products or services.

Chapter 1 reviews recent developments in television display technology. It introduces and explains video recording concepts and standards; discusses the differences between television receivers and monitors; reviews recent innovations in equipment design, including component television and projection television systems; and closes with a discussion of flat panel display technology, high-definition television, digital television, and other developments that have potential future significance.

Chapter 2 discusses videocassette recording systems. It surveys the characteristics of available recording formats, equipment, and supplies; reviews the legality of taping broadcast signals for library, business, and home applications; and discusses the recent and rapid proliferation of prerecorded videocassettes containing entertainment and informational programs. As noted above, this chapter also includes a brief discussion of video cameras.

Chapter 3 deals with video disk systems for consumer and industrial applications, emphasizing analog systems intended for entertainment and education. It describes video disk technologies and equipment; surveys available consumer programming; and discusses the development of interactive learning systems and other information-oriented video disk programs by schools, businesses, and other organizations. The discussion continues in chapter 6 where the use of video disks for document and data storage is treated.

Chapter 4 reviews alternatives to conventional broadcasting for delivering television programming to homes and offices. The chapter begins with a discussion of cable television systems, emphasizing the scope and content of available cable services. Subsequent sections deal with interactive cable systems, subscription television, TVRO satellite terminals, direct broadcast satellite technology, low-power television systems, and pay-per-view television programming.

Chapter 5 deals with videotext systems that deliver information to modified television receivers in homes and offices. It begins with a discussion of videotext technology, in both its teletext and viewdata variants. Subsequent sections describe videotext equipment and transmission; videotext installations and experiments in Europe, the United States, and elsewhere; the types of information available to videotext users; information retrieval techniques; and the development of videotext systems for special applications.

Chapter 6 surveys a group of video-based information systems that are specifically designed for the storage, retrieval, and dissemination of documents by businesses, government agencies, libraries, and other organizations. The chapter begins with a discussion of facsimile systems that use video technology to transmit document images to remote locations. The microfacsimile system, a variant form of conventional facsimile typically implemented as a component in sophisticated document storage and retrieval systems, transmits microfilm images to video display stations, paper printers, or computer-output microfilm recorders. This chapter also describes the use of video disks for document storage, emphasizing recent developments in digital optical video disk technology. A final section discusses the emergence of digital optical data disks for computer-processed information.

Chapter 7 deals with videoconferencing systems that use video and audio technology to conduct interactive meetings among geographically separate groups of people. It reviews the several forms of videoconferencing and discusses their significance in business.

Chapter 8 returns to the subject of video displays introduced in chapter 1, but emphasizes video terminals for the display of computer-generated data. It describes available technology, equipment configurations, and display characteristics for both alphanumeric and graphic applications. The chapter also reviews health considerations associated with the prolonged use of display terminals. While most attention is given to cathode ray tube (CRT) terminals, flat panel display technologies are also discussed.

Because VIDEO-BASED INFORMATION SYSTEMS is a survey of the state of the art, footnotes are omitted. Each chapter, however, contains a list of suggestions for additional reading. Throughout the book, specific products and systems are mentioned and illustrated as examples of particular points raised in the text. Such inclusion does not constitute an endorsement or imply superiority of the product over the competing products of other vendors.

Finally, this book surveys developments in video-based information systems through early 1984, but in a changing field the true state of the art is necessarily elusive. To extend the book's useful life in a field characterized by rapid technological advances and the steady introduction of new products and services, the individual chapters try to establish a conceptual framework that will allow the reader to understand ongoing developments in video-based information systems and to relate new products and services to those available at the time the book was written.

While high technology presents a bewildering array of new products and services, they are often variations or elaborations of basic concepts that have existed for some time. This book emphasizes the basic concepts that are essential to understanding video-based information systems. The reader should view it as a starting point for the study of ongoing technological developments.

CHAPTER 1

RECENT DEVELOPMENTS IN TELEVISION DISPLAYS

While the peripheral video products and information services to be discussed in later chapters currently attract the bulk of professional attention, a television set or other type of video display is the one indispensible component in any video-based information system. Although television sets are a commonplace feature of everyday life and a standard piece of equipment in many offices, libraries, and other work environments, the fundamentals of video display technology are too often taken for granted. While books, magazines, and other media increasingly publicize computer technology and discuss the features and functions of available hardware, comparable treatment is rarely given to television equipment. Yet, for the display of video tapes or video disks, the acquisition of a microcomputer with color graphics capability, or participation in a videotext system, an understanding of television technology and the knowledgeable selection of high-quality television receivers or video monitors with appropriate features are critical to successful system implementation.

Much of the seeming indifference to television set technology may be attributed to the fact that, compared to the recent rapid development of peripheral video devices, television sets have changed little since the early 1960s. Before that time, the design of television receivers changed repeatedly to reflect such important technological developments as the introduction of color broadcasting, the expansion of available broadcast facilities from the 12 very high frequency (VHF) channels to a combination of 82 VHF and ultra high frequency (UHF) channels, and the transition from vacuum tube technology to solid state electronics. By way of contrast, the period from the early 1960s through the late 1970s was characterized by industry consolidation rather than innovation as equipment manufacturers competed for increased market share rather than overall industry growth. While the two major American manufacturers, RCA and Zenith, held over 40 percent of the U.S. market, they faced stiff competition, in terms of both price and performance, from foreign manufacturers, especially such Japanese firms as Sony, Toshiba, Sharp, Hitachi, and Mitsubishi.

The impact of foreign competition was further reflected in the consolidation of previously independent brands. The Dutch electronics manufacturer Philips, for example, acquired the Magnavox, Philco, and Sylvania product lines. The Japanese firm Matsushita, manufacturer of Panasonic video products, acquired the Motorola television product line, renaming it Quasar. Sanyo, another Japanese company, acquired Whirlpool's share in Warwick Electronics, the company that manufactured televisions sold by Sears. By the late 1970s, with an estimated 85 percent of American homes having at least one color television set and an estimated 40 percent having two or more, the American market for television receivers was approaching saturation. During periods of high inflation, television prices remained relatively stable, reflecting lowered demand.

In the early 1980s, however, the American market for television sets was dramatically stimulated by the proliferation and popularity of video games, videocassette recorders (VCRs), video disk players, personal computers, cable television services, and other add-on devices, no two of which can be used simultaneously on one television. Within the home, competition for the television set has increasingly led to multi-set purchases. Sociologically, the late 1970s and early 1980s were likewise characterized by an emphasis on home entertainment motivated in large part by high transportation costs resulting from rising energy prices, coupled with the general impact of inflation on personal recreation budgets. Consequently, at a time when purchases of home appliances are generally declining, industry analysts are optimistic about growth prospects for television sales (figure 1). In the United States, market saturation is now considered to be one color television receiver per capita rather than the former measure of one per household. As demand increases, prices are expected to rise as well.

Faced with the pleasant prospect of an expanding market, television manufacturers have begun to introduce equipment with new features and capabilities. Some of

FIGURE 1

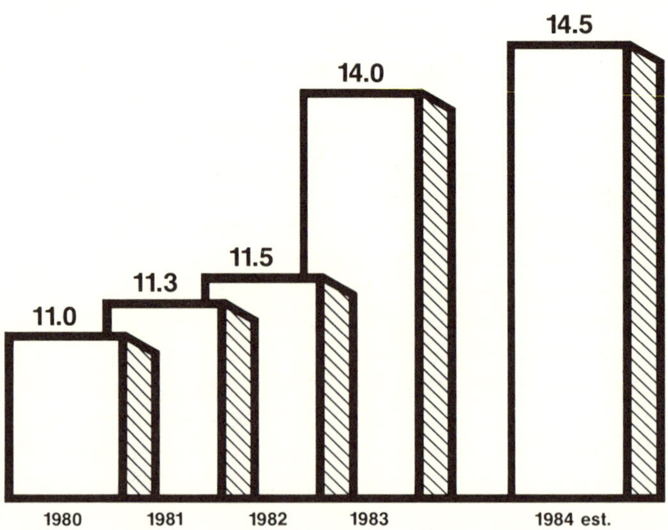

Unit sales of color receivers to dealers (in millions) reflect excellent growth prospects for U.S. television industry. (Source: Electronics Industries Association and RCA Consumer Electronics)

these new features are designed to improve quality and reliability. Others address the increasing demands of video enthusiasts and institutional users for more flexible equipment designed for high performance with peripheral video devices. While the television set is still the least innovative of the video products now available, some changes are evident and more are expected. This chapter surveys these changes, emphasizing their significance for consumer, business, library, and other applications.

Display Characteristics

Video Standards

With most commercially available television sets, the display screen consists of the phosphorescent faceplate of a cathode ray tube (CRT). Images are formed by an electron beam that scans the faceplate, illuminating it in response to an incoming signal received from broadcast or local sources. Depending on the model selected, the CRT may be capable of monochrome or color display. Monochrome television tubes feature a single gun that fires electrons at the CRT faceplate. Most monochrome television tubes are designed for black-and-white display, although video monitors designed for use with microcomputers feature a dark background with a bluish-white, green, or amber phosphor. Most color television tubes feature three electron guns, one for each of the three primary colors—red, blue, and green. A well-known exception is the Sony Trinitron tube, which uses a single gun to produce three differently colored beams.

In any case, the amount and nature of the illumination in any given portion of the displayed television image is determined by the characteristics of the incoming signal. Individual video images, called *frames*, are a composite of very small points of light called *picture elements*—often abbreviated as pixels or, simply, pels. These pixels are arranged in horizontal lines called *scan lines*. These scan lines are displayed on the video screen in an organized pattern called a *raster*. The pixels begin at the upper left corner of the screen and continue in successive horizontal lines to the lowest right corner. To maintain a viewable image, the phosphorescent surface of the television screen must be periodically recreated or "refreshed" by redisplaying the pixels or replacing them with new ones, thereby changing the frame. The illusion of moving images is created by slight differences in successively displayed frames. The sharpness or resolution of the displayed video image varies directly with the number of horizontal scan lines, while a flicker-free image is sustained by sufficiently frequent frame changes.

To ensure compatibility among the signals broadcast by different stations and the television receivers of different manufacturers, the number of scan lines per frame and the frequency of frame changes are specified by video standards. In addition to specifying signal formats for television broadcasts, these standards affect the design of videocassette recorders, video disk players, video cameras, microcomputers, and other peripheral devices that generate signals for video display. While they are all based on the raster-scanning method of image formation, prevailing video standards differ in the number of scan lines provided per frame and in the frequency with which frames are changed. Three video standards are currently in use in various parts of the world:

1. The U.S. standard—which is also used in Canada, Mexico, Japan, the Caribbean, much of Latin America, Saudi Arabia, and a few other parts of the world—was developed in 1941 by the National Television Systems Committee and is consequently termed the NTSC standard. As applied to both black-and-white and color signals, it provides for 525 horizontal scan lines per television frame with 30 complete frame changes per second. Each frame is actually divided into two fields, each consisting of 262.5 scan lines, which are alternately replaced at a rate of 60 times per second.

2. The two major European video standards provide more horizontal scan lines, and consequently higher resolution, than the American NTSC standard. The United Kingdom, West Germany, some other Western European countries, and parts of South America, Asia, and Africa adhere to the Phase Alternation Line (PAL) standard for color television broadcasting. It provides for 625, rather than 525, horizontal scan lines. As a further advantage, it places primary responsibility for color control on the broadcasting station, thereby minimizing the need for color adjustment at the receiver. By way of contrast, television receivers conforming to NTSC standards typically include controls that enable the viewer to establish satisfactory color values, hue, and saturation. PAL standards were based on an earlier 625-line standard for black-and-white television broadcasting developed by the Comité Consultatif International des Radiocommunications (CCIR). While it has adopted PAL standards for color broadcasting, the United Kingdom continues to conform to older 405-line standards for black-and-white transmission.

3. In 1967, France implemented the Sequential Couleur à Memoire (SECAM) television broadcasting format which, like the PAL standard, provides for 625 horizontal scan lines. It differs from the PAL standard in its control procedures and other characteristics. Color selection, hue, and saturation are completely controlled at the point of transmission, and the SECAM receiver requires no color adjustment and has no controls for that purpose. The SECAM standard is also used in the USSR and in parts of the Middle East. France, like the United Kingdom, had an earlier format for black-and-white broadcasting based on 819 horizontal scan lines per frame, the highest resolution of any nonexperimental television system. That standard is in the process of being phased out in favor of the SECAM format.

The three major television broadcasting standards are incompatible with one another and, as a further complication, there are slight differences in the implementation of the PAL and SECAM standards from country to country. Certain South American countries, for example, have adopted a 626-line variant of the PAL format. As might be expected, a television receiver designed to accept signals conforming to one standard cannot work with the others.

Where multistandard reception is required, manufacturers such as Barco and Panasonic offer combination NTSC/PAL/SECAM receivers. These devices are, at present, expensive and address a limited market because few persons travel with television sets. Some consumers may, however, want to use multistandard receivers to view videocassettes obtained from relatives or friends in other countries. Similarly, consumers or libraries with serious video collections may require such multistandard television receivers to display video cassettes or video disks produced in non-NTSC formats. Prerecorded PAL-format video cassettes containing European programming are currently available for sale in the United States, and, given the popularity of video cassette recorders in Europe, their availability may increase. Similarly, Europeans may want to acquire videocassettes or disks recorded in the NTSC format. In such applications, of course, the user must acquire a videocassette recorder appropriate to the particular television standard. At the time this chapter was written, multistandard videocassette recorders were not available in the United States.

Receivers vs. Monitors

The familiar television set is a video display device that is specifically designed to receive television broadcast signals. Integral VHF, UHF, and/or cable channel tuners are provided for this purpose. Video and audio signals from local television stations are impressed for broadcasting on a radio frequency (RF) carrier and enter the receiver through its antenna. The television's tuner selects the desired channel, amplifies the video and audio signals, and directs them to the screen and speaker.

Unfortunately, amplification of the incoming video and audio signal is accompanied by corresponding amplification of any impairments or distortions present in the signal. The result is a loss of image resolution. As discussed above, the NTSC standard specifies that each television frame consists of 525 horizontal scan lines. Of these, forty-one scan lines contain no image information, but are reserved for control and synchronization, leaving a maximum of 484 scan lines that can theoretically be displayed on the video screen at one time. A significant percentage of these is lost, however, to signal impairments, improperly adjusted receivers, the common manufacturing practice of magnifying images displayed by new receivers to allow for eventual picture tube shrinkage, and the so-called scanning factor in which image details fall between scan lines. As a result, the highest quality conventional television receivers will only display slightly more than 300 scan lines, while the typical medium-priced television set will display about 240 scan lines. Inexpensive or poorly adjusted receivers may display as few as 175 scan lines.

Several recent developments in video display technology are designed to minimize the degradation of images received from broadcast sources. Manufacturers now equip their most advanced models with special "comb" filters that prevent interference between incoming color and brightness signals thereby significantly enhancing the sharpness of displayed images. Inline picture tubes, a feature associated with the best television receivers, typically require less color convergence and maintain color purity longer than ordinary tubes. Different manufacturers use proprietary picture tube designs that are claimed to improve image quality. As an example, Mitsubishi's "Diamond Vision" technique treats the picture tube with light-absorbing chemicals thereby permitting the accurate reproduction of a wider range of colors with more subtle differentiation of shades than is possible in ordinary room light with conventional television receivers. Similarly, Toshiba claims that its "Blackstripe" picture tube increases image brightness by as much as 18 percent. A number of television receivers feature a photocell-activated control that automatically adjusts the display's brightness to compensate for variations in ambient light. Several newer sets automatically adjust colors to compensate for uneven picture tube wear.

To minimize the need for the frequent color adjustments typically associated with the NTSC video standard, some newer and more expensive television receivers incorporate special electronic circuitry that permits the utilization of the Vertical Interval Reference (VIR) signals broadcasted by most stations. VIR signals, which accompany the visible picture signals, contain color and contrast information. A television receiver equipped with VIR circuitry will automatically adjust color and tint to levels established by the broadcasting station. VIR is a particularly useful feature in schools, libraries, hospitals, and similar installations where the television set is mounted on a wall or other inaccessible location and/or where viewer adjustments are not possible or desirable. In most cases, a manual override is provided to accommodate individual preferences and to disable the VIR controls when images are being displayed from video tapes, video disks, or other nonbroadcast sources.

While these image-enhancing features are significant, some degradation of broadcast video signals through simplification is unavoidable. Unfortunately, a conventional television receiver also requires that video and audio signals from any attached videocassette recorders, video disk players, video cameras, microcomputers, or other nonbroadcast sources be converted to a radio frequency carrier for reception through the television's antenna poles to which these devices are attached. Such devices have an RF modulator that functions as a miniature television transmitter, broadcasting a low-power radio frequency signal to the receiver. This signal conversion is accompanied by impairments that degrade the quality of the displayed video image and any accompanying sound. This degradation is especially obvious when the television receiver serves as the display device in a microcomputer configuration. In such applications, the impaired image quality limits the number and size of characters that can be displayed on the receiver's screen at one time.

Where such nonbroadcast video sources are involved, video monitors are generally preferred to television receivers. Because they accept video and audio signals directly from peripheral devices through input jacks rather than an antenna, video monitors eliminate the need for RF conversion and its accompanying signal degradation. The typical result is a noticeably sharper image with resolution routinely exceeding 300 horizontal scan lines. This higher resolution is especially important when the monitor displays images generated by a microcomputer or video disk system. The higher resolution offered by video monitors is less significant when videocassette recorders are used because, as will be discussed in the next chapter, the resolution of VCR images is typically lower than images conventionally broadcast.

Video monitors have long been available for professional use. The recent proliferation of video peripheral devices has, however, stimulated the demand for video monitors suited to a broader spectrum of applications. Microcomputer display devices constitute one of the fastest growing markets for video monitors. An increasing number of monochrome and color monitors is available for such applications. Color monitors are also available for use with video disk players, videocassette recorders, and video cameras. The least expensive color monitors are designed to accept composite video signals that combine all color and synchronization information. More expensive color monitors—called "red-blue-green" or, simply, RBG monitors—contain separate input jacks for each of the primary video colors plus an additional jack for the input of synchronization signals. RBG monitors are especially appropriate in microcomputer applications requiring high quality graphic displays. The microcomputer system must, however, be capable of generating an RBG signal. Most microcomputers generate composite video signals only. The characteristics of video displays designed for computer-generated data will be discussed more fully in chapter 8.

Note that conventional video monitors, whether monochrome or color, lack a tuner and cannot receive broadcast television signals. While this limitation is not typically significant to the video production professional, it will constrain a consumer, business, library, or other organization seeking a multifunction video display device. To meet the requirements of such applications, several manufacturers have recently introduced combination receiver/monitors that feature an integral VHF, UHF, and/or cable channel tuner plus input jacks for the direct connection of peripheral video devices. Usually, output jacks are also provided for the attachment of auxiliary audio speakers or additional video monitors.

Component Television

As videocassette recorders, video disk players, microcomputers, cable television, and emerging videotext systems have expanded the range of available video information sources, television set manufacturers and users have begun to reconsider the appropriateness of traditional equipment configurations. Historically, television receivers have incorporated a tuner, display, and audio system in a single chassis. While this integrated configuration has proven convenient and economical, it necessarily compromises flexibility and performance. Videocassette recorders, video disk players, and other peripheral devices must, as previously discussed, be attached to the receiver's antenna poles. Where multiple peripherals are involved, their connection can involve a confusing tangle of wires, and the selection of a particular video program source may require some plugging and unplugging of equipment. In addition, the conversion of incoming signals to RF form can degrade image quality.

Video monitors, as previously noted, can simplify equipment connections and eliminate RF conversion through the use of input jacks, but most video monitors lack the tuner required for the reception of broadcast or cable television signals. Combination monitor/receivers represent one approach to such multifunctionality. Component television systems offer another.

As with audio systems which the user develops after selecting a particular configuration of equipment from a specified range of compatible devices, component video systems offer high performance plus maximum flexibility in design (figure 2). They also permit the upgrading of specific components without wholesale system replacement as the user's needs change. While the range of available video components is not as broad as it is in audio systems, the typical component television system consists of three separate but interconnected elements:

1. The display device is a high-quality video monitor with a minimum resolution of 330 horizontal scan lines when receiving broadcast signals and higher when operating with a video disk player, a microcomputer, or a videotext system. With signals generated by such local video sources, some newer models claim resolution approaching 400 horizontal scan lines. Resolution aside, the

FIGURE 2

Unlike preconfigured receivers, component television systems consist of separate monitors, tuners, and audio systems. (Source: Teknika)

monitor typically measures 19 to 25 inches diagonally, with some manufacturers offering a choice of several sizes. As with conventional video monitors, component monitors provide input jacks for the attachment of peripheral devices. The monitors of several manufacturers will also accept direct RBG color input from appropriately configured microcomputers or videotext systems.

2. The system's major central component is a tuner/source selector that is typically a microprocessor-based device designed to tune broadcast signals to permit the display of information from other video sources. As will be discussed later in this chapter, most models feature cable-ready tuners. The source selector is essentially an input distribution system. It supports the connection, via jacks, of two or more videocassette recorders, video disk players, video game consoles, microcomputers, or other peripheral devices. Available source selectors can typically control four to eight peripheral devices. Dials or switches allow the operator to select the particular video source to be used at a given time. Some tuner/source selectors also provide multiple electrical sockets into which various peripheral devices can be plugged, thereby minimizing the need for wall outlets.

3. The component television's audio subsystem consists of an amplifier and speakers. Depending on the manufacturer, the amplifier may be built into either the tuner/source selector or the monitor. As will be discussed later in this chapter, some manufacturers also provide an AM and/or FM radio tuner and amplifier, although this approach is most often taken by the audio equipment manufacturers who have recently introduced video product lines. The component television's speakers are usually separate, and, as with the video monitor, a given manufacturer may offer a choice of several models that vary in size, quality, and price.

First introduced in Japan in 1980, component television systems are now available in the United States from such manufacturers as Sony, Teknika, NEC, Kloss, Proton, Mitsubishi, Panasonic, Pioneer, Sharp, Sanyo, RCA, Zenith, Fisher, and Jensen. Specific components offered by the various vendors may or may not be compatible with one another. With retail prices beginning at around $1,000 for an entry-level system including a 19-inch color video monitor, two small audio speakers, and a VHF/UHF tuner/source selector, the comparatively high cost of a component system is initially likely to restrict their appeal to video enthusiasts interested in high performance. Industry analysts expect, however, that—as sales volume increases—the future cost of component systems will compete more favorably with those of conventional television receivers and receiver/monitors. It is also likely that the number of users willing to pay premium prices for flexible, high-quality display systems will increase with the continued proliferation of video peripheral devices and varied forms of video programming.

Small-Screen Television

Through 1982, most television receivers and video monitors sold in the United States were table-top color display devices with 19-inch or 12- to 13-inch diagonally measured picture tubes. In 1983, some manufacturers began using slightly larger Japanese-made picture tubes, which measure 14 or 20 inches diagonally and feature a more rectilinear shape and a flatter screen than earlier models. The 19- or 20-inch television receiver or monitor is typically preferred for use with videocassette recorders and video disk players. The 12-, 13-, and 14-inch models are well suited to color display in microcomputer systems. Intermediate sizes—15 or 17 inches, for example—are also available, but there is relatively little demand for them. Color console models are available with screens as large as 26 inches, and several manufacturers have recently restyled such devices to make their overall dimensions more compact. Often, however, such console televisions are designed as pieces of furniture and, as such, they are primarily intended for consumer applications.

While most video applications are best served by a color display device, black-and-white television receivers remain available and, as will be discussed later in this book, there is a substantial market for monochrome video monitors designed for use with microcomputers. The typical black-and-white television receiver features a 12- to 13-inch screen. Although larger models are selectively available, there has been little demand for them.

Although most conventionally sized screens are well suited to the majority of business and library applications, there recently has been considerable consumer interest in very small television receivers (figure 3). Relying on miniaturized electronic circuitry, such compact televisions are designed for portability and will operate with an integral battery pack, enabling them to be used as field monitors.

FIGURE 3

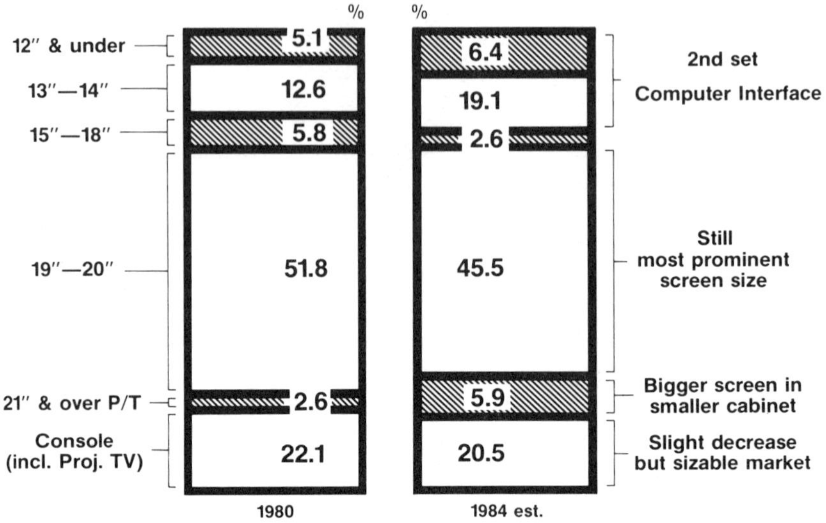

Statistics on color television screen sizes show continued dominance of 19-inch models with growing popularity of smaller screens, often for microcomputer applications. (Source: Electronics Industries Association and RCA Consumer Electronics)

Typical screen sizes, measured diagonally, range from 3.75 to 6 inches. For general consumer applications, they may be sold as self-contained devices or configured with an AM/FM radio and/or an audio cassette recorder as a kind of portable entertainment center. Technicolor Audio-Visual has even offered an integrated unit containing a small-screen television and a videocassette recorder.

Several companies have recently introduced television receivers with very small screens, and an increasing number of such devices should become commercially available during the mid-1980s. As will be discussed later in this chapter, some models abandon the relatively bulky cathode ray tube used in conventional video displays, relying instead on alternative display technologies. By way of contrast, the much publicized Sony Watchman employs a variant form of CRT technology to achieve a very compact design. With conventional television receivers and video monitors, the surface of the cathode ray tube is illuminated by an electron gun located behind and perpendicular to the screen. With the Watchman, the electron gun is located beneath the CRT and parallel to it. Electrons are fired into a deflection plate, which directs them to the screen. The CRT itself is just .6 of an inch thick, and the device's overall dimensions are 3.5 inches wide by 7.75 inches high by 1.25 inches thick.

At the time of this writing, such very compact television sets were limited to black-and-white reception. The smallest available color receiver featured a 1.5-inch screen. Other compact color models feature screen sizes ranging from 2.5 to 5 inches. Whether color or black-and-white, however, business and library applications of small-screen television appear limited, although they can be used as field

FIGURE 4

A hand-held television receiver features a 2-inch screen and makes extensive use of miniaturized electronic circuitry. (Courtesy: Sinclair Research Limited)

monitors in videotaping operations. In addition, prices have been inflated by high development costs, limited production, a wide range of accessories, and other factors, so that small-screen televisions often cost more than their 19-inch counterparts.

Multi-screen Television

One of the most interesting applications of small screens is in multi-screen television receivers. One such device—the Sampo Tri Screen, model 9519—combines one 19-inch color screen with two 5-inch black-and-white screens (figure 5). The three screens can be used to display different video channels simultaneously, although only the large screen has audio capability. The Sampo Tri Screen might be used, for example, to simultaneously monitor the three networks' coverage of elections or other news events, the user switching the appropriate channel to the large screen as desired. As an alternative to the reception of broadcast signals, any of the screens can display the output of a video camera, videocassette recorder, microcomputer, or other peripheral device.

Other vendors have experimented with multi-screen television. Sharp, for

FIGURE 5

The Model 9519 triple-screen television can receive broadcast signals or operate with closed circuit cameras. (Courtesy: Sampo Corporation of America)

example, once offered a split-screen television receiver called Dualvision, and has shown a prototype model of a 26-inch color receiver capable of displaying nine channels simultaneously. As an alternative to scanning channels successively, the device can be used to preview available channels quickly before selecting one for full screen display. Other companies, like Toshiba and Hitachi, have demonstrated prototype models of four-screen television receivers, but the uncertain market for multi-screen devices has undoubtedly restrained development efforts.

Decoders that display closed captions for hearing-impaired persons are a variant form of split-screen television device. An increasing number of television programs of educational and cultural significance are broadcast with closed captions. These captions are displayed in a window in the bottom portion of the television image (figure 6). In addition to the obvious consumer application, closed caption decoders are of interest to schools and libraries with programs oriented toward handicapped persons. At the time this chapter was written, closed caption decoders were being sold exclusively by Sears and are designed for attachment to customer-owned television receivers. As will be discussed in chapter 5, several videotext experiments grew out of research in closed captioning technology.

FIGURE 6

Closed captioning systems for hearing impaired persons rely on special decoders. (Courtesy: Intelmatique)

Projection Television

While small-screen televisions provide an interesting example of the potential portability of information and entertainment made possible by miniaturized electronic circuitry, recent developments in large-screen "projection" television will likely prove of greater importance to businesses, libraries, and other organizations interested in displaying information from video sources to groups. Unlike a conventionally designed television that uses a stream of electrons to display images on the phosphorescent surface of an integral cathode ray tube, projection television displays images on a separate screen. Screen size varies from model to model. The current range is 4 to 10 feet measured diagonally, with most available devices featuring 5- to 6-foot screens. Several models can also project video images on a wall.

While it has attracted much recent attention, the projection approach to video display dates from the 1940s, although the images projected by early models were of marginal quality. The first practical projection televisions were developed by Advent Corporation in the early 1970s, but attracted few consumers or institutional customers. Since the 1970s, however, the introduction and widespread acceptance of videocassette recorders, video disk players, video games, and other peripherals has stimulated consumer interest in large-screen television. Some video enthusiasts, for example, have designed "home theaters" in which a large-screen television is used for the group display of prerecorded videotapes and video disks as well as programming available through conventional broadcast and cable channels. In academic and business training applications, large-screen television permits the convenient group discussion of information displayed from microcomputers, interactive video disks, and similar sources.

The increased interest in projection television has stimulated the introduction of new models and the refinement of existing ones. Over the past several years, many major television manufacturers have added one or more projection models to their product lines. The most primitive form of projection television involves the installation of a simple image magnifier on the front of a conventional television set. As might be expected, these devices cost much less and provide much lower image quality than televisions built specifically for projection. True projection televisions use either front or rear projection techniques.

Front projection models, the oldest and most fully developed product group, feature an opaque silver or white screen, which may be mounted on a wall, supported by an integral floor stand, or combined with the image projector in a single television console. Such integral projection systems require less space than models employing a separate projector and screen. When not in use, the integral screen may be concealed within the television console. Separate component systems, however, tend to have larger screens than integrated models, offer somewhat better image quality, and require considerable space (figure 7). In business and other organizational applications, however, space limitations are typically less of a problem than in consumer households. As a general rule, the minimum acceptable viewing distance for any display device is three times the screen height. Thus, a room intended for the installation of a television screen measuring 3.5 feet high (about 6 feet diagonally) should provide seating at a minimum distance of 10.5 feet. To meet space constraints, several models feature retractable screens.

Rear projection televisions resemble conventional console-model televisions, but they do not include a phosphorescent screen. Instead, the video image is projected via mirrors onto the rear of a translucent screen, which typically measures 4 to 5 feet diagonally. The image is viewed from the front.

Regardless of the specific projection method employed, a three-tube projection system is the industry standard for highest image quality. Each of the tubes projects one of the three primary video colors—red, blue, and green. In a variant approach, some vendors employ two projection tubes—one for green, the other for both red and blue. Consumers, business systems analysts, librarians, and others who have not recently seen projection television will be pleasantly surprised by both the number of models currently available and their significantly improved image quality. Newer models offer bright pictures with footlamberts measuring in the 80 to 120 range. (The higher the number, the less the room lights need to be dimmed for viewing.) Available projection televisions offer most of the features associated with the highest quality conventional televisions. For maximum flexibility, some vendors even offer component configurations consisting of a projection monitor with a separate tuner/selector and audio subsystems.

But, while they have improved greatly, projection televisions remain subject to some important limitations. Projected images are, for example, more sensitive to variations in ambient light and viewing angle than those generated by conventional television display technology. The models with the largest screens are typically most sensitive to ambient light. Front projection models are typically more sensitive to

FIGURE 7

A front projection television system with curved, wall-mounted screen. (Courtesy: Kloss Video)

viewing angle than rear projection devices. Regardless of model, room lights may have to be subdued and the viewer seated directly in front of the screen for best results. In addition, the larger screen provided by projection television will necessarily magnify any impairments or "noise" in the video image. As a final limitation, prices for projection televisions range from 5 to 20 times those of conventional 19-inch television receivers with comparable features.

Design Trends

Convenience Features

Television manufacturers are increasingly using microprocessors, electronic memories, and related components to implement features that enhance the flexibility of their equipment, simplify operation by minimizing the need for picture or color adjustments, and improve reliability. Some of these convenience features may appeal to a specific segment of the consumer market, but have no immediately apparent business or library application. As an example, Zenith offers an optional feature called Space Phone, which allows the television viewer to make and answer telephone calls using the television speaker and a microphone in place of the telephone handset. Television sound is muted while the telephone feature is in use and, for outgoing calls, the dialed telephone number appears on the television screen. This feature should not be confused with Picturephone, a variant and experimental form of videoconferencing in which the user can both hear and see the person at the other end of the telephone line. Picturephone is described more fully in chapter 7. Space Phone merely minimizes interrupted viewing by having the television serve as an extension telephone.

Business and library applications of so-called programmable television receivers are likewise difficult to discern. These receivers incorporate microprocessors and electronic memories, but—despite the connotation of computer-like versatility and flexibility—their capabilities are limited to a few straightforward functions of potential consumer interest. They can, for example, be pre-set to turn on or change channels at specific times. Two channel locations can likewise be entered into the television's internal memory, thereby permitting the rapid switching between two different programs using a single button on a remote control unit. When certain television shows are inappropriate for viewing by children, specified channels can be temporarily "programmed out," thereby preventing their reception during hours when the parent cannot directly supervise the child's viewing habits.

Once a relatively esoteric accessory, remote control devices are now quite common accessories with medium-priced and expensive television sets. A convenience in most consumer applications, they are a necessity for many handicapped and bedridden persons. Remote control devices can likewise prove useful in business and library applications involving group viewing or where the television receiver is mounted on a wall or other inaccessible location. Inexpensive remote control devices are connected to the television receiver by a cord. More expensive models are of the infrared type and are "full featured" in the sense that they incorporate all of the controls available on the television set itself. The newest and most sophisticated remote controls are "universal" devices, which permit specified television receivers, videocassette recorders, video disk players, and other video devices from a given vendor's product line to be activated from a single source.

Tuner Design

While the features described above can prove convenient in certain situations, a more significant group of capabilities is designed to improve the overall sharpness and color fidelity of the television picture, minimizing the need for adjustments when programs or channels are changed. Such features are especially important, for example, where a business or library will establish viewing rooms with television sets available for individual use or where television receivers will be purchased by school or academic libraries for student viewing of educational programs.

Television sets manufactured during the 1960s and 1970s featured mechanical tuners with rotary dials for the selection and adjustment of individual channels. In most cases, an automatic fine tuning (AFT) feature minimized the need for repeated adjustments once a channel was properly tuned. While sets with mechanical tuners and rotary channel selectors are still being manufactured, state-of-the-art television receivers feature electronic tuners with quartz crystals that eliminate the need for AFT. These electronic tuners are typically activated by pushbutton channel selectors or calculator-style numeric keypads that permit the direct entry of desired channel numbers. Several available television sets feature scan-type tuners that successively seek out and display only those channels actually used for broadcasting in a given area. A significant advantage of electronic tuners is that they eliminate moving parts and are consequently more reliable than older mechanical ones.

Conventional television tuners, whether electronic or mechanical, can receive twelve VHF and seventy UHF channels. An increasing number of newer television receivers feature tuners that can also access certain cable television channels, assuming of course that the television is connected to a cable facility. Such television receivers are described as "cable ready." The various cable systems to be discussed more fully in chapter 4 transmit signals at frequencies that a conventional television tuner is unable to receive. When an ordinary television receiver is connected to a cable system, the cable service company typically installs a converter box as an alternative to the television's integral tuner. The television tuner is permanently set at a designated channel—usually 2, 3, or 4, depending on local usage—and all subsequent channel selection is performed via the converter box. It thus makes little sense to pay the higher price for a television receiver with a sophisticated electronic tuner if it is to be used for cable reception because the receiver's integral tuner will be disabled. As a further limitation, the installation of the cable converter box usually eliminates the use of any remote control device purchased with the television, and it may also complicate the installation of videocassette recorders, video disk players, microcomputers, or other video peripheral devices.

Cable-ready television receivers address these limitations by permitting the direct attachment of cable facilities and tuning of cable channels, thereby eliminating the need for the separate converter box. The specific channels to be tuned will vary with the nature of the cable service operating in a given locality and with the capabilities of a given cable-ready receiver. In addition to the twelve VHF and seventy UHF channels, most cable-ready television sets can receive the nine "midband" cable channels designated by letters A through I and the so-called superband channels designated by letters J through W, for a total of 105 channels. Some 127-channel cable-ready televisions will also receive the "hyperband" channels designated W + 1 through W + 17 plus the additional midband channels designated A − 1 through A − 5. Newer cable-ready receivers can tune 160 or more channels. With certain cable television companies, customers with cable-ready television sets may obtain a slight reduction in monthly service charges equivalent to the rental charge for the cable converter box. As a further advantage, cable-ready television sets can also be equipped with remote control devices. As previously noted, such devices cannot usually be operated when a cable converter box is installed.

An important limitation of cable-ready tuners is that they cannot access those "premium" channels, like Home Box Office, which intentionally encode their broadcast signals to prevent reception by nonsubscribers. To view such channels, the cable-ready television receiver must still be equipped with a converter/decoder box provided by the cable company. As a further constraint, cable-ready receivers may not provide sufficient buttons to tune all of the channels offered by larger cable systems. In such situations, tuning must be limited to the most commonly viewed stations. Television receivers with calculator-style numeric pads for the direct entry of channels offer greater flexibility in this respect.

FIGURE 8

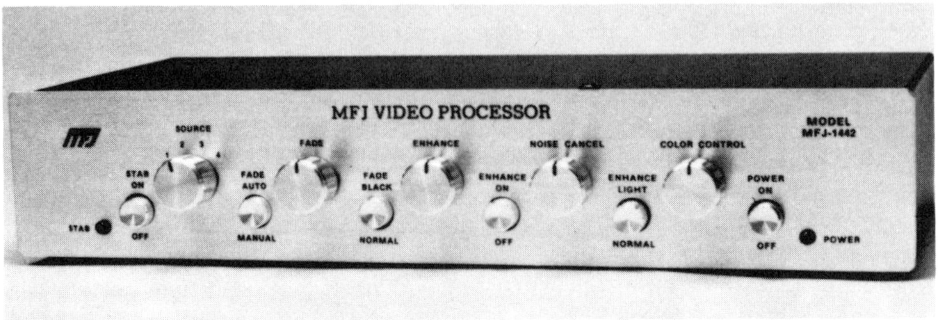

Signal processors increase detail and edge sharpness by accentuating the high frequency and contrast components of video images. (Courtesy: MFJ Enterprises)

Image Enhancement

As video systems have matured and attracted serious users interested in improved image quality, manufacturers have responded with capabilities designed to enhance image quality within the limitations of prevailing video resolution standards. As discussed earlier in this chapter, some newer television receivers are equipped with special comb filters and VIR circuitry that can significantly improve the brightness and color fidelity of displayed images. An increasing number of television receivers are also equipped with a photocell-activated control that automatically adjusts the display's brightness to compensate for variations in ambient light.

Over the past several years, a number of companies have introduced signal processors designed for attachment to television receivers. One group of these signal processors, termed "image enhancers," accentuates the high frequency and contrast components of an incoming video signal, thereby increasing detail and edge sharpness (figure 8). Since any impairments present in the signal will also be accentuated, these devices typically include noise cancellation circuitry. Another device, termed a "color and luminance amplifier," will modify and, in most cases, enhance the color and brightness of video signals. While these devices can be used with video signals received from broadcast or cable sources, they may prove most useful in enhancing the display of images recorded on video cassettes. In such applications, they can make marginally viewable or otherwise degraded images useable.

Future Developments

Alternative Display Technologies

As noted earlier in this chapter, the cathode ray tube remains the dominant video display device, but scientific and technical literature is filled with research that discusses alternative display technologies. While CRT displays are well understood and relatively inexpensive to manufacture in large quantities, they are bulky, consume considerable power, and are inherently vulnerable to geometric image distortions attributable to the varied distance and angles that the electron beam must traverse to illuminate the center and edges of the phosphorescent screen. Compact cathode ray tubes, as used in the Sony Watchman, can be produced, but such devices are presently limited in utility. Alternative display technologies, collectively termed "flat panel" displays, promise potentially compact design, light weight, low-power consumption, and freedom from geometric distortion. While these advantages are important to designers of television receivers, interest in flat panel displays is perhaps strongest in the data terminal applications to be discussed in chapter 8.

Compact television receivers using liquid crystal displays (LCDs) became commercially available in 1983 after several years of demonstration in prototype. Widely utilized in wristwatches, digital clocks, calculators, and some handheld computers, liquid crystal displays link and align organic molecules to alter light reflections in response to electrical signals, thereby producing dark images on a light background (figure 9). LCD television receivers—developed by Seiko, Casio, Sinclair, Hitachi, Toshiba, Sharp, and Sanyo—are extremely compact and can be viewed outdoors. LCD displays actually gain brightness as sunlight increases. Carrying portability to the extreme, several companies have developed wristwatch-style televisions based on LCD technology. For the television set designer, the compactness of LCD displays

FIGURE 9

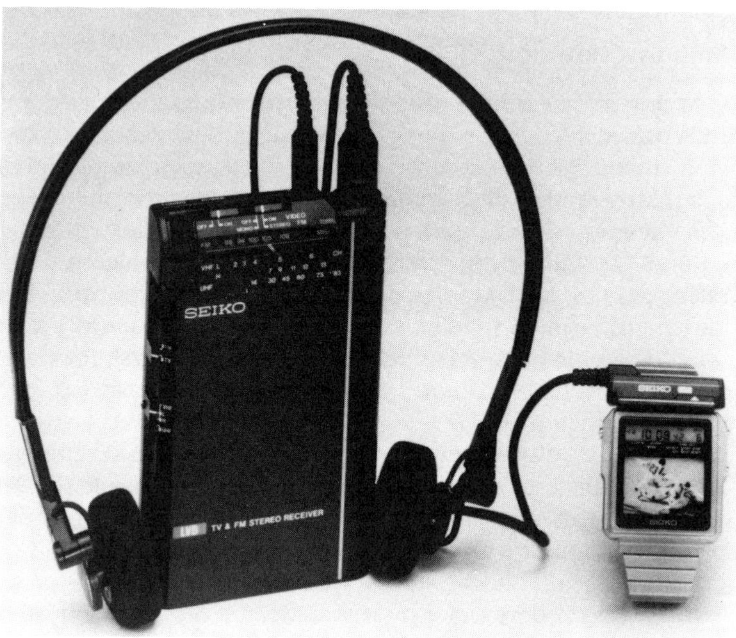

A wristwatch television receiver uses LCD technology and an attached tuner with headphones. (Courtesy: Seiko)

permits the development of truly portable devices that consume relatively little power, although several companies are reportedly working on LCD television receivers with 19-inch screens. The LCD devices now available are limited to monochrome display only because color reception would require the prohibitively expensive development of sets with three separate layers or crystals. A further constraint characteristic of all flat panel displays is that the competitive economic advantages of LCD technology over conventional cathode ray tubes has not been demonstrated.

The other types of flat panel displays either generate images from glowing substances or, like LCDs, alter light reflection patterns in response to an electrical signal. In the former group, gas plasma displays are used in some commercially available data terminals and microcomputers manufactured by such companies as IBM, Burroughs Corporation, and Grid Systems. As will be described more fully in chapter 8, images are created when discharged neon gas, mixed with argon and xenon, causes areas of the display screen to glow in one or more colors. A number of Japanese and American companies are reportedly working on television receivers that employ gas plasma technology, and a prototype model has been demonstrated by Nippon Hoso Kyokai (NHK), the Japanese Broadcasting Corporation.

Another flat panel technology, thin-film electroluminescent displays, apply electrical voltage to intersecting wires, causing a glow that forms an image. Presently available for applications involving computer generated data, prototype models indicate some potential for television display. Other flat panel technologies, to be discussed in chapter 8, generally lack the rapid response required for the display of moving video images.

High-Definition Television

Obviously, as described earlier in this chapter, the more horizontal scan lines, the sharper and more detailed the resulting video images; but neither the 525-line NTSC standard nor the 625-line PAL and SECAM standards provide image quality approaching that of motion picture films. As previously noted, the images actually displayed on television receivers are comprised of just 40 to 80 percent of the total transmitted lines. As will be discussed in chapters 6 and 8, high-resolution video displays offering 1,000 to 2,000 or more horizontal scan lines are employed in specially designed business systems and in technical applications involving computer-generated graphics. There has been some recent discussion, however, of the possibility of high-resolution commercial television or, as it is increasingly termed, "high-definition television" (HDTV).

As early as 1974, Matsushita Electric, the Japanese manufacturer of video products, and NHK, the Japanese Broadcasting Corporation, demonstrated HDTV systems displaying 1,125 scan lines per image. More recently, CBS has demonstrated similar capabilities in several American cities and has petitioned the Federal Communications Commission to allocate broadcast frequencies to HDTV. Prototype HDTV systems have also been developed by researchers at Sony, Mitsubishi, and other companies. At 1,100 scan lines per television frame, the resulting images approach motion picture quality in their presentation of detail (figure 10A–B). As a further advantage with broad information processing implications, a video format offering

FIGURE 10A & B

Compared to conventional NTSC broadcast standards (A), high definition television images (B) provide much greater detail. (Courtesy: NHK Technical Research Laboratories)

1,100 or more scan lines per frame is suitable for the display of a wide range of textual information, including images of typewritten or printed documents.

But while high-definition television may be technically possible, there are several significant impediments to its commercial success. Because high-resolution television signals contain more detail than conventional television signals, they will require a greater allocation of space or "bandwidth" within the television broadcast spectrum. Existing television channels are spaced at distances of 6 megahertz within the broadcast spectrum. A single high-definition channel would require the bandwidth of five such channels. Unfortunately, such large amounts of bandwidth are not available within the existing broadcast spectrum, although high-definition television signals might be transmitted via the cable or direct broadcast satellite (DBS) methodologies to be discussed in chapter 4. Alternatively, high-definition television programming might be initially developed for videocassettes, video disks, or other nonbroadcast sources.

At the time of this writing, it was thought that high-production television would be primarily used for the production of "video movies," replacing conventional 35mm motion picture film. The implementation of such applications will probably be accompanied by a potentially beneficial redesigning of video screens. The screens of currently available television receivers have an aspect ratio of 4 to 3 or 1.33 to 1, meaning that they are one-third wider than they are high. Before 1953, motion pictures were produced in that same aspect ratio. Most films produced since that time, however, have aspect ratios ranging from 1.66 to 1.85, with occasional wide-screen films being created at 2.21, 2.35 (CinemaScope), or 2.62 (Cinerama). Films with aspect ratios greater than 1.33 must be modified prior to broadcasting or distribution on prerecorded videocassettes or video disks. This modification essentially involves the selection of a portion of each frame for inclusion in a video image. Some visual material must necessarily be omitted. In most cases, material is simply omitted from the borders of the film image, but with very wide-screen films, only about half of the film image can be displayed in a video frame. Often, critical components of an image must be left out. Researchers and others interested in the use of video media for viewing and studying films have complained that these modifications, coupled with the smaller size of conventional television screens, may significantly alter a film's artistic character and overall impact. Addressing these objections, demonstrations of high definition television have used screens with aspect ratios of 1.67, 2.00, or 2.67 for a theater-like effect suitable for group viewing.

Digital Television

Even assuming that problems of available transmission bandwidth could be overcome, high-definition television signals would not be compatible with the existing installed base of television receivers, necessitating their upgrading or replacement. Some industry analysts contend that the introduction of HDTV should be accompanied by a radical rethinking of television receiver design and methods of transmission.

Historically, the television broadcast industry has used costly, high bandwidth transmission in order to keep television receivers simple and affordable. Prevailing broadcasting methods transmit the picture elements in successive frames as analog signals. Considerable recent attention has been given to the possibility of digital television transmission in which the individual picture elements that constitute a television frame would be encoded by a predefined sequence of bits. The resulting digital signal would prove less vulnerable to transmission impairments, but digital transmission would also permit the use of signal compression techniques or other innovative methods of transmission. These techniques, which are currently being used in the facsimile and videoconferencing systems described in chapters 6 and 7, allow more information to be transmitted within existing bandwidths. If, for example, digital television receivers were equipped with internal memories capable of storing one or more frames, the broadcast signal need only contain the changes that distinguish successive frames rather than entire replacement frames.

Given the striking departure that digital transmission would represent, it is unlikely to be implemented soon, if at all. Yet, at the time of this writing, several manufacturers already announced digital television receivers that can process conventional analog video signals. As discussed earlier, an increasing number of television receivers incorporate microprocessors and other electronic circuitry, although these components are primarily intended to improve convenience and minimize viewer adjustments. With so-called digital television receivers, computer-like circuitry performs essential signal processing operations. It accepts an incoming analog signal, converts it to digital form, enhances and filters it, then converts it back to conventional analog form for display. As an added advantage, digital televisions may also be able to receive the teletext signals discussed in chapter 5.

By early 1983, several vendors had demonstrated prototype digital television receivers, with commercial availability scheduled for mid-1984. One model, developed by the Standard Elektrik Lorenz division of ITT combines about 400 discrete components on a single integrated circuit. Sony has demonstrated a digital television receiver that conforms to prevailing NTSC 525-line broadcast standards, but rather than interlacing two fields of 262.5 scan lines each as conventional receivers do, it scans the entire video frame at a rate of 60 times per second. The result is a sharper picture that is especially well suited to textual display in microcomputer and videotext applications. Prototypes of such "single pass" digital receivers have also been developed by ITT, NHK, and others.

Video Sound

Many of the same analysts who criticize prevailing video resolution also deplore the low quality of the audio portion of video programming. Even though it is no longer possible to purchase a nonstereo phonograph (other than certain models for children), television sound is exclusively monophonic, and the typical television set is equipped with one very small speaker capable of a limited range of frequency response. While improved technology has enhanced the size and quality of television images, the accompanying sound remains weak. A comparable situation prevails in the motion picture field. While some movie theaters are equipped with stereo sound systems, most offer monophonic sound with a very limited audio response range and significant distortion. In general, visually oriented information systems have placed very little emphasis on sound as an auxiliary information carrier. This is most obviously the case in display-oriented computer systems where audio output is rare.

Yet there are significant applications for enhanced sound in video-based systems. Leaving computer systems aside, more sophisticated sound systems will enhance the presentation of television concerts, operas, musical films, and variety shows. As will be discussed in chapter 4, several cable television services, such as Home Box Office and Showtime, are increasingly including popular music concerts as part of their regular offerings, and classical music is an important component of the programming offered by the so-called arts networks. Music Televison (MTV), a Warner Amex cable offering, is the visual counterpart of radio broadcasting, offering rock-oriented, single-song promotional pieces, longer concerts, and music-related news twenty-four hours a day. Recognizing the potential of video music, the National Academy of Recording Arts and Sciences has established a Grammy Award category for "Video of the Year." As a further development to be discussed in chapters 2 and 3, stereo videocassettes and video disks are increasingly available. These "visual records" may eventually become an important component in consumer and library collections of sound recordings.

In a well-known approach to the enhancement of television sound, the Public Broadcasting System (PBS) occasionally broadcasts the audio portion of televised concerts in stereo over local FM radio stations. This technique, called "simulcasting," is also used by such cable services as the Movie Channel and the previously mentioned MTV. In such cases, the user's FM radio receiver is connected to the cable line. For those viewers who do not want to use separate video and audio systems for the reception of such simulcasts, several manufacturers offer television sets or component television systems with FM stereo receivers. This combined equipment configuration is especially characteristic of the growing number of audio companies, like Jensen and Fisher, who have introduced video product lines. In some cases, these systems include a microprocessor-controlled audio-video receiver that can be tuned to AM and FM radio stations or VHF, UHF, and cable video channels (figure 11). Noise reduction and stereo synthesis circuitry may also be used to enhance non-stereo video soundtracks.

FIGURE 11

An audio-video amplifier features an integral monitor and supports the attachment of videocassette recorders, video disk players, stereo sound systems and other peripheral devices. (Courtesy: Akai)

Stereo television broadcasting, which has been available in Japan and West Germany for several years, represents the ultimate solution to the problem of video sound. As a further potential advantage of significance for educational applications, stereo television broadcasting might be used for the transmission of a dual-language sound track. In mid-1983, the Federal Communications Commission approved stereo television broadcasting for the United States, although the required investment in additional broadcasting equipment will likely delay implementation for several years. In mid-1984, ABC announced plans to begin limited stereo broadcasting on a test basis, while NBC has indicated that it will begin some stereo broadcasting during the 1985 television season.

In anticipation of these developments, "stereo-ready" television sets with built-in speakers and amplifiers began appearing in mid-1984. Other models are equipped with output jacks which will direct unprocessed audio signals to a stereo decoding device. Several companies have likewise announced stereo adapters for existing television sets. To improve the quality of existing television sound, noise reduction circuitry, stereo synthesis capability, and similar features are also provided by a growing number of conventional television sets. For their most expensive models, manufacturers are increasingly providing larger, more powerful audio speakers that respond to a broad range of frequencies and include treble and bass controls. Some television receivers also feature audio output jacks for the connection of external speakers. As previously discussed, several component television systems will support the attachment of high-fidelity speakers of varying sizes and responsiveness. Other companies offer audio equalizers, which filter and enhance video soundtracks to produce synthesized sound effects. Some of these devices serve as an interface between a television receiver and a stereo amplifier and speaker system. Others feature an integral amplifier and support the direct attachment of high-fidelity speakers. Mixed results may be obtained in either case. The simplest stereo synthesizers merely direct most of the low frequencies to one speaker and most of the high frequencies to the other. The resulting stereo effect may seem artificial. More sophisticated stereo synthesizers divide audible sound into multiple frequency bands, portions of which are directed to each speaker for a more realistic effect.

As a final point, it has been suggested that stereo broadcasting capability might be offered through cable systems. Unfortunately, the addition of such stereo capability requires a considerable increase in the power of a broadcast signal. Such a power increase can result in several problems, including severe interference with the signals broadcast by adjacent channels. Elimination of such interference would require considerable and expensive modifications of existing cable systems.

Additional Readings

The books and articles listed below provide more detailed information about specific aspects of television display technology. Emphasis is placed on publications that discuss the scientific underpinnings of television display systems. Although some of the material is technical, much of it can be understood by well-educated persons who lack formal technical training. With a few exceptions, publications describing specific products are avoided. While such product surveys are important, they become outdated too quickly to be meaningful in a bibliographic list. Monthly issues of *Video, Videoplay*, and *Video Review* magazines are the best sources for such product-specific information. All three magazines regularly publish articles dealing with the major product groups discussed in this chapter.

CLOSED-CAPTION SYSTEMS

Wells, D. R. Captioning for the deaf—A PBS progress report. *SMPTE Journal* 89: 656–58 (September 1980).

FLAT-SCREEN TELEVISION

Credelle, T. L. Large-screen flat panel television display. *BKSTS Journal* 64: 456–62 (September 1982).

———. Large-screen flat panel television: A new approach. *RCA Engineer* 26: 75–81 (July-August 1981).

Harris, M. A. Fiber optics pipes form a flat screen TV. *Electronics* 56: 49–50 (June 16, 1983).

NHK Display Devices Research Group. Gas discharge panels for displaying color television images. In B. Kazan, ed., *Advances in Image Pickup and Display*, vol. 6, pp. 90–177. New York: Academic Press, 1983.

Smith, K. Electrons make U-turn in flat CRT. *Electronics* 55: 81–82 (October 20, 1982).

HISTORY OF VIDEO TECHNOLOGY

Fielding, R., ed. *A Technological History of Motion Pictures and Television*. Berkeley: University of California Press, 1983.

Sterling, C., and Shiers, G., eds. *Technical Development of Television*. Salem, New York: Ayer Company, 1976.

PROJECTION TELEVISION

Schiecke, K. Projection television: correcting distortions. *IEEE Spectrum* 18: 40–45 (November 1981).

SMALL-SCREEN TELEVISION

Aldersley-Williams, H. Flat out for pocket TV. *New Scientist* 98: 282–85 (May 5, 1983).

———. Liquid crystal television: Here at last. *Electro-Optics* 15: 55–58 (May 1983).

Kokado, N., et al. Pocketable liquid crystal television receiver. *IEEE Transactions on Consumer Electronics* 27: 462–77 (August 1981).

Labrunie, G. LCD pocket TV developments in Japan. *Displays* 2: 301–3 (1981).

TELEVISION ACCESSORIES

Adler, R., Desmares, P., and Spracklen, J. Ultrasonic remote control for home receivers. *IEEE Transactions on Consumer Electronics* 28: 123–28 (1982).

Perry, T. S. Component television. *IEEE Spectrum* 20: 38–43 (June 1983).

TELEVISION TECHNOLOGY

Berkhoff, E. J., Kraus, V. E., and Raven, J. G. Applications of picture memories in television receivers. *IEEE Transactions on Consumer Electronics* 29: 251–59 (1983).

Clark, D. 3D comes to colour TV. *New Scientist* 96: 510–11 (November 25, 1982).
Crane, R. J. *The Politics of International Standards: France and the Color TV War*. Norwood, New Jersey: Ablex Publishing, 1979.
Drysdale, J. K. Video 90. *RCA Engineer* 26: 75–81 (July-August 1981).
Fink, D. G. Forces at work behind the NTSC standards. *SMPTE Journal* 90: 498–502 (1981).
Fischer, T. What is the impact of digital TV? *IEEE Transactions on Consumer Electronics* 28: 423–30 (1982).
Fisher, R. *Digital Applications in Television Receivers*. New York: Focal Press, 1983.
Grob, B. *Basic Television and Video Systems*. New York: McGraw-Hill, 1984.
Harshbarger, J. H. Standardization of the television raster for non-broadcast applications. *SMPTE Journal* 9: 797–807 (1982).
Lerner, E. J. Digital TV: Makers bet on VLSI. *IEEE Spectrum* 20: 39–43 (February 1983).
MacKellar, J. C. Television receiver design. *IEE Proceedings, Part A* 129: 493–506 (September 1982).
Mokhoff, N. Continuing quest for 3-D televison. *IEEE Spectrum* 18: 48–51 (February 1981).
Steele, F. H. Capturing the living image. *IEE Proceedings, Part A* 128: 9–17 (1981).
Takano, Y. Recent advances in color picture tubes. In B. Kazan, ed., *Advances in Image Pickup and Display*, vol. 6, pp. 1–89. New York: Academic Press, 1983.
Yashima, I., et al. Development of the TV receiver for cars. *IEEE Transactions on Consumer Electronics* 28: 437–46 (1982).

VIDEO RESOLUTION

Alinott, J. W., and Collins, R. N. Quality rating of television pictures: Comparison of results obtained by laboratories in different countries. *IEE Proceedings, Part F* 130: 289–95 (June 1983).
Fujio, T. High definition television systems: Desirable standards, signal forms, and transmission systems. *IEEE Transactions on Communications* 29: 1882–91 (1981).
Kriss, M. A., and Liang, J. Today's photographic imaging technology for tomorrow's HDTV system. *SMPTE Journal* 92: 804–18 (1983).
Kubo, T. Development of high definition TV displays. *IEEE Transactions on Broadcasting* 28: 51–64 (1982).
Lu, C. High definition TV comes at high cost. *High Technology* 3: 45–48 (July 1983).
Miyahara, M. Improvements of television picture quality by eliminating disturbances caused by interlaced scanning. *IEEE Transactions on Communications* 31: 902–6 (1983).
Parker, D. W. Hi-fi television. *Television* 20: 14–16 (1983).
Rzeszewski, T. S. A compatible high definition television system. *Bell System Technical Journal* 62: 2091–111 (1983).
Sandbank, C. P., and Moffatt, M. E. B. High definition television and compatibility with existing standards. *SMPTE Journal* 92: 552–61.
Southworth, G. R. A high definition still-frame television system. *SMPTE Journal* 92: 834–42 (1983).
Steber, G. R. High resolution SSTV. *QST* 67: 11–13 (August 1983).
Yuyama, I. Fundamental requirements for high definition television systems. *NHK Technical Manager* 32: 14–20 (June 1982).

Zidek, L. M. Microcomputers in TV receivers. *Electronic Technology* 17: 35–38 (February 1983).

VIDEO SOUND

Hautsch, F. Stereo sound for German TV network. *Siemens Review* 49: 11–13 (March-April 1982).

Jurgen, R. K. Stereophonic sound for television. *IEEE Spectrum* 19: 30–33 (September 1982).

Mowrer, W. Stereo TV now. *High Fidelity* 33: 52–53 (November 1983).

Numaguchi, Y. Multichannel sound system for television broadcasting. *IEEE Transactions on Consumer Electronics* 27: 366–71 (1981).

Ocker, L. W., Simanton, J. R., and Wegner, C. R. TV multichannel sound—Savior or sacred cow? *IEEE Transactions on Consumer Electronics* 27: 361–65 (1981).

CHAPTER 2

VIDEOCASSETTE RECORDERS AND VIDEO CAMERAS

In terms of hardware, an information processing system may consist of up to four groups of components: an input mechanism, processing circuitry, and output device, and some form of storage. Viewed in this manner, a television set includes an input mechanism—the antenna or, in the case of a video monitor, input jacks—for the reception of broadcast signals, cable transmission, and/or signals from attached peripheral devices; internal signal processing circuitry; and an output device—the CRT or other video screen. Notably missing is an internal or auxiliary storage component that permits the recording of incoming signals for later use and the display of previously recorded programming. While, as discussed in chapter 1, future television sets may ultimately be equipped with internal frame storage, the provision of auxiliary storage in a video system is presently accomplished through the attachment of videotape recorders and video disk players. Of the two, videotape recorders are the more versatile devices, permitting both recording and playback. Video disk players, to be discussed in the next chapter, are exclusively designed for the playback of prerecorded programming and cannot be used to record broadcast or other signals.

The possibility of videotape recording of broadcast signals was first demonstrated in the early 1950s when Bing Crosby Productions equipped an audio recorder with stationary video heads to sequentially record a video signal down the length of magnetic tape, a method termed "longitudinal recording." Unfortunately, the recording of an acceptable signal required very fast tape movement, resulting in impractically low storage densities. A standard 2,400-foot reel of magnetic tape, for example, might hold as little as four minutes of video programming.

In the late 1950s, Ampex Corporation—and subsequently RCA—resolved this problem, introducing a machine in which the magnetic tape and the recording heads both moved in opposite directions, toward one another. Because the recorder used four video heads, the recording process was termed "quadraplex," and it has become the standard for high quality applications in network television studios.

But quadraplex recorders are complex and expensive. The development of simpler, less expensive helical recorders in the early 1960s permitted the extension of videotape recording to a broader spectrum of industrial, institutional, and—

ultimately—consumer applications. The helical recording process takes its name from the spiral-like manner in which the videotape is wrapped around the machine's recording heads. Unlike the quadraplex process in which video information is recorded perpendicular to the edges of the tape, the helical process records individual frames as slanted stripes of magnetic pulses. While the tape used by quadraplex recorders measures two inches wide and is typically wound on reels in 2,400-foot lengths, available helical recorders use videotape in various widths and packaging. Reel-to-reel helical recorders that use one-inch videotape are manufactured by such companies as Ampex, Fernseh, Hitachi, Marconi, NEC, Philips, RCA, Sony, and 3M. They are designed for professional use in industrial and institutional video production facilities.

While the one-inch helical scan recorders offer simplicity and economy when compared to quadraplex models, they utilize open reels of tape with their attendant handling problems. The U-Matic videotape format, introduced by Sony in 1971, utilizes a three-quarter–inch tape conveniently packaged in plastic cassettes. Designed for professional applications, it is utilized by public, school, and other libraries with video production facilities. In addition to Sony, U-Matic format recorders are offered by such companies as NEC, HVC, Panasonic, and Teac.

The introduction of videocassette recorders (VCRs) for professional applications set the stage for the development of even simpler, less expensive videotape machines for consumer use. But cartridge and cassette-oriented models introduced in the late 1960s and early 1970s were not successful, and the now-defunct systems sold under such trade names as Instavision, Cartravision, Betacord, V-Cord, and the VX Series Great Time Machine are typically only remembered by a handful of

FIGURE 12

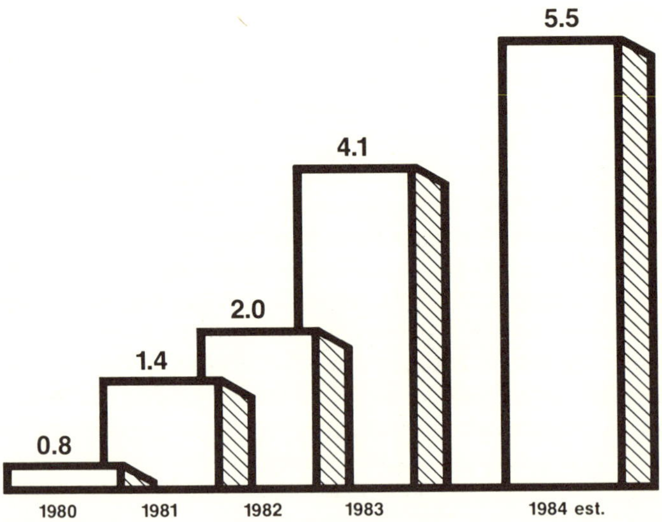

Industry sales to dealers (in millions of units) reflect the rapid growth of the U.S. market for videocassette recorders. (Source: Electronics Industries Association and RCA Consumer Electronics)

embittered customers. In 1975, however, Sony introduced a machine that ultimately proved to be the first in a still developing series of consumer-oriented videocassette recorders—the Betamax. Two years later, the Japanese Victor Company (JVC) introduced the competing VHS videocassette format. Today, Beta and VHS format videocassette recorders are offered by several dozen companies (figure 12). While they are primarily marketed to individual consumers, they are suitable for business applications, and they are an indispensible component in any library program to develop collections of prerecorded video presentations. They can also be used with video cameras for production work, and industrial models are available for serious production applications.

This chapter begins with a discussion of the available videocassette recording formats and a review of the basic functions and special features of available equipment. Later sections will discuss the increasingly wide range of available prerecorded videocassettes and will briefly describe some recent developments in video camera technology. The discussion is limited to equipment conforming to the previously described NTSC video standard used throughout North America, although most of the capabilities and features described are also encountered on equipment designed for use in PAL and SECAM video systems.

Videocassette Formats

Beta vs. VHS

Excluding the U-Matic cassette recorders, which are designed for professional use, and the defunct formats mentioned above, there are six videocassette recording formats offered for consumer and organizational applications: Beta, VHS, CVC, VHS-C, V-2000, and 8mm. Of the six, VHS and Beta dominate the market so completely that the other formats are relegated to special situations or limited market segments.

While both the Beta and VHS formats use one-half–inch videotape stored in a plastic cassette, they are otherwise incompatible. As previously noted, the Beta format was introduced in 1975, and, while it is most closely associated with the Sony Corporation, it is also used in videocassette recorders manufactured and/or marketed by such companies as Sanyo, Toshiba, NEC, Zenith, and Sears. All Beta-format recorders are manufactured in Japan, although they are sold in the United States under familiar domestic brand names. All VHS-format videocassette recorders are likewise manufactured by such Japanese firms as Matsushita, JVC, Hitachi, Mitsubishi, Sharp, and Akai. In the United States, their products are marketed under such brand names as Canon, Curtis Mathes, Fisher, General Electric, Jensen, Kenwood, Magnavox, Minolta, Olympus, Panasonic, J. C. Penney, Pentax, Philco, Quasar, RCA, Sansui, and Sylvania. At the time this chapter was written, such Korean electronics firms as Gold Star and Samsung, and German companies like Schneider and Grundig, had announced plans to begin manufacturing VHS-format videocassette recorders for the American market.

The incompatibility of the Beta and VHS formats poses problems for the consumer, business, or library interested in purchasing a videocassette recorder and/or developing a collection of prerecorded videocassettes for circulation or in-house

use. As might be expected, proponents of each format claim superiority. But while many of these claims are subject to often heated debate, it is possible to clarify the major issues in format selection by delineating the essential characteristics of the two formats in terms of recording time, image quality, loading mechanism, and market strength.

With both Beta and VHS systems, the recording time per cassette is a function of both tape length and tape movement speed. Beta format cassettes measure 6.1 inches wide by 3.8 inches high by 1 inch thick and are widely available in three tape lengths: the L-500 cassette contains approximately 450 linear feet of videotape; the L-750 cassette contains a thinner tape of about 730 linear feet; and the L-830 cassette uses an even thinner tape of about 810 linear feet. Shorter Beta cassettes can be purchased for special applications.

The first Beta recorder, the Sony Betamax SL-7200, operated at a tape movement speed of 1.5 inches per second, yielding one hour of recording capacity per L-500 cassette. That speed, now termed Beta I, provided excellent quality, but proved impractical for many consumer applications, because the typical two-hour movie or similar program would require two cassettes. Recording at the Beta I speed is still possible with Beta machines designed for industrial applications. Some newer consumer models can play previously recorded Beta I cassettes, but cannot record at the Beta I speed. For recording, newer Beta format machines offer a choice of two switch-selectable operating speeds: Beta II (.79 inches per second) and Beta III (.53 inches per second). The Beta II speed provides three hours of video programming with an L-750 cassette and 3.66 hours with the longer L-830 cassette. The slower Beta III speed provides 4.5 hours of video programming with an L-750 cassette and 5.5 hours with an L-830 cassette. It should be noted, however, that tapes recorded at the Beta III speed by different machines are not always compatible.

The VHS cassette measures 7.4 inches wide by 4 inches high by 1 inch deep and can contain tapes in various lengths. The most popular type of VHS cassettes, generically designated T-120, contains 800 feet of video tape. As discussed later in this chapter, VHS cassettes with shorter tape lengths are available for camera work or other applications. As with Beta-format machines, most VHS units offer a choice of two or three selectable operating speeds. The two speeds invariably provided are Standard Play (SP), in which the tape moves at 1.31 inches per second for two hours of video programming per T-120 cassette, and Extended Long Play (ELP), sometimes called "Super Long Play" (SLP), in which the tape moves at .44 inches per second for six hours of video programming per T-120 cassette. A useful intermediate speed, termed Long Play (LP), provides tape movement at .66 inches per second for 4 hours of video programming per T-120 cassette. Some VHS recorders omit the LP speed in both the recording and playback modes. Others will record at SP and ELP only, but can play back at all three speeds for compatibility with other recorders operating in the LP mode. Several manufacturers have recently introduced a VHS cassette, generically designated T-160, which contains about 1,060 feet of thinner tape for up to 8 hours of video recording at the ELP speed. These thinner tapes may not be suitable, however, for use with older VHS recorders.

At all operating speeds and tape lengths, the VHS format offers greater video programming capacity per cassette than the Beta format. But with both formats, any increase in programming capacity per cassette is accompanied by degraded image quality. Conversely, the fastest operating speeds can record a wider spectrum of signals. They provide both the highest resolution and the lowest recording capacity per cassette.

There is some variation, however, in the image quality offered at the comparable Beta and VHS recording speeds. Leaving the rarely encountered and low-capacity Beta I format aside, most analysts agree that the VHS SP (2-hour) speed offers the highest image quality with properly adjusted recorders. Proponents of the Beta format argue that the Beta II and Beta III speeds offer higher resolution than the VHS LP and ELP speeds, respectively, although—as will be discussed later in this chapter—many newer VHS recorders feature an additional set of video heads designed to improve quality at the ELP speed.

Beta recorders feature a U-shaped loading path in which approximately two feet of video tape is wound around a series of rollers on its way to and from the video head. VHS recorders use a shorter but more sharply angled M-shaped loading path. Beta proponents argue that the U-shaped loading path places less cumulative stress on the tape and minimizes the potential for improper threading, jamming, or ripping—an especially important consideration when thinner tapes are used.

In addition, the VHS loading mechanism requires that tape be returned to the cassette to minimize stress during fast forward and rewind operations. Some delay is inherent in the consequent loading and unloading of tape. Because Beta recorders do not require such loading and unloading, they respond more quickly to changes in operating modes.

As a related point, Beta's loading mechanism has facilitated the introduction of freeze-frame, variable motion, and other special display features discussed later in this chapter, although VHS manufacturers have exercised considerable ingenuity in developing comparable features. At the time of this writing, however, Beta machines were the only devices capable of supporting an automatic cassette changer.

While some claims to technical superiority by the two dominant formats are based on subjective determinations, there is no doubt about their relative market strengths. In the United States, VHS recorders currently outsell Beta models by at least three to one, and the VHS format typically holds 65 to 80 percent of the market in most European countries. The consumer considering the purchase of a videocassette recorder typically wants it to be compatible with those of friends and neighbors who are more likely to have a VHS model than a Beta device. The consumer's bias for the VHS format is further reflected in the selection of prerecorded videocassettes available for sale and rental in video stores and other retail outlets. To meet user demand, such stores typically stock multiple VHS-format copies of new titles, but will have only one or two, if any, Beta-format copies. This, in turn, reinforces the prospective customer's decision to purchase a VHS machine—a decision bolstered by the greater number of companies committed to the VHS format, their consequently more formidable presence in retail outlets, and the seemingly greater variety of available models.

If a business, library, or other organization is purchasing a videocassette recorder for completely self-contained applications—the in-house recording of special events using a video camera, for example—then the choice of a recording format is not critical. If, however, the organization expects to exchange videocassettes with other organizations or to view prerecorded videocassettes, the VHS format is the best choice where only one recorder will be purchased. Tapes recorded in one format can be copied to the other if VHS and Beta machines are both available. The incompatibility of formats poses special problems for libraries interested in developing a collection of prerecorded videocassettes for circulation. To provide the broadest service, titles will need to be acquired in both formats, with multiple-copy VHS purchases for very popular titles. If only one format will be maintained, it should be on VHS.

Other Formats

While the VHS and Beta formats dominate the market and consumer attention, three other videocassette formats have been developed. Of these, the Compact Video Cassette (CVC) format is perhaps the best known. Developed in Japan by Funai and introduced in the United States by Technicolor Audio-Visual, the CVC format is specifically designed for application requiring compact, portable recording equipment. Unlike the half-inch Beta and VHS formats, it utilizes one-quarter-inch video tape packaged in a cassette measuring just 4.1 inches wide by 2.6 inches high by .5 inches thick—approximately the size of the familiar Philips-type audio cassette. For high-quality output, the recording speed is 1.26 inches per second—just slightly slower than the VHS SP speed—and tape is supplied in two lengths: 188.5 feet (58 meters) for 30 minutes of recording time, and 377 feet (116 meters) for 60 minutes of recording time. These comparatively short recording times, combined with the absence of speed selection capability on currently available equipment, are a potential disadvantage of the CVC format, but, at the time this chapter was written, longer tapes were reportedly in development.

CVC recorders, as noted above, are specifically designed for portability and for use with a video camera, as opposed to the taping of television broadcasts, and some models lack the tuner required for such taping. One model, the Technicolor 212, measures just 10 inches wide by 10 inches deep by 3 inches high and weighs 7 pounds. As noted in chapter 1, Technicolor has introduced a CVC recorder with an integral color television receiver. Despite their attractive compactness, however, CVC recorders have not enjoyed significant consumer interest. In late 1982, Technicolor discontinued its consumer product line, although it will continue to sell CVC systems through professional video outlets.

A potentially significant deterrent to consumer acceptance of CVC systems is the compactness of recently introduced Beta and VHS portable recorders, which are described later in this chapter. To facilitate the design of compact portable recorders while maintaining compatibility with the popular VHS format, JVC has introduced the VHS-C cassette, which uses half-inch video tape, but is approximately the same size as the CVC cassette. The VHS-C format contains 40 meters of tape for 20 minutes of recording at the VHS SP speed. It is specifically designed for camera work, and JVC has introduced a portable recorder that measures 7 inches wide by 8 inches deep by 3 inches high and weighs just over 4 pounds. For compatibility with conventional VHS playback equipment, the VHS-C cassette can be inserted into a special adapter.

The fifth videocassette format, the V-2000, was developed by Philips, the Dutch electronics firm, and is used in equipment offered by the German electronics manufacturer Grundig. It employs half-inch video tape, but uses both sides of the cassette, recording signals in two quarter-inch tracks with a maximum recording time of four hours per side. Grundig has reportedly also developed a compatible mini-cassette for use in a portable system.

Although the Grundig recorders offer a number of interesting features, including front-loading and the ability to search for programming by recording time, it is difficult to see how the V-2000 format can win a significant market share against the firmly entrenched Beta and VHS formats in the United States. It is possible, however, that the V-2000 format will fare better in Europe where the videocassette recorder market is more open to innovation.

While the half-inch Beta and VHS formats enjoy the lion's share of the market, there has been much recent discussion of an emerging 8mm cassette that is being loosely termed the Ultra Compact Machine (UCM) format. As their name suggests, such systems are primarily designed for applications requiring portability. Under the direction of the Japanese Ministry of Trade, such companies as Sony, Matsushita, JVC, and Hitachi—as well as the Dutch firm Philips—are working on UCM-format cameras and cassette recorders. In January of 1984, General Electric, RCA, and Eastman Kodak became the first companies to announce the commercial availability of such products in the United States. The General Electric and Eastman Kodak systems are manufactured by Matsushita. The RCA system is manufactured by Hitachi. With the support of such major vendors, 8mm systems will certainly have the potential to challenge and possibly displace the VHS and Beta formats, although, by the time they gain substantial market acceptance, those formats will be even more firmly entrenched. Given these present and future problems of compatibility, a few industry observers have suggested that videocassette recorders in all formats may eventually be made obsolete by the introduction of video disk recorder/players for consumer use. As will be noted in chapter 3, Matsushita currently offers a video disk system capable of direct recording, but its high cost limits its use.

Equipment Characteristics

Stationary vs. Portable Recorders

Regardless of recording format, the typical videocassette recorder consists of two basic components: a recording/playback deck that, as the name implies, records video and audio signals on a specially formulated magnetic tape; and a tuner/timer which permits the manual and/or automatic recording of broadcast video programs. Available videocassette recorders are generally categorized as either stationary or portable models. Stationary models are designed for table-top operation in an office, home, or studio. With most stationary machines, the recorder/playback deck and tuner/timer are integrated in a single chassis, although as component television systems gain popularity, users may be attracted to the advantages of a separate tuner/timer in eliminating redundant components and thereby reducing overall system costs.

When cost is considered in relationship to performance, stationary units are preferred to portable ones in applications limited to the recording of broadcast signals and the playback of prerecorded cassettes. The size of available stationary units varies slightly with the design of the cassette insertion system. Older models, many of which are still being sold, employed a top-loading mechanism that requires a somewhat taller design than that of newer front-loading units. A typical top-loading stationary VHS recorder measures approximately 18 inches wide by 14 inches deep by 5.5 inches high, while a comparable top-loading Beta unit is perhaps one-half inch smaller on all dimensions. Front-loading units for both formats are about 2 or 3 inches shorter. As a functional rather than an aesthetic advantage where shelf or table space is limited, the front-loading design allows other video peripherals to be stacked on top of the recorder. At the time of this writing, all VHS recorders and most Beta models required the manual insertion and removal of cassettes. For use with certain Beta recorders, Sony offers its BetaStack changer, which is capable of automatically loading and unloading up to four cassettes for over 20 hours of continuous recording or playback.

In addition to their consumer appeal as a substitute for home movie equipment, portable videocassette recorders will prove most attractive to organizations that intend to use video cameras for taping special events or for other forms of local video programming. Unlike the integrated stationary units discussed above, the typical portable recorder is a two-piece system that consists of separate but interconnectable recorder/playback and tuner/timer components. The recorder/playback deck operates from a battery pack and is designed to go into the field with a video camera. The typical battery charge lasts about one hour. The tuner/timer remains connected to a television receiver or video monitor where it is used for the taping of broadcast signals, to supply AC electrical power to the recorder/playback deck, and to recharge the battery pack.

Some vendors of portable recorders sell the recorder/playback deck and tuner/timer separately, while others require the simultaneous purchase of both components. The separate purchase of components permits a lower initial cash outlay as well as greater flexibility in the development of equipment configurations in applications where, for example, multiple recorder/playback decks might be used in conjunction with a single tuner/timer. Components from different manufacturers, however, cannot generally be intermixed, even within the same recording format. At the time this chapter was written, only Sharp offered a one-piece portable with recorder/playback deck and tuner/timer integrated in a single chassis resembling a large portable radio.

The overall size and weight of portable recorders has fallen steadily over the past several years. At the time of this writing, the most compact Beta-format decks measured approximately 8.5 inches wide by 12 inches deep by 3 inches high and weighed less than 9 pounds, including the battery. Conventional VHS-format portable recording decks are of comparable size. Portable recording decks designed for the ultra compact VHS-C format measure approximately 7 inches wide by 8.5 inches deep by 3 inches high and weigh about 4 pounds, including the battery.

Just several years ago, videocassette recorders typically compromised capabilities to gain portability. Today, however, portable and stationary recorders offer comparable features, although portables typically cost 10 to 20 percent more than equivalent stationary models.

Basic Features

A casual survey of available videocassette recorders, whether stationary or portable, reveals a seemingly bewildering array of Beta and VHS models. But, as discussed earlier in this chapter, the large number of available brands are actually manufactured by a small number of Japanese companies. Thus, with the exception of slight variations in external appearance and in the number and placement of operating controls, the comparably priced models offered by the various vendors will typically prove more alike than different. To choose wisely it is necessary to understand the range of both basic and additional features currently offered.

In terms of basic capabilities, all available models will record broadcast signals and play back previously recorded videocassettes (figure 13). The user can watch one program while taping another or tape and view the same program simultaneously. As with audio cassette recorders, tape movement controls permit fast advance and rewinding. A "pause" feature, provided with all models, stops tape movement briefly. It can be used to avoid recording portions of a broadcast signal or to interrupt playback without unthreading the tape. Because the recorder's video heads remain in contact with the tape during the pause operation, some additional wear will result. To keep tape wear to a minimum, some recorders will automatically deactivate the pause mechanism after several minutes.

In addition to broadcast television signals, most videocassette recorders will accept input from a video camera or another videocassette recorder and will deliver an output signal to an attached television receiver, video monitor, or videocassette recorder. The copying of previously recorded cassettes is accomplished by connecting two recorders and transmitting the recorded material from one to the other. The two recorders need not be of comparable format, provided that they conform to the same television broadcast standard (NTSC, PAL, or SECAM, as discussed in chapter 1). Thus, a VHS and a Beta recorder can be connected for copying tapes.

Most videocassette recorders include an audio input jack to attach an external microphone. An "audio dubbing" control permits the superimposition of a new soundtrack on a previously recorded cassette. All videocassette recorders also include a digital clock, which is used to initiate automatic recording as discussed below.

FIGURE 13

A full-featured, stationary videocassette recorder offers wireless remote control, front-loading design, electronic tape counter, and stereo capability. (Courtesy: NEC)

Tuner/Timers

The VCR's tuner/timer permits the manual or automatic recording of broadcast video programming. While the two components are typically integrated, they perform different functions. The tuner, like its television receiver counterpart, is used to select a particular broadcast channel for recording. The earliest videocassette recorders, some of which are still available at low prices, included a mechanical tuner activated by a rotary dial. Most newer models, however, feature an electronic tuner activated by pushbutton selectors.

With stationary videocassette recorders, the tuner is typically built into the VCR chassis. Most portable recorders feature a separate but compatible tuner/timer unit (figure 14). In some cases, it is possible to use a different tuner, such as one provided with a component television system, but such devices often have more primitive timers than those designed specifically for VCR applications.

Regardless of configuration, the number of tunable channels varies somewhat from model to model. As with television receivers, all available VCR models permit the tuning of VHF channels 2 through 13 and UHF channels 14 through 83. Like many newer television receivers, an increasing number of videocassette recorders feature cable-ready tuners that can tune a predetermined range of cable channels, although additional accessories may be required to establish an appropriate connection with particular cable systems.

While a particular videocassette recorder may be able to receive a wide range of

FIGURE 14

Portable VCRs feature separate record/playback and tuner/timer units, stacked here for convenience. (Courtesy: Pentax)

channels, the number of channels that the VCR is prepared to tune at a given time is limited to the number of tuner buttons provided. Most available devices provide 14 to 16 tuner buttons located on the front panel of the VCR. When pressed, these buttons light up to reveal the particular channel in use. In most cases, the vendor presets these buttons to tune local VHF and UHF channels. The number of available buttons is usually more than sufficient for the channels available in most localities. Additional controls allow the operator to perform fine tuning, tune additional channels, or change the channels tuned by particular buttons. This retuning capability is especially important with cable-ready tuners, since the number of cable channels available in a given locality often exceeds the number of tuner buttons provided. In such cases, the available buttons must be configured to tune the 14 or 16 most frequently viewed channels, and specific buttons can be retuned as required.

The VCR timer is used for automatic recording of broadcast signals at night or other times when the machine is unattended. Using controls provided for that purpose, the operator sets the recorder's internal clock to begin and end recording at particular times. The specific channel to be tuned is also indicated. Timer sophistication varies directly with the price of the VCR. The least expensive recorders offer a simple "single day/single event" timer that can be set to record automatically one program in a 24-hour period. A more sophisticated "multi-day/single event" timer can be set to record automatically the same program each day for as many as ten days—assuming, of course, that the available supply of blank tape is adequate. The most sophisticated timer configuration—termed "multi-day/multi-event"—provides for the unattended recording of two or more programs in two or more days. For each program, the operator indicates the day, the starting time, the stopping time, and the channel to be tuned. The specific number of days and events accommodated varies from model to model. At the time this chapter was written, the most widely provided options were 14 days/4 events or 14 days/8 events, although some models permit the unattended recording of 8 events over as many as 27 days. Again, the available tape supply may limit the utility of these multi-day timers.

Operating Speeds

As discussed above, both Beta- and VHS-format machines can record at multiple speeds, allowing the operator the option of extending cassette capacity through slower tape movement. As previously noted, this results in greater density of recording with a consequent degradation of image quality—although, in applications where the recorded material is of ephemeral significance, the user is often willing to sacrifice quality for economy. By way of review, all available Beta-format recorders can both record and play back at the Beta II and Beta III speeds. With a high capacity L-830 Beta cassette, these speeds provide 3.66 or 5.5 hours of recording programming, respectively. Some models can also play tapes recorded at the Beta I speed, but no newer consumer VCRs can record at that speed. Beta I recording capability remains available, however, with certain industrial models.

All available VHS recorders permit both recording and playback at the standard play (SP) and extended long play (ELP) speeds for either two or six hours of program capacity per T-120 cassette. As previously noted, the intermediate long play (LP) speed permits four hours of recording per cassette, but some VHS machines do not support LP operation. Others will play back, but not record, at the LP speed. The

FIGURE 15

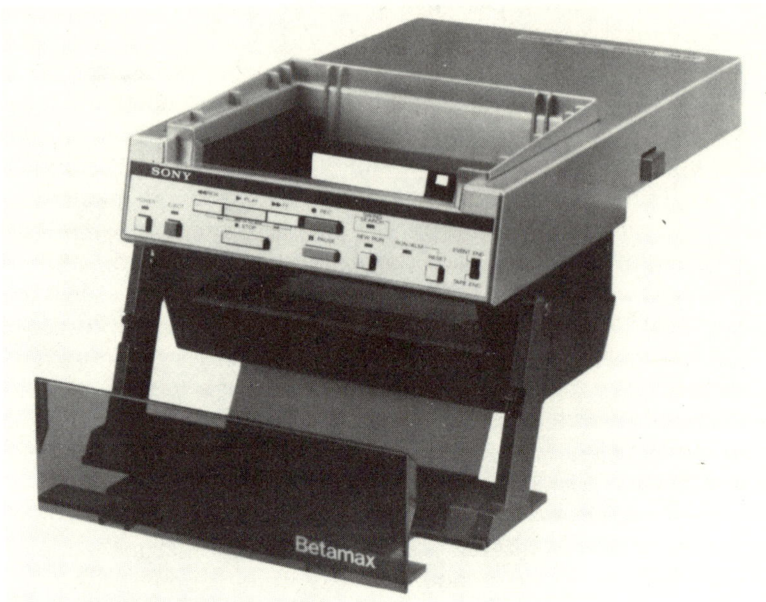

Designed for certain Betamax models, the BetaStack Autochanger will automatically load up to four cassettes providing up to 20 hours of continuous recording or playback. (Courtesy: Sony Corporation)

Autochanger attachment for certain Betamax models allows a series of four cassettes to be played automatically (figure 15).

With the least expensive VHS machines, the video heads are optimized for operation at the SP speed, and selection of the ELP speed involves a significant degradation of image quality. Over the past several years, however, this problem has been addressed by the development of VHS machines with two pairs of video heads, the second pair being specifically designed for high performance at the ELP speed. The quality of ELP recording is greatly improved with these machines. As might be expected, however, these four-head recorders are about 25 percent more expensive than their conventional counterparts.

With both Beta and VHS models, levers or buttons are provided for the selection of the desired recording speed. The machine automatically selects the appropriate playback speed for previously recorded cassettes.

Tape Indexing

The recording of multiple programs or program segments on a given cassette poses problems of retrieval. Videotape is a serially accessed information storage medium that requires the operator to advance past irrelevant portions of a tape to reach the desired segment. The previously mentioned fast-forward and rewind controls facilitate rapid tape movement, but some indexing mechanisms and procedures are necessary to identify the portions of a tape where particular program segments begin. The least expensive videocassette recorders provide a mechanical odometer, which measures elapsed footage from the start of the cassette. At the time a recording is made, the operator notes the odometer readings for particular program segments. These readings are then written or typed on an adhesive label that can be affixed to the front or side of the cassette. At playback time, the operator consults the label, inserts the cassette into the recorder, resets the odometer to zero, and advances the tape to the indicated odometer reading. This method, while it does not provide precise retrieval, should position the tape very near the beginning of the desired program segment.

As an alternative to the mechanical odometer, a small but growing number of videocassette recorders can place codes on tape to identify individual program segments. At retrieval time, these codes are automatically counted to advance the tape to a specified segment. This electronic indexing capability has been a common feature with industrial videocassette recorders for several years. Its recent appearance on consumer models reflects the increasingly sophisticated requirements of VCR users.

Special Effects

Most available Beta and VHS recorders are equipped with a "scan" feature that allows tape to be advanced or reversed at faster than normal speeds while maintaining a viewable image. In this respect, scanning differs from the previously discussed fast-forward and reverse controls, which do not maintain viewable images. Scanning is primarily used to locate particular program segments or to skip quickly over uninteresting portions of a program. The scanning speeds supported by available models range from 2 to 30 times normal, with some models offering several different speeds. It is important to note, however, that the scanning feature may not operate with tapes recorded at all speeds. As an example, some relatively inexpensive VHS recorders do not permit viewable scanning at the SP speed.

Other special effects are selectively offered, their availability varying directly with recorder price. Slow motion—the opposite of scanning—causes video images to be played at a fraction of normal speed. At the time of this writing, the available slow motion range was one-half to one-thirtieth of normal. Slow motion is primarily useful with prerecorded instructional cassettes where the particular steps involved in the performance of some task or activity can be examined in detail. Frame advance and freeze-frame, which permit the individual display of recorded images and the prolonged display of a single frame, are merely variations of slow motion carried to the extreme.

As with fast scanning, it is important to note that these special effects may not operate with tapes recorded at all speeds. With conventional two-head VHS-format machines, noise-free special effects are normally only possible with tapes recorded at the ELP speed. More sophisticated four-head VHS-format machines can typically support special effects with tapes recorded at both the SP and ELP speeds. Beta recorders typically support noise-free special effects in the Beta III mode only, although a few models provide them in the Beta II mode as well. Several Beta recorders incorporate a second pair of video heads just to accommodate the special effects.

Remote Control

Even the least expensive stationary videocassette recorders are equipped with a remote control unit, although it will probably be attached to the VCR by a cord and will include only a small number of playback controls (usually forward scanning, reverse scanning, and pause). More expensive models feature wireless, infrared remote control units that provide controls for most or all recording and playback operations. The most sophisticated units permit remote activation of slow motion, freeze-frame, and other special effects. Such remote control units are especially useful in instructional applications.

Audio Capabilities

In terms of audio output, the typical videocassette recorder is subject to the previously discussed limitations of the television's speaker system, complicated by the fact that VCRs are optimized to record video rather than audio signals. In addition, videotapes are not ideally formulated for audio signals, and typical tape movement speeds are too slow for high fidelity audio recording. While high quality audio cassette recorders move tape at about 1.8 inches per second, VHS tape movement speeds range from 1.31 inches per second in the SP recording mode to just .44 inches per second in the ELP mode. With Beta recorders, tape movement speeds range from .79 inches per second in the Beta II mode to .53 inches per second in the Beta III mode.

But the emerging integration of video and audio programming, previously discussed in chapter 1, has had an impact on the design of videocassette recorders, most notably in the development of VCR equipment capable of stereo output. Stereo videocassette recorders for industrial applications have been available for several years, but they are most often used for the production and playback of bilingual programming. By way of contrast, consumer-oriented stereo VCRs are primarily designed for the playback of prerecorded musical programming and motion pictures with stereo soundtracks. They can also be used for the recording of TV-FM simulcasts. Interest in them has recently been stimulated by the stereo cable broadcast programming discussed in chapter 4 as well as competition from the stereo video disk systems described in chapter 3.

Stereo VCRs do not have an integral amplifier and speakers, but are instead designed for connection to an external stereo system using ordinary phonograph connectors plugged into the VCR's audio output jacks. With an ordinary videocassette recorder, a greater level of sound can be achieved through this type of connection, but the dual-channel effect that is characteristic of stereo recording will be absent. Several video equipment vendors offer stereo synthesizers, however, which provide somewhat enhanced audio output in such configurations.

Consumer-oriented, VHS-format stereo videocassette recorders were first introduced in 1981, and the availability of prerecorded stereo videocassettes has increased steadily since then. Like their audio cassette counterparts, stereo VHS-format videocassette recorders feature noise-reduction circuitry designed to minimize hissing and other sounds. The specific noise-reduction technique employed varies from system to system. Some recorders use the well-known Dolby process in either its B or C variants. Others feature the CX noise reduction process developed by CBS or the Dynamic Noise Reduction (DNR) approach developed for portable stereo audio cassette players. These methods are, at best, only partially compatible with one another, and advertisements and packaging for prerecorded stereo videocassettes do not always indicate the particular noise-reduction methods that were used. As a further point of confusion, some allegedly stereo videocassettes actually feature motion pictures with rechannelled monophonic sound.

It is also important to note that stereo videocassettes require careful handling. With VHS-format cassettes, the entire stereo soundtrack is recorded in just 1mm along the top edge of the videotape where it can easily be damaged by improper threading or a misaligned cassette housing. Actually, the 1mm audio recording portion of a prerecorded, VHS-format stereo videocassette is divided into two tracks of .35mm each, with a .30 separation band between them. Users accustomed to high-fidelity sound will find the resulting audio response disappointing, even when noise-reduction techniques are employed. Some critics contend that nearly comparable results could be achieved with Dolby-enhanced monophonic tapes.

Beta-format stereo recorders have gone through two stages of development. Through 1982, several manufacturers offered stereo recorders utilizing a Dolby-like technique called Beta Noise Reduction (BNR). Like their VHS counterparts, these machines recorded the stereo signal in a narrow band along the top edge of the tape. They were sold in Europe and Japan, but were never available in the United States. In early 1983, however, Sony introduced a new audio recording technique called "Beta Hi-Fi" in which the stereo soundtrack is recorded as part of the video signal, thereby providing much greater audio responsiveness. In fact, the frequency response range, signal-to-noise ratio, and harmonic distortion characteristics of the Beta Hi-Fi process are comparable to or exceed those of high-quality audio cassette and open-reel tape recorders. Most Beta recorder vendors will offer comparable models, and Sony intends to support the Beta Hi-Fi format with prerecorded concerts, motion pictures with stereo soundtracks, and a series of short cassettes, called "Video 45s" containing a few musical selections. Because Beta Hi-Fi cassettes also contain a conventional audio soundtrack, they are compatible with monophonic Beta recorders.

Special Configurations

Several manufacturers offer videocassette recorders that are modified for special applications. As an example, GYPR Products offers a VHS-type recorder for use with a video camera in time-lapse surveillance applications. A number of companies offer videocassette recorders and supporting equipment for interactive educational and industrial applications. As an example, the Sony Programmable Auto Search Control will locate over sixty different program segments within a videotape, while the Sony Video Responder is a computer-based accessory that poses questions, identifies answers as correct or incorrect, and selects subsequent programming based on those responses. Among other vendors, GenTech offers interface cards, cables, and software that permit microcomputer control of a videocassette recorder. These

FIGURE 16

Designed for industrial applications, GenTech's interactive television system combines VCR and microcomputer technology. (Courtesy: Ball Communications)

interactive VCR configurations (figure 16) approximate the capabilities of the video disk players discussed in the next chapter—subject, of course, to the serial approach and other limitations of all tape-oriented systems.

Maintenance

Videocassette recorders should be operated and stored in a reasonably clean environment. When not in use, the machine should be covered to minimize the infiltration of dust and other contaminants. If protected from abuse, a videocassette recorder should operate reliably and require little user maintenance. As previously noted, industrial models are somewhat more ruggedly constructed than their consumer counterparts, although consumer models are often acceptable for business and library installations.

One particular group of VCR components—the video heads and related rollers and capstans—do require periodic cleaning by the user. During recording and playback, videocassettes deposit coating particles and other debris on the video heads, and dust sticks to the heads, rollers, and capstans. A number of vendors offer cleaning kits to remove these contaminants. Some of these kits include a solvent that the user must swab onto the indicated parts after opening the recorder chassis. Alternatively, a cassette containing a special tape or other dry polishing material can be inserted and "played" to remove grit and residue from video heads and other parts without opening the recorder. Because both methods clean by abrasion, they should only be used when necessary. Unfortunately, there is little agreement concerning the recommended cleaning intervals. Some sources suggest cleaning after 20 to 40 hours of use. Others recommend cleaning at 100- to 300-hour intervals. Perhaps the most sensible approach is to clean the video heads when image degradation becomes noticeable.

Regardless of the frequency of cleaning, every recorder's video heads will require eventual replacement. Typically, such replacement should be expected after 1,000 hours of use, although longer head life has been reported. Head replacement must be performed by trained personnel and usually costs several hundred dollars. Most vendors offer maintenance contracts that cover the cost of head replacement as well as other required repairs.

Supplies and Programs

Blank Videocassettes

Broadly described, the videotape used by videocassette recorders consists of a polyester ribbon coated with magnetic iron oxide particles in a binder material. Videotapes are manufactured by many of the same companies that produce magnetic tapes for computer and audio applications. Examples include BASF, Fuji, JVC, Maxell, Memorex, PD Magnetics, RKO, Sony, TDK, and the 3M Company. Regardless of manufacturer, the polyester ribbon, or tape backing, must be durable enough to withstand the stress imposed by tape transport mechanisms. The composition of the magnetizable coating varies—some manufacturers using ferric oxide, others preferring chromium dioxide or beridox particles. Individual brands differ in such characteristics as signal-to-noise ratio (as manifested in the amount of graininess and "snow" in displayed images), dropouts (coating imperfections that result in momentary distortions or streaking), and frequency response (which affects the sharpness and detail of recorded images). Varied results may be experienced with the same brand of videotape used in different recorders, and, regardless of brand, the potential for image distortion is greatest at the beginning and end of a given cassette. Discussions of videotape quality appear periodically in *Video Review*, *Video*, and other consumer-oriented video magazines.

In addition to their conventional product lines, an increasing number of manufacturers offer high-grade cassettes made with finer magnetic particles that are more densely packed and highly polished. The result is an improved image, freer of color distortions, snow, skewing, jitter, and other impairments. The improvement is especially noticeable at the slowest recording speeds (VHS ELP or Beta III). As a further advantage, high-grade tapes are made with an improved binder system that typically reduces particle shedding, with corresponding reductions in video head wear. The somewhat greater cost of high-grade cassettes may consequently be offset by a lengthening of the interval between video head replacements.

Regardless of the type of tape used, the videocassette itself is an injection-molded plastic shell designed for compatibility with VHS or Beta recorders. Cassettes may vary in quality from one manufacturer to another. The more expensive cassettes typically have more rugged, carefully constructed shells that are assembled to close tolerances for improved performance and longer life. It is also possible to purchase "professional" cassettes with very durable, industrial-strength shells. As might be expected, such stronger shells cost 10 to 20 percent more than conventional videocassettes.

Regardless of manufacturer, the available types of VHS-format cassettes are generically labelled with alphanumeric codes that indicate their recording capacities in minutes at the SP speed: T-30, T-60, T-90, T-120, and T-160, although a given manufacturer may not offer all types. T-120 cassettes, the most popular length, permit two hours of recording in the SP mode, four hours of recording in the LP mode, and six hours of recording in the ELP mode. Because two hours is the typical length of televised motion pictures and specials, a single T-120 cassette can store one, two, or three such programs, depending on the recording speed selected. The T-30, T-60, and T-90 tape lengths avoid waste in video camera work or other applications with shorter recording requirements. Generally, however, cassettes containing shorter tapes are significantly more expensive per recording minute than longer ones, since packaging and marketing costs are relatively fixed. Thus, for example, a given manufacturer's T-120 cassette may sell for a nondiscounted price of $25 or 20.8 cents per minute of SP recording, while the same manufacturer's T-30 cassette costs $16 or 53.3 cents per minute. T-160 cassettes, which can record up to eight hours of program material in the ELP mode, are potentially the most economical length, but such cassettes have thinner tape that is not recommended for use in older machines. They are intended for new VHS recorders that feature gentler tape movement mechanisms.

While VHS designations indicate tape recording capacity, Beta cassettes are typically labelled with generic designations —L-125, L-250, L-370, L-500, L-750, and L-830—that indicate their approximate tape length in feet. The actual length is about 3 percent less than the designation. The L-750 cassette, for example, contains 728 feet of tape, while the L-830 contains 807 feet. Both the L-750 and L-830 cassettes use thinner tapes than do the L-500 or shorter cassettes. Thin tapes are more easily scratched and offer less tensile strength, but, as previously discussed, the Beta recorders' tape loading and movement mechanisms are inherently less stressful than those of VHS models.

As previously indicated, an L-830 cassette permits 3.66 hours of recording time in the Beta II mode and 5.5 hours in the Beta III mode. As with VHS cassettes, the longer tape yields the lowest cost per minute of recording time. For example, an L-830 cassette may sell for a nondiscounted price of $24 or 12 cents per minute in the Beta II mode, while an L-250 cassette sells for $12.50 or 20.8 cents per minute of Beta II recording. While variations in pricing and the prevalence of substantial discounts make any generalizations suspect, VHS cassettes are typically less expensive than their Beta counterparts for an equivalent recording capacity at the LP, ELP, Beta II, and Beta III speeds. As previously noted, the Beta I mode—the counterpart of the VHS SP recording speed—is no longer available on new consumer units.

CVC cassettes, the quarter-inch format discussed earlier, are supplied in two lengths offering 30 or 60 minutes of recording capacity. At the time of this writing, the approximate retail price of a 30-minute CVC cassette was $9 or 30 cents per minute.

Unlike VHS and Beta devices, CVC machines do not support multiple recording speeds for variable capacity within a given length of videotape.

Regardless of their recording formats or length, videocassettes should be stored in a controlled environment where the temperature ranges between 65 and 80 degrees Fahrenheit at relative humidities of 40 to 60 percent. Rapid, significant deterioration of recorded information can be expected in storage conditions outside of these ranges. To protect them against dust or other harmful contaminants, videocassettes should be stored in containers. Most consumer-type videocassettes are sold with a cardboard slipcase for this purpose. Professional-type videocassettes are often sold with a plastic storage box, and such boxes can be purchased separately if desired. Tapes should be rewound before storage, and shelved vertically to prevent warping. Vertical storage also minimizes the adverse effects of gravity on tracking signals and prevents downward settling of the tape. The tape storage area should be well removed from loudspeakers and other sources of residual magnetism.

Regardless of the storage conditions provided, videocassettes are inevitably subjected to wear during viewing, and dropouts or other signs of deterioration may become evident after as few as twenty uses. Tape wear is accelerated by the use of fast forward, freeze frame, pause, and other special visual effects.

Videotaping and Copyright

Since their introduction in the mid-1970s, videocassette recorders have permitted the recording of broadcast television signals in two commonly encountered types of applications: (1) where two television programs of interest are broadcast at the same time, one of the programs can be viewed while the other is recorded for later playback, and (2) a program televised at an inconvenient time can be recorded for viewing at the user's convenience. Of particular interest in consumer applications, such "time-shifting" frees the viewer of constraints imposed by the broadcast television schedule and is one of the main reasons for purchasing a VCR.

In late 1976, however, Universal City Studios and Walt Disney Productions brought a copyright infringement suit—the so-called Betamax case—against the Sony Corporation, its advertising agency, a group of California video retailers, and one private individual selected as representative of all VCR owners. The plaintiffs charged that the home taping of copyrighted television broadcasts violates the "fair use" provisions of copyright law and has a potentially detrimental effect on their future earnings from the sale of television reruns. In 1979, the United States District Court ruled in favor of the defendants, holding that the home taping television broadcasts for private, noncommercial viewing constitutes "fair use" within the framework of existing copyright legislation. The court further held that, even if home taping did constitute a copyright infringement, manufacturers, vendors, and users would not be liable for damages. Although Sony and the Beta format were specifically involved, the decision applied to all videotape recorders and formats.

In October 1981, however, the Ninth Circuit U.S. Court of Appeals reversed the 1979 District Court Ruling, holding that the home taping of television broadcasts does violate copyright law. It directed the lower court to develop a method for computing damages and a compensation scheme. Among suggested methodologies were a continuing royalty to be paid to television copyright holders by videocassette recorder manufacturers and a tax on blank videocassettes. Through 1983, the Appeals Court decision had the force of law, although it was only binding within the jurisdiction of the Ninth Circuit (California, Arizona, Oregon, Hawaii, and Kansas) and was not enforced by the arrest or prosecution of any VCR users. In January 1984, the Supreme Court of the United States overturned the Appeals Court decision, ruling that the taping of broadcast signals did not constitute a copyright violation. The decision was applauded by VCR vendors, but widely criticized by television producers and other broadcast industry representatives who must now lobby for congressional modification of existing copyright legislation.

The district, appellate, and supreme court decisions are concerned with home taping only and do not address the taping of broadcast signals by libraries, educational institutions, or other nonprofit organizations. The Copyright Law of 1976 recognizes that off-the-air taping of television programs for nonprofit educational use by teachers in classrooms may be permissible under fair use provisions, which permit the reproduction of copyrighted material for teaching, research, or similar purposes. The law is unclear, however, concerning the limits that should be placed on this practice, and the House of Representatives' copyright committee report (No. 94-1476, sec. 107) suggested the need for more detailed guidelines reflecting the requirements and concerns of the various interested parties. Recognizing the educational significance of much of their programming, public broadcasting stations have generally allowed off-the-air taping for classroom use, although they typically require the destruction of the tapes after a specified period of time. The Public Broadcasting Service, Great Plains National Instructional Television Library, Public Television Library, and the Agency for Instructional Television have issued a joint statement of policy that permits the videotaping of broadcast signals by students, faculty, and staff members of accredited, nonprofit educational institutions. Such videotape recordings must be used solely for classroom instruction or related educational activities and only in the educational institution for which they were made. As a further constraint, all videotape recordings must be destroyed after seven days.

Of potentially great library significance is the use of videocassette recorders to "collect" television programs for research or related educational purposes apart from their use in a specific classroom situation. As examples of possible applications, many libraries—and such library-related institutions as archives, historical societies, and museums—maintain special collections of news photographs and other graphic materials that might be significantly enhanced by the addition of videotapes of major news events and public affairs programs. Similarly, college and school libraries could record and store such programs, making them available for assigned viewing or individual study by students in political science, history, journalism, communications, and other courses. Televised motion pictures, plays, musical presentations, and other programs of cultural significance might likewise be recorded to support instruction in literature, theater arts, cinema studies, and the humanities in general.

In addition to these obvious applications, ordinary television programs and their accompanying advertisements—perhaps more than any other form of information—reflect popular culture and prevalent social values. As such, a thoughtfully assembled collection of videocassettes of popular television series might prove of great interest to sociologists, psychologists, cultural historians, and other researchers, both now and in the future. Prior to the widespread availability of videocassette recorders, such collections could only be assembled by a handful of specialized repositories working in conjunction with television producers—perhaps the best known example being the Vanderbilt University library's collection of videotaped news broadcasts. Given recent developments in video recording technology, however, a video collecting program can now be initiated with a minimal capital investment.

Regardless of their potential educational or research value, commercial television producers have generally opposed the establishment of such videotape collections. In 1973, before the revision of copyright legislation, CBS sued Vanderbilt University for taping and editing news programs for scholarly purposes. That suit, which was withdrawn in 1976, led to a provision in the revised copyright law that permits the taping and lending of a limited number of copies of "audiovisual news programs"—including local, regional, and network newscasts; on-the-spot coverage of news events, interviews concerning news events; presidential addresses; and congressional hearings—by libraries and archives. The provision does not apply to general public affairs programs, documentaries, or magazine-format news programs. Libraries and archives performing such taping must be open to the public or to researchers other than those affiliated with the library itself. The making and lending of such videotape recordings must not result in a direct or indirect commercial advantage. All videotapes produced must carry a copyright notice. This provision is an adjunct to the American Television and Radio Archives Act, which authorizes the Librarian of Congress to record news broadcasts and distribute such recordings to other libraries for use by researchers.

Other than the possible educational uses and news programs discussed above, the recording of television broadcasts for commercial or noncommercial purposes is illegal, although the detection of violations and subsequent enforcement are admittedly difficult. As a technological approach to the problem of unauthorized videotaping, several companies have experimented with anticopy detection circuitry, which could be incorporated in videocassette recorders. Originally developed by the sound recording industry to protect record and tape sales, these devices respond to a code present in broadcast signals that indicates copyright material and disables the machine's recording capabilities. No marketing plans have been announced.

Prerecorded Videocassettes

In 1976, when the copyright infringement proceedings discussed in the preceding section were initiated, there were an estimated 160,000 videocassette recorders in individual homes and, in the absence of any significant number of licensed prerecorded cassettes and reasonably priced video cameras, the taping of broadcast signals represented their sole application. By the fourth quarter of 1981, when the Appeals Court ruled the home taping of television broadcasts illegal, there were an estimated 2.6 million videocassette recorders in individual homes, and sales had increased 87 percent over the previous year. This significant increase in the sale of VCR hardware was accompanied by a rapid expansion of the number and variety of prerecorded VHS and Beta videocassettes available to consumers. Borrowing terminology from the computer field, these prerecorded cassettes are widely described as "software," although they more accurately correspond to the data rather than the programs processed by computers.

Except for program material in the public domain, producers of prerecorded videocassettes are licensed by the copyright holders of the original material (in some cases, the producer is also the copyright holder.) While they can be readily copied by any consumer or institution equipped with two videocassette recorders, such copying is forbidden by copyright legislation, and most prerecorded videocassettes bear a prominent notice of copyright protection accompanied by a warning concerning penalties for infringement. Some videocassette producers have also sought technological defenses, encoding their cassettes in a manner that prevents unauthorized copying but does not interfere with playback. Of particular significance for libraries, educational institutions, and related organizations is a statement appearing on many prerecorded videocassettes indicating that they are intended for "home use only" by individuals, their families, and social acquaintances. Producers of such prerecorded videocassettes maintain that copyright legislation grants the copyright holder the exclusive right to public performance of a work. They further cite congressional interpretations that extend such protection to performances in such "semi-public" places as schools, camps, clubs, prisons, hospitals, and libraries. Organizations wishing to exhibit copyrighted cassettes publically must secure a license from the copyright holder. Questions of public performance aside, an increasing number of libraries have been acquiring prerecorded cassettes for collection development purposes. Like other library materials, these cassettes may either be viewed in the library or circulated for predefined periods of time.

Whether they will be used in homes, schools, offices, libraries, or other locations, prerecorded videocassettes can be divided into two broad groups: those primarily intended for entertainment, and those designed for educational or other nonentertainment purposes. While a comprehensive survey is beyond the scope of this book, the following discussion provides a brief overview of available materials in both categories. A growing number of published catalogs, guides, indexes, and other reference works provide detailed information about individual titles. Useful examples include the *Video Source Book* and *Video Tape/Disc Guide Series* (Syosset, New York: National Video Clearinghouse); *Consumer's Handbook of Video Software* (New York: Van Nostrand); James L. Limbacher, *Feature Films on 8mm, 16mm, and Videotape* (New York: Bowker); *Chicorel Index to Video Tapes and Cassettes* (New York: American Library Publishing Company); *The Home Video Sourcebook* (New York: Collier Books); the *NICEM Index to Educational Videotapes* (Los Angeles: National Information Center for Educational Media); *The Videolog: Programs for Business and Industry* (New York: Esselte Video); *Media Review Digest* (Ann Arbor: Pierian Press); and *The International Index to Multi-Media Information* (Pasadena: Audio Visual Association). Program reviews can be found in such publications as *Booklist* (Chicago: American Library Association); *Library Journal* (New York: Bowker); *Film Library Quarterly* (New York: Film Library Information Council); *Sightlines* (New York: Educational Film Library Association); and *Science Books and Films* (Washington, D.C.: American Association for the Advancement of Science).

Feature films constitute the most numerous category of entertainment-oriented, prerecorded videocassettes. Their consumer appeal is obvious. For the public library system that furnishes films to schools or individual borrowers or for the academic library that supports a film studies program, movies on videocassettes represent a potentially more convenient and economical alternative to conventional film collections. In the typical production procedure, a film negative is converted to a one-inch videotape master from which several working copies are made. These one-inch working copies are converted to half-inch cassettes, using a series of "slave" recorders. Some smaller production companies begin with film prints rather than negatives and produce a three-quarter–inch master and working copies. In either case, the conversion process is performed in "real time"—that is, a two-hour film requires two hours to transfer to cassette. Most production companies use high-quality blank videocassettes, although the specific brand may vary. Generally, a given title will be produced in both the VHS and Beta formats.

The production of prerecorded videocassettes for the home market is a rapidly expanding facet of the entertainment industry. The number and variety of available titles is increasingly broad. Pornographic films, which constituted a very substantial percentage of available titles in the late 1970s, still represent an important and profitable segment of the prerecorded cassette market, but, as videocassette recorders have been acquired by a broader spectrum of users, the ratio of pornographic to nonpornographic titles has declined significantly. Nonpornographic feature films now outnumber pornographic consumer-oriented prerecorded cassettes, and their producers are the video counterpart of book publishers. Chief among them are the video production subsidiaries established by American motion picture and television studios. Examples include Columbia Pictures Home Entertainment, ABC Video Enterprises, MCA Videocassette, MGM/CBS Home Video, Paramount Home Video, Twentieth Century Fox Video, Walt Disney Home Video, and Warner Home Video. Other companies—including Thorn EMI Video, Electronic Video Incorporated, Vestron Video, and Time-Life Video—have acquired production and distribution rights to selected motion picture titles. These producers place considerable emphasis on recent films, with most titles becoming available on videocassette within three to six months of their release as motion pictures. This puts prerecorded videocassettes in competition with the cable television movie channels discussed in chapter 4. The relatively sudden emergence of new video technologies has forced a reexamination of the sequence in which motion pictures have traditionally been distributed to the theatrical aftermarket. For example, several companies have released selected titles on rental-only videocassettes prior to their availability on cable or broadcast television. After several months of testing the market, these rental-only cassettes are recalled, the film is released in theaters or on cable television, and the "rental-only" cassettes reappear later for sale.

In addition to recent titles—that is, those films produced since the late 1970s when prerecorded videocassettes first became widely available—videocassette producers have released a number of older films. The larger companies have tended to emphasize the most popular post-1960 color films; older films with well-known actors of demonstrated general appeal; horror; cult; martial arts; and other films intended for special audiences; and well-known titles by famous directors. Given the recent emphasis in cinema studies on the "auteurist" view that the director is the cinematic counterpart of a book's author, this last group of videocassettes is of special interest to individuals, libraries, and educational institutions seeking to develop collections of films for serious study. Typically, works by American directors are more readily available than those by foreign ones, and surprisingly few foreign language films have been issued on cassette. Foreign films pose the additional problem of translation for English-speaking audiences. Some foreign-language films are released in dubbed versions, while others use subtitles—the latter method being preferred for serious study. To aid the perspective purchaser, some producers indicate the type of translation in advertisements or on the cassette package. In some cases, a choice of versions is offered for a given title. A few prerecorded cassettes are available with closed captions for persons with hearing impairments.

While the major videocassette producers emphasize newer releases and selected older films of proven appeal, several companies specialize in videocassette releases of older films and, in some cases, television programs. Such companies include the Nostalgia Merchant, Reel Images, Video Dimensions, Weiss Global Enterprises, Blackhawk Films, Video Yesteryear, Video Classics, Admit One Video, and Blay Video. Their offerings include silent films, with an emphasis on comedies; classic black-and-white sound films produced from the 1930s through the 1950s; B-movies; musicals; westerns; horror films; movie serials; and cartoons. In an interesting approach to the release of older films, Warner Home Video has introduced its "Night at the Movies" series, which features selected titles from the 1950s, each accompanied by a cartoon, newsreel, and preview of coming attractions as they would have appeared in a motion picture theater at that time.

As a point of interest to librarians, educational institutions, and individual researchers developing videocassette collections to support serious cinema studies rather than mere entertainment, there may be significant differences between the theatrical and video versions of a given film. As noted in chapter 1, the video aspect ratio—that is, the relationship between the height and width of the television screen—differs markedly from that employed for motion pictures. As a result, videocassette producers must scan or edit each scene to select the portions of the film image to appear on tape. While a film's content is rarely altered by such scanning, the director's artistic intentions may be distorted or otherwise affected. This is especially the case with wide-screen films.

Films with running times longer than the two-hour capacity of conventional videocassettes pose additional problems. For the large number of films that run slightly longer than two hours, a cassette with additional tape can be used. But where the running time exceeds 160 minutes, other techniques must be used. From the standpoint of the serious film student, the preferred alternative is to use two cassettes for such longer films, but this approach involves additional production, packaging, and handling expenses, which the producer may be reluctant to undertake. In a much less satisfactory approach, the film itself may be shortened. In some cases, the final credits are abbreviated or omitted entirely. In others, one or more scenes may be removed. A third approach, called "time compression," involves a slight increase in the film's playback speed. While the content remains intact, the pace and overall artistic impact are affected.

While some videocassettes contain edited versions of motion picture films, others may contain additional scenes omitted from theatrical releases. These additional scenes may contain sexual or violent material censored from the theatrical version. Alternatively, they may feature additional substantive content. This is the case, for example, with the multi-cassette program entitled *The Godfather: The Complete Epic* (Paramount, 1981). It is based on a broadcast television program entitled *The Godfather Saga*, which contained footage omitted from the theatrical releases of *The Godfather, Parts 1 and 2*. The cassette version contains additional scenes omitted from the television program, making it a "video original." As a further point of confusion, the two original *Godfather* films are also available on cassette in their theatrical versions.

While motion pictures remain the most numerous category of entertainment-oriented videocassettes, a growing number of titles features music, dance, theatrical presentations, and sports programs. Interest in music programming has increased significantly with the introduction of the stereo videocassette recorders discussed earlier in this chapter. Producers of videocassettes containing classical music have concentrated on opera, ballet, and similar programs where music is enhanced by visual content. Several popular and rock music artists have produced videocassettes that combine music with visual imagery to achieve effects not possible with sound recordings alone. Such cassettes contain video programming similar to that offered by the MTV cable channel discussed in chapter 4.

A relatively new type of entertainment-oriented videocassette—the "video magazine"—is patterned after television programs that treat a variety of subjects in an anthology-like format. Issued at periodic intervals, it may combine interviews, film clips, still visuals, animation, narration, and music to deal with such diverse topics as art, health, sports, sexual relations, and politics. Just as conventional prerecorded cassettes are the video equivalent of printed books, these video magazines are the counterpart of serial publications.

While entertainment-oriented programming is the dominant category of prerecorded videocassettes available to consumers, an increasing number of the educational films produced for schools are also available on videocassettes. These educational cassettes can be divided into two broad groups: documentaries and instructional programs. Documentary cassettes—the video counterpart of nonfiction books—typically deal with historical, biographical, geographical, scientific, or cultural topics. Instructional cassettes—the video counterpart of how-to books—combine sound and moving imagery to demonstrate procedures or convey other information. Typical titles deal with health, physical fitness and sports, home and automobile repair, gardening, cooking, hobbies, and such self-improvement topics as speed reading and personal stress reduction. Instructional cassettes are also available to teach sign language, manual spelling, or other sign systems. Some instructional cassettes are available with closed captioning or signing for hearing-impaired persons.

Prerecorded videocassettes designed for business and professional audiences constitute a special and increasingly popular variant of informational-instructional cassettes. Some of these programs are of general business interest. Others deal with specialized facets of business or professional practice. The latter group includes the growing number of highly technical instructional programs intended for the continuing education of physicians, engineers, computer specialists, and other professionals. General interest cassettes address a broader range of business and related interpersonal concerns. Some of the most popular examples are essentially video versions of best-selling business books or continuing education seminars. They often take the form of lectures or discussions by well-known authors. Common topics include management skills, interpersonal relations, sales training, effective communications, productivity improvement, stress management, improved listening skills, and time management.

Video Cameras

The taping of broadcast signals and the playback of prerecorded cassettes represent two of the three primary applications of videocassette recorders. The third is the production of original programming using a video camera, a market that has recently experienced significant growth in the United States (figure 17). Broadly defined, a video camera is a photosensitive device that converts the light values of a scene into a varying series of electrical signals suitable for recording on videotape and/or display on a video monitor. Available video cameras vary considerably in capabilities and complexity, with corresponding variations in price from several hundred to tens or hundreds of thousands of dollars. In the latter group are video cameras designed for professional production work and which are, consequently, beyond the scope of this discussion.

While the focus of this book is on the use of video systems rather than the production of video media, this section will briefly survey the characteristics of video cameras suitable for consumer, business, library, or other use in such nonprofessional applications as the taping of family and community events, meetings, lectures, workshops, or other special activities. The discussion will be limited to equipment costing less than $1,500. Devices in that price range are primarily marketed as a more convenient alternative to conventional photographic motion picture cameras. When compared to motion picture cameras, however, video cameras offer the substantial advantages of immediately viewable images, integral sound recording, and a reasonably priced, high-capacity recording medium that requires no external development and is reusable.

FIGURE 17

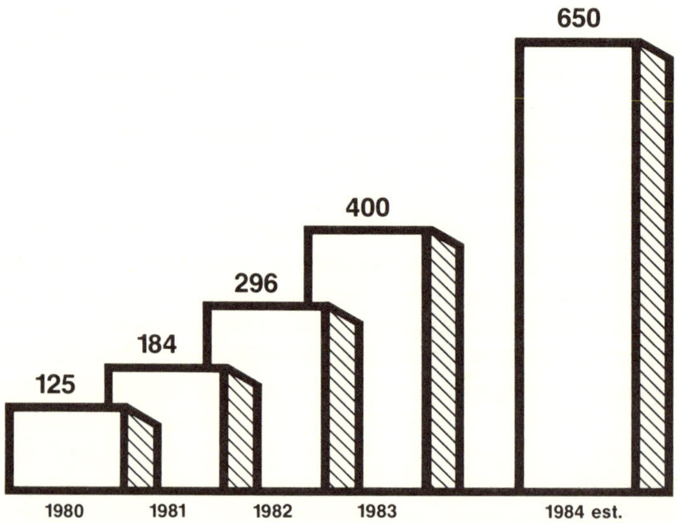

Unit sales to dealers (in thousands) indicate significant recent growth in the U.S. market for video cameras. (Source: Electronics Industries Association and RCA Consumer Electronics)

Within the scope of the broad definition presented above, a video camera consists of six major components: a viewfinder, a lens, an iris, an image pick-up tube, various image adjustment controls, and a microphone. As in conventional photography, the viewfinder is used to monitor the scene being recorded. The least expensive video cameras have a reflex-type optical viewfinder—sometimes termed a "through-the-lens" or TTL viewfinder—which uses an eyepiece and mirrors to permit the viewing of a scene as it appears to the camera's lens. More sophisticated and expensive cameras, including most newer models, feature an electronic viewfinder—a small, typically 1.5-inch diagonal, closed-circuit video monitor that displays the scene as it will be recorded on tape, thereby facilitating decisions about composition, focus, and other image attributes. In some models, this kind of viewfinder can be used in the field as a monitor for playing back what has been recorded. The electronic viewfinder may either be built into the camera chassis or provided as a separate module that can be attached to the top or either side of the camera as desired. While the detachable configuration provides greater flexibility, the integral electronic viewfinder permits a more compact camera design. Regardless of configuration, electronic viewfinders offer better performance than optical ones, but they increase the camera's cost, weight, and power consumption.

Video cameras that are primarily designed for indoor use under conditions of low illumination are typically equipped with an *f*1.4 lens for a wide iris opening. The width of the iris opening determines the amount of light that enters the camera. Video cameras designed for outdoor use or recording in brightly lit rooms are typically equipped with a narrower *f*1.6, *f*1.8, *f*1.9, or *f*2.0 lens. To adjust the iris opening for a given level of illumination, most newer cameras are equipped with both an automatic iris control and a conventional manual iris ring. But, while the size of the iris opening can be reduced, its maximum width is determined by the lens' *f*-setting. It is therefore essential for the camera to be equipped with a lens appropriate to the lowest levels of light expected during the filming. Most camera manufacturers also provide specifications that indicate their minimum illumination requirements in foot-candles. To simplify operation further, most viewfinders include indicator lights that alert the user to conditions of inappropriately low or high illumination.

Many newer video cameras are equipped with zoom lenses, the most common ratios being 3:1 and 6:1. Zoom capability may be manually controlled or power-activated. Some cameras offer a variable-speed power zoom. A potential disadvantage of power zoom is its audible hum, which may be recorded by the camera's microphone. Macro lenses, which permit close-up photography, are likewise common. Some video cameras are equipped with an industry standard C-mount lens assembly that permits the attachment of any C-mount compatible lenses, including those designed for conventional still or movie cameras. A simple adapter may be required for such attachment, however. As a further limitation, C-mount lens assemblies are typically incompatible with power zoom, since motorized lenses are difficult to detach.

The video camera's image pick-up tube is the critical component that converts incoming light to the electrical signals required for recording. While video cameras designed for professional production work feature expensive Image Orthicon or Plumbicon pick-up tubes, most consumer-oriented video cameras utilize a Vidicon tube or one of its several variants. Developed by RCA in the early 1950s, the Vidicon tube is smaller, less complex, and requires lower illumination levels than tubes used in cameras designed for broadcast applications. Vidicon tubes suffer certain limitations, however, the most important being image retention with its accompanying streaking and smearing effects. Several manufacturers have introduced variations of the Vidicon tube, which are claimed to minimize these effects. These Vidicon variants are marketed under such trade names as Saticon, Newvicon, and Trinicon. Sophisticated video cameras are now available with a variety of options (figure 18). In 1982, Hitachi became the first manufacturer to offer a tubeless, solid-state camera which uses a single chip of metal oxide silicon (MOS) as an image sensor. Most other camera manufacturers have since announced one or more tubeless models. The solid-state design offers advantages commonly associated with integrated electronic circuitry, including lighter weight and lower power consumption (figure 19). It also eliminates problems of image retention and offers excellent resolution.

In addition to the iris adjustment controls discussed above, consumer-oriented video cameras have additional controls for the establishment of focus, color temperature, and white balance. As with conventional cameras, focus can be manually adjusted by adjusting a ring until the viewfinder image is sharp. An increasing number of models feature an automatic focus capability that eliminates the need to refocus when using the zoom lens. Depending on the camera, automatic focus may depend on infrared sensing or ultrasonic sound detection. Both methods base focus decisions on the nearest subject and are consequently unsuitable for scenes that contain both near and far subjects.

FIGURE 18

Sophisticated video cameras feature infrared focusing, multispeed zoom lenses, character generators, and hand grip controls which initiate recorder operations. (Courtesy: JVC Company of America)

FIGURE 19

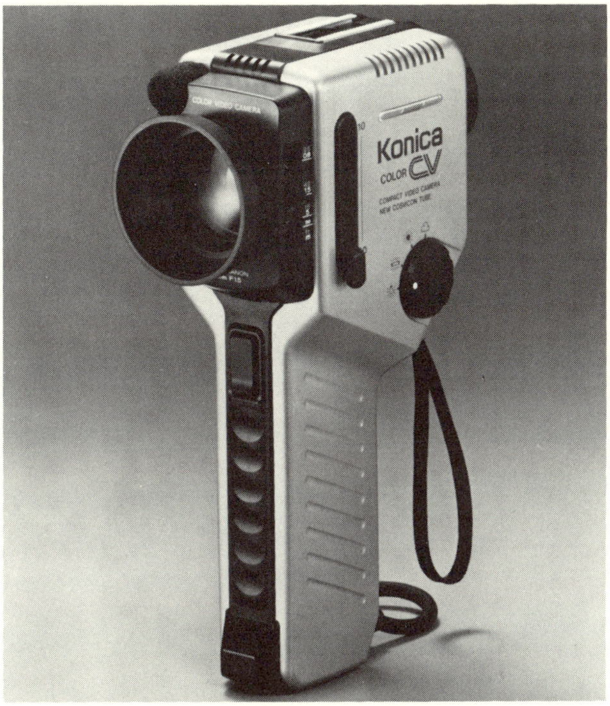

The most compact video cameras weigh less than two pounds and will operate with most VHS or Beta recorders. (Courtesy: Konishiroku Photo)

All cameras need to be adjusted to compensate for differences in the heat given off by different light sources and for the varying percentages of the three primary video colors in light. In most cases, this is simply accomplished by setting a switch or dial to labelled positions corresponding to indoor lighting, outdoor sunlight, or outdoor shade. To further ensure proper color reproduction, the camera is aimed at a white object and adjusted until white is properly dissolved in the viewfinder. Since white is a composite of the primary colors, proper white balance will result in appropriate adjustment of the other colors.

For audio recording, consumer-oriented video cameras may be equipped with either a small condenser microphone mounted in the camera chassis or a telescoping boom-type microphone mounted on the top of the camera. The latter type is preferred because it is further removed from the audible hum generated by the camera's power zoom mechanism. In some cases, the boom microphone is detachable. As an alternative to the camera's integral microphone, an external microphone can be plugged into the videocassette recorder.

To increase the attractiveness and competitive position of their products, vendors of video cameras have incorporated additional special features designed to simplify operation further. Examples include a multifunction remote tape transport control that initiates single frame advance, forward and reverse visual scanning, and other tape movement operations at the camera rather than at the videocassette recorder; a standby switch to conserve battery life; adjustable handgrips and shoulder rests; the ability to switch from positive-appearing to negative-appearing images; automatic fade-out and fade-in controls for professional looking production; and even an internal character generator for the recording of titles on tape.

As with videocassette recorders, cameras sold under a variety of brand names are actually manufactured by a relatively small number of companies. Consequently, the prospective customer will be faced with several groups of essentially similar devices that differ primarily in the placement of operating controls and the availability of special features. With the introduction of its Betamovie System in 1983, Sony became the first manufacturer to offer a camera and recorder integrated in a single unit (figure 20A). With their compact cassettes, 8mm video cameras offer similar capabilities (figure 20B). All conventional cameras, however, are designed for

FIGURE 20

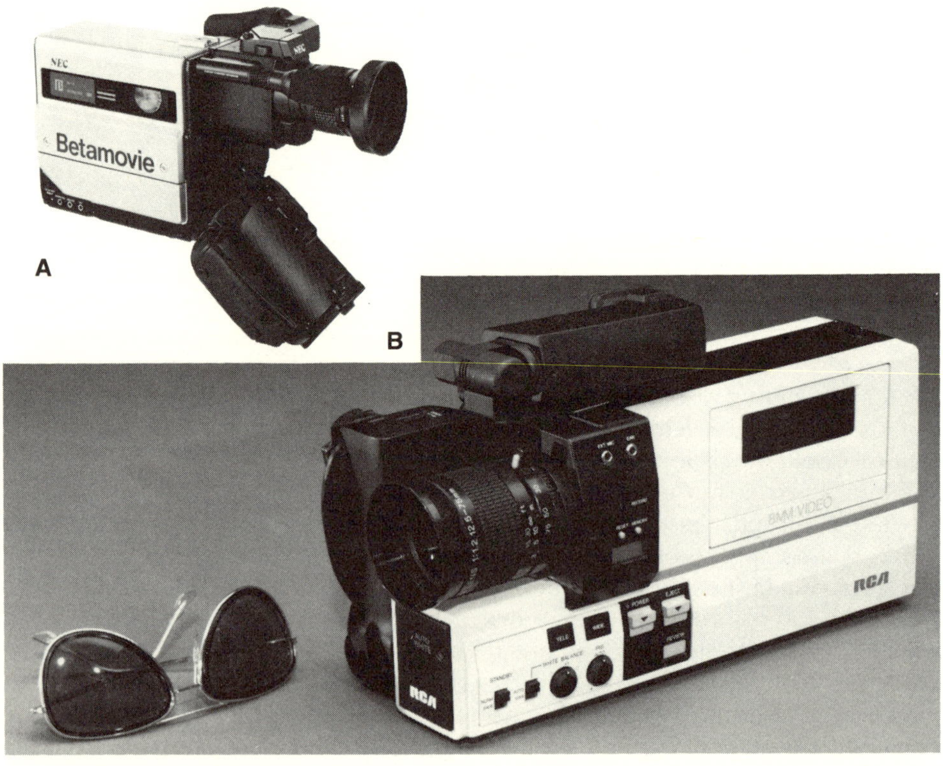

While conventional video cameras require an external VCR, the Betamovie camera (A) features an integral recorder (Courtesy: NEC); (B) 8mm video systems likewise combine camera and recorder in a single, compact unit. (Courtesy: RCA Consumer Electronics)

attachment to the input jack of a separate videocassette recorder that contains the tape supply. For the greatest flexibility, a portable recorder/playback deck is the preferred equipment configuration for camera work, although stationary recorders can be used indoors.

Most videocassette recorder vendors also market one or more compatible video cameras. Problems can arise, however, when the cameras and recorders of different vendors are used together. In some cases, certain features may be disabled or the operation of some controls and indicator lights may be altered. Adapters are available to permit the interconnection of Beta cameras to VHS recorders and VHS cameras to Beta recorders, but, again, some functions may be affected. A demonstration before purchasing video cameras and recorders is strongly advised.

Additional Readings

BUSINESS APPLICATIONS

Budd, J. F. *Corporate Video in Focus: A Management Guide to Private TV.* Englewood Cliffs, New Jersey: Prentice-Hall, 1983.

McDonald, F. Use of videotaping in documenting confessions. *Police Chief* 50: 42–43 (February 1983).

Moffett, K. M. Using videocassette recordings for project documentation. *International Journal of Instructional Media* 10: 285–90 (1983).

Sambul, N. J. *The Handbook of Private Television: A Complete Guide for Video Facilities and Networks Within Corporations, Nonprofit Institutions, and Government Agencies.* New York: McGraw-Hill, 1982.

EDUCATIONAL APPLICATIONS

Copeland, P. CAVIS—From concept to system. *Media Education and Development* 16: 58–73 (June 1983).

Iuppa, N. V. *A Practical Guide to Interactive Video Design.* White Plains, New York: Knowledge Industries Publications, 1983.

Kaplan, D. *Video in the Classroom: A Guide to Creative Television.* White Plains, New York: Knowledge Industries Publications, 1980.

LIBRARY APPLICATIONS

Bahr, A. *Video in Libraries: A Status Report.* White Plains, New York: Knowledge Industries Publications, 1979.

Boyle, D. Documentary video classics—A core collection. *Sightlines* 16: 16–18 (Spring 1983).

Burk, L. C., and Esteves, R., eds. *Video and Cable Guidelines.* Chicago: American Library Association, 1980.

Coleman, J. S. Alternatives in building a video collection. *North Carolina Libraries* 40: 33–36 (Spring 1982).

Ellis-King, D. Video and television viewing facilities in Dublin public libraries. *AV Librarian* 9: 28–29 (Winter 1983).

Gitlin, M. Developing video collections: What are the alternatives? *Film Library Quarterly* 15: 3–11 (1982).

Gothberg, H. M. *Television and video in libraries and schools*. Hamden, Connecticut: Library Professional Publications, 1983.

Harlan, P. Videotapes in libraries: Principles and realities. *New Jersey Libraries* 15: 13–15 (Summer 1982).

Murray, J. B. Oral history/video documentation at the Schomburg center. *Film Library Quarterly* 15: 23–27 (1982).

Pinion, C. F. Video home lending services in public libraries. *AV Librarian* 9: 18–23 (Winter 1983).

Rogers, J. V. *Nonprint Cataloging for Multimedia Collections*. Littleton, Colorado: Libraries Unlimited, 1982.

Schmezer, M. Videocassette and recorder circulates at Morgantown public library. *West Virginia Libraries* 35: 32–33 (Fall 1982).

PRERECORDED VIDEO CASSETTES

A number of catalogs, guides, and reviews were noted in this chapter, p. 50.

Bensinger, C. *The Video Guide*. 3d edition. Indianapolis: Howard W. Sams, 1982.

Hulse, E., and Trost, M. How movies are remade for video: In search of the perfect print. *Video Review* 3: 56–59 (May 1982).

Jacobs, B. Video singles: Could they be the biggest hits in music? *Video Review* 4: 45–48 (January 1983).

Wollman, J. Learning from video: A guide to how-to tapes. *Video* 7: 64–66, 104–6.

VIDEO ACCESSORIES

Jacobs, B. Complete shopper's guide to videophile add-ons: Enhancers and proc amps. *Video Review* 4: 36–39 (November 1983).

VIDEO CAMERAS

Millerson, G. *Video Camera Techniques*. New York: Focal Press, 1983.

Reifsnyder, A. Color cameras. *Video Review* 4: 24–30 (June 1983).

Sato, S., Takeuchi, K., and Yoshida, M. Recording video camera in the Beta format. *IEEE Transactions on Consumer Electronics* 29: 365–75.

Slovick, M. Tubeless—A new image for video cameras. *Video* 7: 74–75, 122–23 (April 1983).

VIDEOCASSETTE EQUIPMENT

Apar, B. *The Home Video Book*. New York: Watson-Guptill, 1982.

Bishop, J. M., and Bishop, N. H. *Making Home Video: An Illustrated Guide to Getting the Most from Your Videocassette Recording Equipment*. New York: Putnam Publishing Group, 1980.

Chesire, D. *The Video Manual*. New York: Van Nostrand Reinhold, 1982.

Duton, M., and Owen, D. *The Complete Home Video Handbook*. New York: Random House, 1982.

Gerson, R. The launch of the 8mm age. *Video Review* 5: 20, 122 (March 1984).

Grosswirth, M. *Home Video*. New York: Doubleday, 1981.

Kybett, H., and Dexnis, P. *Complete Handbook of Home Video Systems*. Reston: Reston Publishing, 1982.

Langman, L. *The Video Encyclopedia*. New York: Garland Publishing, 1983.

Lovece, F. The 8mm metamorphosis. *Video Review* 4: 29–30, 126 (July 1983).

McNitt, J., ed. *The Home Video Sourcebook*. New York: Macmillan, 1982.

Rosen, F. W. *The Home Video Primer*. New York: Focal Press, 1983.

Utz, P. *The Complete Home Video Book*. Englewood Cliffs, New Jersey: Prentice-Hall, 1983.

Utz, P. *Video User's Handbook*. 2d edition. Englewood Cliffs, New Jersey: Prentice-Hall, 1982.

VIDEO RECORDING TECHNOLOGY

Sadashige, K. Overview of longitudinal video recording technology. *SMPTE Journal* 89: 501–4 (1980).

Trundle, E. *Beginner's Guide to Videocassette Recorders*. New York: Focal Press, 1983.

Videotape recording glossary. *SMPTE Journal* 89: 731–34 (October 1980).

Wheeler, J. Long-term storage of videotape. *SMPTE Journal* 92: 650–54 (1983).

Woodcock, R. All about VCR heads. *Video* 4: 50–51, 82 (March 1981).

Woodcock, R. Super 8 versus video: A direct comparison. *Video* 6: 89–90, 111, 113 (September 1982).

Zaludek, J. P. Videotape—Past, present, and future. *SMPTE Journal* 91: 356–60 (1982).

VIDEO SOUND

Feldman, L. Beta hi-fi: Better audio for video. *Audio* 67: 53–56 (May 1983).

Kono, T., et al. Video recording and playback systems—Beta hi-fi VCR. *IEEE Transactions on Consumer Electronics* 29: 141–52 (1983).

Lovece, F. Super sound machines: Beta and VHS hi-fi. *Video Review* 4: 36–40 (March 1983).

VIDEOTAPES

Discussions of blank videotape quality appear periodically in *Video Review*, *Video*, and other consumer-oriented magazines.

VIDEOTAPING AND COPYRIGHT

Miller, J. K. *Applying the New Copyright Law: A Guide for Educators and Librarians*. Chicago: American Library Association, 1979.

Schwartz, T. A. How extensively may you use copyrighted TV programs in the classrooms? *Journalism Education* 38: 13–15+ (Spring 1983).

Sinofsky, E. R. *Off-Air Videotaping: Issues, Decisions, Implications*. New York: Bowker, 1983.

CHAPTER 3

CONSUMER AND INDUSTRIAL VIDEO DISK SYSTEMS

Videotape—whether packaged on reels or in cassettes—is one of two forms of auxiliary storage for video information. Video disks are the other. As the name suggests, a video disk is a platter-type storage medium shaped much like a phonograph record. While specific video disk technology varies from system to system, the information itself is recorded as a sequence of video frames, each composed of the raster of picture elements or pixels described in chapter 1. To view the recorded information, the disk is inserted into a device called a "player" which is, in turn, attached to a television receiver or video monitor.

Unlike cassette recorders, available consumer and industrial video disk players cannot record broadcast or other video signals. They are exclusively designed for the playback of previously recorded disks created by a mastering process. Compared to videocassette systems, video disks offer better image quality and generally more advanced features at lower prices, but videocassette recorders enjoy significantly greater market penetration, which is largely attributable to their recording capabilities. Definitive statistics are unavailable, but, despite growing sales of video disk players (figure 21), VCR installations are thought to outnumber video disk installations by more than 10 to 1. It is possible, however, that future video disk systems will offer recording capabilities that will make videocassette recorders obsolete. At the time this chapter was written, such systems were available on a limited basis. Since 1981, for example, the Panasonic Industrial Company—a division of Matsushita Electric Corporation—has offered devices capable of recording up to 15,000 black-and-white or color video frames on an 8-inch disk, using video cameras. Panasonic disk recording systems conform to the NTSC resolution standards discussed in chapter 1, making them suitable for a wide range of graphic images. As with videotape, disk recording occurs in real time, and a separate processing step is not required. The recording is a series of still frames, but it can be played back as moving images. These video disk recording systems are designed for business, educational, and related applications. As will be discussed in chapter 6, Matsushita and several other companies have also developed high-resolution video disk recording systems for business documents and data. At present, however, video disk and videocassette systems address different requirements, as evidenced by the sizeable percentage of

FIGURE 21

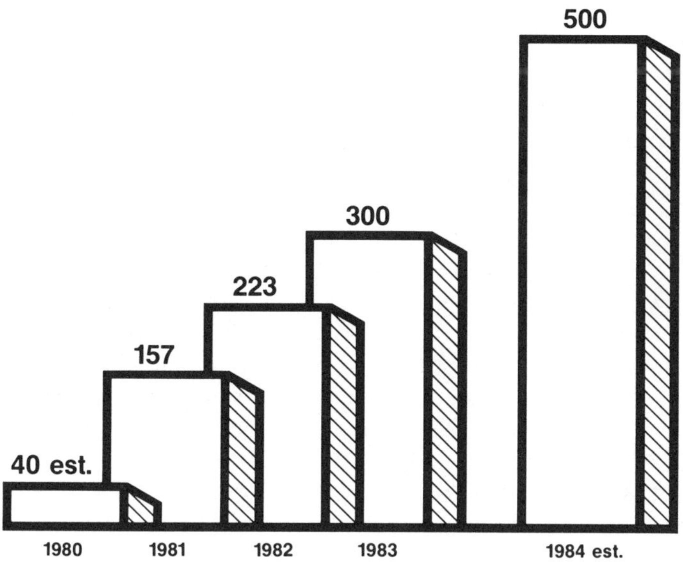

Video disk player sales to dealers (in thousands) indicate growth, but significantly lower sales volume than for VCRs. (Source: Electronics Industries Association and RCA Consumer Electronics)

video disk system owners who also own a videocassette recorder. This chapter emphasizes systems that use prerecorded video disks in various consumer and industrial applications.

While the commercial prominence of video disk systems is recent, the idea of recording video information on a platter-like surface dates from the late 1920s when primitive television signals were recorded on waxed phonograph records. Although these early video disks were actually sold commercially for a brief period of time in the mid-1930s, the first viable application of video disks occurred in 1965 when the Magnetic Video Recording Company developed a video disk system designed to record television signals for instant replay in the broadcasting of sports events. These systems, which remain in use, employ a magnetic disk similar in appearance to computer disks, with the information content of individual video frames recorded in successive tracks. Conforming to prevailing NTSC standards for the frequency of frame changes in broadcast television, the disk spins at 30 revolutions per second and a read/write hand moves across the disk surface at varying speeds to permit normal viewing, slow motion, stop motion, or other visual effects. These broadcast video disk systems offer only a few minutes of recording capacity, and, given their high cost, they stand in the same relationship to consumer-oriented video disk systems as the previously discussed quadraplex videotape recorders do to VHS and Beta videocassette equipment.

In the mid-1970s, the German firm Telefunken and the British company Decca jointly produced a consumer-oriented video disk system based on phonograph technology in which video signals were encoded as bumps in grooves on an 8-inch platter. As with conventional phonograph records, the bumps were read by a stylus. The system, called TelDec, was conceived as a means of providing consumers with inexpensive prerecorded video programming, but it suffered several significant limitations, including unreliability and limited recording capacity per disk. Introduced in West Germany in 1975, it remained on the market through 1980. It was never available in the United States. During the same time period, the Japanese firm Matsushita also developed and subsequently abandoned a video disk system based on phonograph technology.

In the late 1970s, a major breakthrough in video disk technology occurred with the introduction of the optical video disk (OVD), which departed from previously prevalent phonograph-oriented approaches in utilizing lasers to read information recorded as pits beneath the surface of a plastic disk. A consumer-oriented video disk system was introduced by Magnavox, a subsidiary of North American Philips, in 1978. Other vendors followed with consumer and industrial systems. In 1980, RCA introduced a variant approach to the design of a stylus-type video disk system called the "capacitance electronic disk" (CED) system. In 1983, a second stylus-type system—the video high density (VHD) disk—was introduced in Japan by the Japanese Victor Company after several years of considerable advance publicity. These three technologies and their applications are discussed in the following sections of this chapter.

Video Disk Technology

Optical Video Disks

Of the three video disk recording technologies, the optical video disk—sometimes called the LaserVision (LV) or, simply, the laser disk system—is the most popular, is the most sophisticated, and can address the broadest range of consumer, business, and institutional applications. As indicated above, video disks contain encoded video and accompanying audio information. The video disks discussed here are properly termed "analog optical video disks" because the individual picture elements that compose successive television frames are represented by variations in the size and spacing of microscopic pits recorded in spiraling tracks. As will be discussed in chapter 6, digital optical video disks represent information by the presence or absence of uniformly sized pits. They are primarily intended for document storage in business and library applications.

Available analog optical video disks measure 12 inches in diameter and are created by a mastering process in special production facilities. A laser is used to transfer program material from such media as conventional photographic film or videotape to a photosensitive master glass disk. This master disk is then used to create one or more intermediates from which individual plastic copies are stamped. In concept and economics, then, video disk production is essentially a publishing process in which an edition of multiple copies is "printed" at one time. The cost of creating the master—typically, several thousand dollars, exclusive of the often substantial cost of producing the original program material itself—is recovered through the sale or amortization of relatively low-cost duplicates. Several companies have experimented with the photographic replication of optical video disks as an alternative to stamping, but such production techniques were not in commercial use at the time this chapter was written.

As previously noted, the information recorded on optical video disks is read by a specially designed player equipped with a laser that is used to detect the presence and characteristics of the microscopic pits in the disk surface. Two different types of optical video disks are currently available: reflective and transmissive. They offer similar recording capacities and playback capabilities, but differ in the type of disk material used and in their intended applications. The most highly publicized and widely encountered optical video disks are of the reflective type, so called because they feature a reflective layer above the disk's rigid plastic base material. As described above, video signals are encoded as microscopic pits recorded in concentric tracks beneath the disk's surface. Variations in pit size and spacing determine the characteristics of reflected laser light as the disk is played or read. These reflections are detected by the player's optical system and electronic circuitry, which converts them to a video image. For moving images, successive frames are read at a rate of 30 per second, and the resulting signal is transmitted to an attached television receiver or video monitor for display. For still-frame display, a given frame is read repeatedly at that same rate.

Reflective optical video disks also feature a protective coating that renders the recorded information impervious to dirt, grease, fingerprints, and scratches, making the separate protective carrier used with other types of video disks unnecessary. Reflective optical video disks are consequently sold, like long-playing phonograph records, in illustrated cardboard sleeves and can be handled rather casually—an important advantage in business, library, and other institutional applications where disks will be used by relatively untrained persons in a variety of situations. Because reflective optical video disks are read by a laser rather than by a contact stylus, their information content is not eroded or otherwise affected by repeated use. The rigid plastic disks may crack if dropped, however, and they should be stored upright to prevent warping.

Reflective optical video disks may be recorded in either of two formats:

1. In the constant angular velocity (CAV) format, a disk can store the equivalent of 48,000 to 54,000 television frames per side. Each frame is individually and randomly addressable by number, and individual disk segments—called "chapters"—can be encoded for rapid access. The display speed can be varied to achieve slow or fast motion effects. Still frames can also be displayed or intermixed with moving frames within a single disk. The CAV format is indispensible for the interactive video disk applications discussed later in this chapter, but it suffers a significant disadvantage for conventional program material: CAV disks rotate at 1,800 revolutions per minute for a total playing time of 30 minutes per side when the disk contains motion pictures rather than still frames. Since the running time of most feature films is 90 minutes or longer, they will occupy two or more CAV disks. Like a phonograph record album, the disk must be turned over or changed every half hour.

2. The constant linear velocity (CLV) format—sometimes called the "extended play" format—overcomes this inconvenience. It varies the disk's rotational speed from 600 to 1,800 revolutions per minute to provide 60 minutes of playing time per side, thereby allowing most movies to be contained on a single disk. With the CLV format, however, individual frame addressability and such special visual effects as freeze-frame and slow motion are eliminated. Only chapter coding and approximate frame access are permitted. The CLV format is consequently incompatible with interactive program materials.

Regardless of format, reflective optical video disks feature dual audio tracks that permit stereo recording. As with video images, audio signals are recorded optically. Dual audio tracks can prove useful in educational applications involving alternative or bilingual explanations of displayed images. An audio jack in the rear of the video disk player permits the attachment of a stereo sound system. For musical programs, newer players feature CX noise reduction circuitry for use with appropriately encoded disks. The CX feature can be disabled when nonencoded disks are played.

At the time this chapter was written, consumer-oriented players for reflective optical video disks were being manufactured by three companies: Pioneer, Magnavox, and Sylvania. Since the last two companies are both subsidiaries of North American Philips, their equipment is identical. With nondiscounted retail prices ranging from $500 to $800, these consumer-oriented reflective optical video disk players are less expensive than most undiscounted VHS and Beta format videocassette recorders, but widespread discounting of all video equipment makes any meaningful cost comparison difficult. Like videocassette recorders, consumer-oriented reflective optical video disk players are easily attached to a television receiver or video monitor. As previously discussed, the use of a video monitor eliminates the potential for interference inherent in the television receiver's RF modulator. It should be noted, however, that—with a horizontal resolution of 340 lines—the sharpness of images displayed from reflective optical video disks is superior to that obtainable with even the best consumer-oriented videocassette recorders and is comparable to that of broadcast television signals.

Consumer-oriented reflective optical video disk players are attractively styled and easily operated (figure 22). The disk is removed from its jacket and mounted in the manner of a phonograph record. While the earliest players resembled a phonograph turntable, newer models feature a more compact, front-loading design. The player automatically directs the laser to appropriate sections of the disk. While the specific capabilities of available models vary somewhat, the most sophisticated and useful features include random addressability by frame or chapter number, with worst case access times of 20 seconds; fast frame display at several times normal speed, with rapid scanning, in forward or reverse, at speeds up to 120 times normal; slow motion display with speeds reduced to as little as one-thirtieth of normal; and still-frame display with the ability to advance one frame at a time. As previously noted, however, these special features will only operate with properly encoded CAV format disks. While most models have operating controls mounted on the player's top or front panel, full-featured remote control units are indispensible for interactive programs that use special visual effects.

While consumer-oriented players can be used for educational and business applications, they are primarily designed for home installations. Reflective optical video disk players specifically designed for industrial applications are manufactured by Pioneer and Sony. These industrial models are several times more expensive than their consumer counterparts and offer faster frame access times and more rapid

FIGURE 22

An optical video disk player with front-loading design and wireless remote controller. (Courtesy: Pioneer)

scanning capabilities. They are also microprocessor-controlled, have internal random-access memories, and can be programmed to perform various frame searching, stopping, and branching operations. During the video disk production cycle, a control program is recorded on the second audio track of the disk, from which it can be loaded into the player's internal memory. Most industrial optical video disk players include a standard interface for attachment to an external computer. Some newer consumer models are also equipped with such an interface, but, at the time of this writing, no prerecorded consumer disks supported computer interaction. Several companies offer alternative interfaces that link an industrial or consumer-oriented player to one of the most commonly encountered brands of personal computer. When so interfaced, a computer program—stored on a floppy disk or other medium—can initiate frame access, vary the display speed, and control other player operations. While it requires additional equipment and special software, this approach is somewhat more flexible than the recording of programs on the video disk itself, since computer-stored programs can be modified to accommodate changes in application requirements. A combined computer/player configuration can also permit the alternating display of information from either the video disk or the computer's memory.

While they receive much less publicity, transmissive optical video disks—developed by Thomson-CSF—share many of the characteristics of reflective optical video disks. They are recorded and read by lasers, are produced by a mastering process, can contain up to 50,000 frames of video information per side, can be searched randomly by chapter or frame, and will display both still frames and continuous motion sequences. But transmissive optical video disks differ from their reflective counterparts in several important respects. They are flexible rather than rigid, and, as such, they can be rolled for easy storage or mailing. Conceivably, they might even be bound into a book, journal, or other publication. Because they are read by transmitted rather than reflected light, both sides of the disk can be accessed without turning the disk over. A microprocessor-controlled player provides 3-second access to individual frames and can interface with a computer. Although several interesting industrial applications have been implemented and remain in operation, Thomson-CSF ceased production and active marketing of transmissive optical video disks and related equipment in 1983. At the time of this writing, its future was uncertain.

Capacitance Electronic Disks

Whether transmissive or reflective, the information recorded on optical video disks is read by lasers rather than by contact. Capacitance electronic disk (CED) systems, by way of contrast, utilize a variant of the familiar stylus-and-groove technology associated with phonograph records as well as the early video disk system discussed in this chapter. With CED disks, video and accompanying audio information is encoded by variations in closely packed, narrow, V-shaped grooves cut into the surface of an electrically conductive plastic disk. Like optical disks, CED disks measure 12 inches in diameter and must be created by a mastering process in special production facilities. Individual copies of a given disk are stamped from a master in the manner of phonograph records. CED systems that use direct recording have been demonstrated in prototype, but are not commercially available.

CED players feature a diamond stylus that, like the needle of a phonograph, rides the grooves of the plastic disk. The stylus and disk together serve as two parallel plates of a capacitor that senses variations in the disk's electrical properties. These variations are interpreted as video and audio signals. Because they are read by contact, CED disks are subject to wear through repeated use. While the exact useful life of a CED disk is uncertain, it has been suggested that disk replacement will be required after several hundred viewings. Although it is automatically cleaned after each use, the CED player's stylus is also vulnerable to wear and tear and will require replacement after several thousand hours.

CED disks are likewise vulnerable to fingerprints, grease, scratches, dirt, and other contaminants. As a result, they are sold in an illustrated protective jacket called a "caddy." To eliminate handling of the disk, the caddy is inserted into a loading slot in the front of the CED player, and the disk is automatically extracted from it. The caddy is then removed and must be reinserted when the disk is to be turned over or removed from the player.

CED technology was developed by RCA, which introduced the first player—under the Selectavision trade name—in early 1981 (figure 23). Since that time, CED players have been introduced by such companies as Hitachi, Toshiba, and Sears. Zenith, Elmo, Montgomery Ward, Sanyo, and Radio Shack discontinued their CED product lines in 1983. Regardless of the player's manufacturer, CED disks rotate at 450 revolutions per minute and feature four television frames per track. They are recorded in one format that provides for 60 minutes of continuous playing time on each of two sides. Unlike optical video disk systems, which can support sophisticated

FIGURE 23

An interactive CED player with disk caddy and remote controller which supports random frame access, high-speed scanning, and other functions. (Courtesy: RCA Consumer Electronics)

interactive applications requiring high-speed random access to specified frames, CED disks are primarily intended for the storage of motion pictures and other "linear" programs. The most widely sold and least expensive CED players do not offer freeze-frame, individual frame access, slow motion, and the other complex visual effects and search capabilities associated with optical video disk systems and the most sophisticated videocassette recorders. Several more expensive models offer high-speed forward and reverse scanning, plus stereo output with CX noise reduction circuitry.

In mid-1983, RCA introduced the first CED player capable of displaying still frames and of accessing individual program segments or chapters within a disk, but these special features are primarily intended for the more convenient playback of musical programs and similar consumer-oriented disks. In addition, CED disks must be specially prepared for freeze-frame display and chapter access. Since distortion-free freeze-frame display requires that the four frames accessed in a single disk revolution be identical, the disk's capacity will be reduced to 27,000 frames. Although several interesting educational programs have been developed, there is no indication that CED systems will be aimed at the broad spectrum of interactive applications currently being addressed by optical video disk systems. As a further constraint, typical CED resolution of 240 horizontal lines per television frame is equivalent to that of the best videocassette recorders, but cannot compare with the 340 lines offered by optical video disk systems. When the same programs are available in the two formats, optical video disks offer consistently sharper images than do their CED counterparts.

Although CED systems may be technologically inferior, a combination of superior marketing, low prices, and a better selection of prerecorded disks has given them a competitive advantage over optical video disk systems in consumer applications. Discounted prices for the simplest CED players begin at less than $200, and prerecorded disks are priced about 25 percent lower than their optical video disk counterparts. Unfortunately, however, CED systems have not proven profitable for its developer, and, in early 1984, RCA announced its intention to discontinue manufacturing and support for CED disks and players sometime after 1987. CED disks and equipment will remain available for sale for the next several years.

Video High Density Disks

Developed by the Japanese Victor Company (JVC), video high density (VHD) disk systems are often described as a kind of compromise between the technological sophistication of optical video disks and the simplicity and economy of CED technology. Like optical video disks, VHD disks are grooveless with video and accompanying audio information encoded as microscopic pits in spiraling tracks, but, as with CED systems, the encoded information is read by a stylus that detects electronic capacitance variations in the disk's pitted surface. To minimize pressure on the disk surface, the stylus' contact area is broader than that encountered in CED systems. Disk and stylus life are still limited, however, although estimates have not been publicized. Like CED disks, VHD disks are supplied in a plastic caddy that is similar to a record album cover. It is designed to protect the disk against fingerprints, scratches, and contaminants. The caddy is inserted into the VHD player and the disk is automatically extracted. The disk itself is never handled.

As with the two competing systems, VHD disks are created by a mastering and stamping process in special production facilities. They are slightly smaller than their optical and CED counterparts, measuring 10 inches in diameter. The claimed advantages of the smaller disk size include a potential reduction in the dimensions of the VHD player and some savings in the cost of petroleum-based disk materials. VHD disks rotate 900 times per minute, and each track contains two television frames of information for a total continuous playing time of 60 minutes per side. Both sides are typically used for recording.

Unlike other video disk systems that feature a one-piece player, the typical VHD equipment configuration consists of two interconnected components: the player itself and an optional random access unit. For applications involving motion pictures or other continuous programming, only the player is required. While the characteristics of specific models may vary, the typical VHD player includes the same kind of operating controls found on videocassette recorders, with such special features as rapid visual scanning and slow motion in both forward and reverse. Still-frame display is provided by replaying a given track repeatedly. But, since two frames are recorded per track, a still-frame display may flicker slightly.

As with optical video disk systems, the random access unit makes VHD technology suitable for interactive applications. It can locate and display specific numbered chapters and frames. It can also locate frames by elapsed time. But unlike optical video disks, which forfeit special visual effects in the long-playing CLV recording format, VHD disks offer special effects with 60 minutes of recording capacity per side.

Demonstration copies of VHD disks have offered excellent image quality, and the player is easily attached to a television receiver or video monitor. The random-access unit, which is an optional accessory, attaches to the player. VHD disks have dual audio tracks for stereo or bilingual programming. Audio output jacks permit the attachment of stereo speakers. As an alternative to conventional phonograph records, there has even been some discussion of applying VHD recording technology to the production of audio-only stereo disks. JVC has demonstrated such an audio high density (AHD) disk system, but—like Matsushita, Sharp, Kenwood, Aiwa, and other Japanese manufacturers of audio products—is currently supporting the compact digital audio disk format developed by Sony and Philips.

While it offers a number of attractive features, marketing plans for the VHD disk remain uncertain. Since 1981, VHD players have been exhibited at various consumer electronics shows. Demonstration models have been completely and attractively styled, closely resembling audio components. In addition to JVC, VHD disk players are expected to be sold in the United States under such familiar brand names as Panasonic, Quasar, and General Electric. European marketing rights are held by Thorn EMI. The planned commercial introduction, originally scheduled for late 1982, has been repeatedly delayed, however, and JVC closed its American VHD programming and equipment operations in early 1983. VHD systems became commercially available in Japan at about that time, and are reportedly selling well. American marketing plans remain uncertain and some industry analysts question whether a disappointingly small video disk market can support a third incompatible format.

Consumer Programming

Linear Disks

Compared to the videocassette recorders discussed in chapter 2, video disk systems typically offer lower cost equipment, better image quality, and, in the case of optical video disks and VHD systems, a broader range of image retrieval and display capabilities. But, as previously noted, available video disk players cannot record broadcast or other video signals. They are limited to the playback of prerecorded disks, which are factory-produced. Thus, regardless of the sophistication and attractiveness of any particular video disk technology, the ultimate success of a given video disk system in consumer applications depends entirely on the availability and characteristics of prerecorded programming. In business and educational applications, by way of contrast, programming is typically custom-developed to meet specific informational or training requirements. Such applications will be discussed later in this chapter.

Despite the many interesting and innovative capabilities of video disk hardware, initial consumer acceptance was significantly impeded by problems of quality and availability associated with prerecorded program materials. A substantial percentage of the earliest optical video disks were defective, the most common complaints being the erratic skipping of frames and the undesired replaying of frame sequences. The recent upgrading of quality control procedures and the use of "clean room" environments have reduced the percentage of factory defects, although optical video disk purchasers continue to report problems with static resulting from dust trapped beneath the protective plastic layer during the manufacturing process. Crosstalk—a second, widely reported problem—results when the player's laser assembly reads two adjacent tracks at the same time. The most common causes are warped disks and improperly adjusted players. CED disk users have reported problems with interference and frame skipping, the latter being caused by dust that causes the player's stylus to skim over the grooves.

Problems of disk availability have been variously attributed to improper geographical distribution patterns and limited factory production capacity. Distribution problems are of greater concern to individual consumers, who want to be able to browse a large disk selection at a local video store, than to libraries, businesses, or other organizations that will purchase disks directly from their producers or from other mail-order sources. Limited video disk production capacity affects both consumers and institutional purchasers. The number of video disk manufacturing plants producing consumer-oriented programs is surprisingly small. In the late 1970s, when optical video disks were first introduced in the United States, they were manufactured by MCA Videodisc and, subsequently, by DiscoVision Associates (DVA), a joint venture of MCA and IBM. In 1982, DiscoVision Associates discontinued operation, and its video disk manufacturing activities were assumed by Pioneer at its Japanese factory in Kofu. But because the Japanese facility will not master R-rated feature films, Pioneer has refurbished DVA's manufacturing facility in California. The 3M Company also operates an optical video disk manufacturing plant in Wisconsin. At the time this chapter was written, CED disks were being manufactured at an RCA facility in Indianapolis and at a CBS factory in Carrollton, Georgia.

For consumer applications, prerecorded video disks can be divided into two broad groups: linear and nonlinear. With conventional linear programs, individual frames are viewed continuously, in the order in which they are recorded on the disk. With nonlinear or interactive programs, the user's interests or information requirements determine the order in which the frames will be viewed. All but a few CED disks and the majority of optical video disks contain linear programs consisting of material derived from another medium—typically, motion picture films. These straightforward programs fulfill the original concept of video disk technology—the production of relatively inexpensive prerecorded video entertainment as an alternative to conventional broadcast television. As with prerecorded videocassettes, most major studios and many independent production companies are releasing films in the optical video disk and/or the CED disk formats. But, while new disks are appearing regularly, the number of available titles remains significantly smaller than the selection available on videocassette. Although many newer titles are being simultaneously issued on both video disk and videocassette, a constantly growing backlist of more than 6,000 consumer-oriented titles is available on Beta and VHS videocassettes. In late 1983, the CED prerecorded disk catalog listed less than 800 available titles. About half as many titles were available on optical video disks. Unlike videocassettes, where almost every title is issued in both the Beta and VHS formats, many video disk programs are available in one format only.

As might be expected with a "publishing-type" medium where the cost of producing a master must be recovered through the sale of a minimum number of copies, catalogs of available optical and CED video disk titles emphasize feature films of broad appeal, supplemented by occasional classic films likely to attract a wide audience. Esoteric titles are notably absent, and few foreign language films are available, even though dual channel audio capability might be effectively used to contain the original language and a dubbed English sound track. Consumers, libraries, and other organizations interested in developing a collection to support serious film studies will generally be better served by the available selection of prerecorded videocassettes, although prerecorded video disks offer the advantage of lower prices. Most video disk titles retail for $25 to $40 each, with CED disks being about 20 percent less expensive than optical video disks. By way of contrast, retail prices for most prerecorded videocassettes begin at around $60, with prices for some titles approaching $100. In an effort to encourage consumer sales and compete with the rapidly growing videocassette rental business, several producers have recently reduced videocassette prices to as low as $30 for a small number of selected titles, thus making them competitive with video disks. Although such lower prices are expected to become more common, most videocassettes remain expensive. The fact that disks are manufactured while videocassettes must be individually copied gives the disk format an enduring cost advantage.

Given the stereo capabilities of both optical and CED systems, it is not surprising that classical and popular musical programs constitute a much publicized and rapidly growing type of consumer-oriented video disks. While they are essentially designed for linear viewing, preprogrammed chapter stops, comparable to the individual bands of a phonograph record album, permit the convenient location of desired musical selections. For musical concerts, stereo optical video disks offer clarity and separation that compares favorably with the best conventional audio recordings. As previously noted, CX encoding is used for noise reduction. Video images greatly enhance the presentation of opera, ballet, and musical theater, making such video disks a potentially interesting addition to consumer and library record collections. As with the music-oriented videocassettes discussed in chapter 2, some video disks that contain popular music are "concept albums" that present a visual elaboration of material that is also available in audio-only form on conventional record albums. As noted in chapter 1, a small but growing number of musical performers have demonstrated an interest in the unique artistic possibilities of such combined audio-video presentations. Others see its future commercial potential, but since the number of consumers who currently own video disk systems is relatively small—and because their demographics differ significantly from those of traditional record buyers—music programs available on video disks must also be released through other video outlets, including cable and broadcast television, in order to recover production costs.

While most manufacturers of consumer-oriented video disks have emphasized entertainment rather than instructional materials, several available titles demonstrate the educational potential of video disk programming for the home market. Utilizing the high image quality of optical video disks, MCA Videodisc offers the *National Gallery: Art Awareness Collection* and a two-program disk entitled *The Louvre/Tut, the Boy King*, which combine still and moving video images with narration and music to display and discuss important works of painting and sculpture. While the images of paintings resemble those readily available in printed art books, the display of sculpture demonstrates the potential advantages of video images over conventional still photography, since the camera can move around a three-dimensional object to show it in close-up and long view from various angles.

Vincent Van Gogh: A Portrait in Two Parts, produced in the optical video disk format by Philips, combines visual images with a soundtrack to present biographical information and critical commentary. Individual paintings can be viewed alone or with a date and title overlay. If desired, the narration can be replaced by a simple musical soundtrack.

Other examples of consumer-oriented video disks that contain material of broad educational significance include documentary films, nature study programs, current events programs, cooking courses, and physical education and sports instruction programs. In some cases, these video disk programs are based on popular books, but go beyond conventional print media in the use of moving images and sound to convey information more effectively. Examples include *The French Chef* disk, which stars Julia Child; Jane Fonda's *Workout* disk; and *Quick Dog Training with Barbara Woodhouse*, all of which are available in the CED format. Others, such as the various Jacques Costeau and Jane Goodall disks offered by MCA Videodisc, are derived from popular television programs.

Nonlinear Programs

The consumer-oriented video disks discussed to this point are primarily designed for conventional linear viewing. Even if the program material itself did not encourage the consecutive display of recorded frames, CED players suitable for direct frame access were not available prior to mid-1983, and models introduced since that time offer only rudimentary frame access capabilities. In addition, CED disks must be specially coded for the special effects that are an indispensible component in nonlinear programming. Optical video disk systems, by way of contrast, are much better suited to nonlinear programming in which the user controls the sequence in which frames will be displayed, but most of the available consumer-oriented optical video disks are recorded in the CLV format. Nonlinear programming relies heavily on freeze-frame, slow motion, random frame access, and other special visual effects and search capabilities that can only operate with optical video disks recorded in the CAV format. At the time this chapter was written, CAV disks accounted for less than 20 percent of available consumer-oriented optical video disks, and some of the best known examples date from the late 1970s when video disk system vendors emphasized their nonlinear capabilities as a means of demonstrating the technological sophistication and potential of their new product.

Produced by Optical Programming Associates, *How to Watch Pro Football* was one of the first consumer-oriented programs to make extensive use of visual effects, programmed repetition, and dual sound tracks to explain professional football strategy through the close analysis of individual plays from both the offensive and defensive standpoints. Of special interest to parents, educators, and children's librarians is the much publicized *First National Kidisc*, developed by the B. Green Company for Optical Programming Associates. It consists of 26 individual program modules designed primarily for preteenage children. The modules are intended for encyclopedic rather than linear viewing, as specific program modules can be randomly accessed to suit the child's interest. They utilize the various special features of CAV disks and consumer-oriented players, combining forward and reverse motion, slow motion, still frame, single frame advance, preprogrammed chapter stops, and dual channel audio. A segment entitled "101 Jokes and Riddles," for example, uses a series of still frames to present riddles and answers. A segment dealing with zoo animals can be viewed in the single-frame, forward-advance mode as a slide show with multiple views of some 40 animals, each preceded by an identification frame. Alternatively, the child can attempt to guess the identity of individual animals by viewing the sequence of frames in reverse order. Dual channel audio is used in segments providing dance instruction and a demonstration of pig latin. A segment entitled "Athletes in Motion" allows the child to study body movements through freeze-frame and slow motion controls. The combination of motion sequences with still frames greatly extends the disk's total playing time. Viewed in continuous motion, a sequence of 540 frames would be displayed in just 9 seconds, but, in the still-frame mode, they might provide half an hour of viewing time.

In early 1983, after several years in which producers of optical video disks concentrated on movies and musical concerts recorded in the CLV format, the number of newly released CAV-format nonlinear disks began to increase slightly, but noticeably. Among available titles, the *Fun and Games* disks, produced by Optical Programming Associates, followed the *First National Kidisc* in presenting program modules dealing with puppet making, tongue twisters, silly songs, hand shadows, and similar activities for children ages 6 through 12. For adults, the *Creative Camera* disk, produced by Pioneer, clearly demonstrates the instructional potential of consumer-oriented, nonlinear video disk programming. Designed as an introduction to single-lens reflex photographic equipment and techniques, it utilizes chapter coding for individual topics. For each program segment, a dual soundtrack offers a choice of basic or more detailed explanation of visual images. Freeze-frame, slow motion, and other special effects are effectively used to reinforce specific points. Similarly, the *Gardening at Home* disk, produced by Xerox, combines moving images, still frames, and textual display in program segments dealing with various aspects of horticulture. Using dual channel audio, the viewer can alternate between basic and highly technical explanations of displayed images. The *History Disquiz*, produced by Arnold Shapiro for King Features Entertainment, utilizes old newsreels as the basis for questions dealing with twentieth century political and social history. Perhaps the most popular of these nonlinear disks—the *Mystery Disc: Murder, Anyone?* program produced by Vidmax—bridges the gap between optical video disk systems and video games as the viewer competes with an on-screen detective to solve a crime based on 16 different scenarios. It is the first in a projected series of game disks in which the program's narrative flow is controlled by the viewer's decisions. Also in 1983, several companies introduced arcade games that utilize optical video disks to provide more spectacular visual effects than are possible with conventional approaches to game design. Some industry analysts view such game programs as critical to the success of video disk systems in consumer applications.

As previously discussed, newer CED players offer special effects suitable for nonlinear programming. At the time of this writing, nonlinear CED disks were just entering the market. Among the earliest available programs, CBS has developed science-oriented instructional disks in the CED format, and RCA has produced several game disks.

Industrial Applications

Interactive Learning Systems

Although video disk systems were originally developed for home applications, initial sales proved disappointing. Consumer response has improved steadily since 1982, but it hardly matches the expectations of the systems' developers. As noted in the introduction to this chapter, disappointing sales may be attributable to a consumer preference for machines that can record broadcast signals rather than merely replay a limited number of available prerecorded programs. Remembering the defunct videocassette formats discussed in the preceding chapter, consumers may also be rightfully wary about the possible obsolescence of a given system resulting from competition among incompatible video disk formats in a limited market. But, even if video disk systems fail completely in the consumer market, many industry analysts believe that they will play an important role in industrial applications. As used in this context, the term "industrial" is not limited to business enterprises, but denotes the broad spectrum of educational and informational applications encountered in corporations, government agencies, schools, libraries, museums, hospitals, and other organizations. As will be discussed in chapter 6, a special group of "industrial" video disk systems are being developed for document and data recording in business, library, and similar applications. This chapter is concerned with systems for the storage of conventional video images.

Because of its elaborate display capabilities, suitability for interactive programming, and ability to interface with external computers, the optical video disk—in either its reflective or transmissive variant—is presently the format of choice for industrial applications. The CED format, as previously discussed, offers only rudimentary interactive capabilities, and is primarily designed for consumer applications involving conventional linear programs, although the low cost of CED players and disks is a potentially attractive feature in educational applications. The VHD format offers random frame access, special visual effects, and other capabilities that are potentially suitable for industrial applications, but VHD systems are not yet commercially available in the United States.

The simplest industrial applications of video disks involve their substitution for conventional motion pictures, videotapes, film strips, or similar audio-visual media in a variety of educational situations. Several elementary and secondary school teachers have reported the successful use of commercially available optical and CED video disks and players as the focal point for discussion in humanities, science, social science, and home economics classes. Many of the consumer-oriented titles described in the preceding section are suitable for this purpose, as are feature films that treat themes discussed in literature and history classes. As with videocassettes, video disk versions of motion pictures can also be used to support cinema studies curricula at the college level—subject, of course, to the limited selection of available titles previously noted.

Although off-the-shelf video disks and consumer players can be used in teaching situations, the most sophisticated educational applications utilize the more rugged and versatile industrial players to display custom-developed programs that realize the full interactive potential of optical video disks. Rather than playing recorded images in linear fashion, these custom-developed, interactive video disks use input processing and branching techniques to display appropriate program segments in response to commands or answers entered at an attached keypad or similar device. In a testing application, for example, specific video segments may be repeated if the user's answers indicate that particular material was not mastered. Alternatively, correct answers may lead to the display of more detailed and difficult material.

As described earlier in this chapter, some industrial optical video disk players are equipped with integral microprocessors and small random-access memories that can be used to load and execute simple computer programs recorded on the video disks themselves. These players are sometimes described as "Level 2" machines to distinguish them from straightforward "Level 1" players that support freeze-frame and other special effects, but cannot perform the answer processing and branching operations characteristic of the best interactive training systems. More sophisticated "Level 3" video disk players are equipped with an industry standard RS-232C electronic interface, which permits control by an external computer. As previously noted, some consumer-oriented players now feature such an interface. Level 3 players can operate as a component in a computer-assisted instruction system where video disks are used to store and display complex, highly animated, color imagery, accompanied by dual channel sound. The video disk program segments support narrative materials, questions, and other textual information stored by the attached computer system. Commands and responses entered at the keyboard of a computer terminal can activate the display of particular video disk program segments. Alternatively, displayed menus of program options can be used in combination with joystick selection mechanisms, light pens, or touch sensitive screens.

While this field of information processing is still in its developing stages, several organizations have produced some interesting educational programs, and new projects are being initiated at a rapid rate (figure 24). The World Institute for Computer-Assisted Teaching, now known as WICAT Incorporated, produced the first interactive educational video disk program—*The Development of Living Things*—in early 1978 from a series of biology films originally produced by McGraw-Hill. WICAT has subsequently developed interactive video disk programs in fields as diverse as medicine and military artillery training. For maximum flexibility and effectiveness, many WICAT programs utilize video disk players linked to microcomputers. These programs make extensive use of special visual effects, branching, and the automatic repetition of specific program segments. They offer advantages commonly associated with computer-assisted instruction: self-paced learning, immediate feedback, and minimal supervision. In a study prepared for the National Science Foundation, WICAT found that video disk training systems offer a significant advantage over conventional lecture/textbook methodologies, providing a firmer grasp of subject content with less student effort. Field tests of video disk programs prepared by Simon Fraser University for elementary school biology instruction likewise indicated a very favorable student response.

The substantial advantages of self-paced learning with minimal supervision make interactive video disks a good medium for continuing education programs intended for physicians and other busy professionals. As a dramatic example of the educational potential of video disk technology, the American Heart Association has developed a sophisticated, highly interactive video disk program designed to provide uniform instruction in cardiopulmonary resuscitation (CPR) techniques. The

FIGURE 24

For educational applications, interactive video disks are typically accompanied by printed manuals and microcomputer software supplied on floppy disks. (Courtesy: Nebraska Videodisc Design/Production Group)

system utilizes an industrial video disk player that operates under microcomputer control, two video monitors, a specially developed random access audio tape recorder, light pens, and computer-controlled mannequins with image sensory devices. One monitor is used for the display of training materials from a video disk. The other displays computer-generated questions with alternative responses which are selected with a light pen. CPR procedures practiced on the mannequins are analyzed by the microcomputer that will automatically display the video disk frames pertinent to a given program.

The growing number of interactive optical video disks developed by the American Medical Association deal with such topics as interviewing techniques for physicians, pulmonary problems, and the management of facial lacerations by physicians not trained in plastic surgery. Through its Miles Learning Center, the Miles Pharmaceutical Company has developed optical video disks that explain surgical procedures, emergency room techniques, and the use of antibiotics. These disks include quizzes that ask the physician to select an appropriate diagnosis or method of treatment. The surgical procedures disks feature an index to critical incidents and allows the physician to control playback speed to examine specific facets of a procedure more closely. Other video disks produced for medical applications contain examples and explanations of specimens or of x-rays, CAT scans, thermograms, and other diagnostic tools. Several organizations have also produced video disks intended for patient education. Dealing with such topics as obstetrics or diabetes, these disks offer a more sophisticated and effective alternative to the videotapes and filmstrips used by some physicians.

In other representative educational applications, the Videodisc Design/Production Group of the Nebraska Educational Television Network has developed closed-captioned video disk programs for hearing impaired persons, as well as a variety of interactive instructional disks dealing with such subjects as Spanish language instruction, metric conversion, city driving, and airline pilot training. Brigham Young University has likewise produced several Spanish language instruction programs that make extensive use of still frames and dual channel audio. Utah State University has produced several experimental educational video disk programs that operate under microcomputer control. One of these programs provides instruction in the use of a library catalog. The University of Utah has produced interactive video disk programs for physics students, which include an oscilloscope lesson and instruction in quantum mechanics. As a support for classroom lectures and a data base of important visual material for researchers, the Department of Physics at Kansas State University has prepared a set of instructional video disks dealing with the physics of automobile collisions. It contains extensive film footage that can be studied at various speeds. The Space Disc series, produced by Video Vision Associates and the Center for Aerospace Education at Drew University, presents a comprehensive collection of space mission film footage and related materials. It is accompanied by a workbook and prepared lecture materials.

Recognizing the potential of video disk technology, the National Education Association and American Broadcasting Company have inaugurated the joint ABC/NEA SCHOOLDISC program, which is intended to produce twenty one-hour programs, each consisting of 10-minute program segments dealing with language skills, science, social science, the arts, and current events. A final segment will provide in-service information for teachers.

A number of government agencies and corporations have produced instructional video disks as an alternative to conventional training films and/or printed training manuals. The Department of Defense in general, and the Department of the Army in particular, have been active users of video disks in a variety of training and recruitment applications. For use in military posts and recruiting stations around the world, the Army Recruiting Command has developed a series of video disk programs that present information on 265 military occupational specialties. Based on favorable experiences with selected training courses, the Army Communication Technology Office is currently in the process of replacing most of its film and videotape training aids with video disks. Among private sector applications, computer companies such as IBM, Data General, and Wang Laboratories have developed instructional video disks for users of their minicomputer and word processing systems. For the continuing education of data processing professionals, Interactive Training Systems Incorporated offers video disk training courses in the UNIX operating system and C programming language. The course is offered in a package that includes a video disk player, a color monitor, and an IBM Personal Computer. In widely publicized applications, optical video disks have been used for orientation and information programs at EPCOT center and the 1982 World's Fair. Video disk orientation and demonstration programs are increasingly encountered at professional conventions and exhibits. Merck Sharpe and Dohme, for example, has produced a video disk program on glaucoma, which has been displayed at medical congresses and opthalmological meetings. Video disks can likewise be used for information display in shopping malls, libraries, museums, and other public places. As such, they compete with the videotext systems to be discussed in chapter 5.

The Architecture Machine Group at the Massachusetts Institute of Technology has provided one of the most dramatic demonstrations of the innovative instructional potential of video disks. Working in a specially designed, computer-controlled viewing room equipped with projection television, video monitors, audio speakers, joysticks, and other operating controls, MIT has developed its Spatial Management System that can display geographical information in various degrees of detail. As an example, maps and pictures of the city of Aspen, Colorado, are stored on optical video disks. Under computer control, the user can specify the display of area overviews or individual street locations—in effect, taking a simulated drive through the city. In a practical application of this concept, the Advanced Research Projects Agency of the Department of Defense has used video disks to reproduce the floor plans of U.S. embassy buildings for use as a military training aid in the event of terrorist attacks.

In addition to their specifically instructional applications, optical video disks can be an effective medium for the presentation of marketing information. In the most extensive and widely publicized of such applications, General Motors Corporation has equipped 10,000 automotive sales dealers with specially prepared video disks, industrial video disk players, and television receivers. The disks can be used to give customers an initial overview of a particular product or to provide specific information about such matters as individual automotive components, warranties, financing, and insurance. Random frame access capability allows the sales person to quickly direct the customer's attention to specific disk segments, while the freeze-frame feature permits the prolonged examination of individual visual images. To facilitate sales to non-English-speaking customers, dual channel audio provides a second sound track in a foreign language. General Motors has also replaced its 8mm training films with interactive optical video disks.

Ford Motor Company has implemented a similar customer orientation program for its dealers and is also using video disks to train service personnel. In another well-publicized marketing experiment, Sears produced portions of its 1981 summer catalog on optical video disks for use in selected stores. Demonstrating the potential of video disks in specialized sales applications, the Power Systems Group of Combustion Engineering has prepared computer-controlled programs that explain its nuclear products and services. The video disk, which contains over 1,000 still frames plus a dozen narrated video segments resembling television commercials, minimizes the need to transport expensive equipment to customer sites. Combustion Engineering has also produced interactive video disks for the training of maintenance workers in the assembly and installation of coolant pump seals for nuclear reactors.

Disk Preparation

While the industrial applications described above demonstrate the simplicity and versatility of video disks as an effective medium for education and information transfer, video disk programs can prove difficult, time-consuming, and expensive to produce. While actual mastering and stamping prices are reasonable, the production of program content may entail considerable expense, and typically requires the services of one of the relatively small number of consultants experienced in video disk programming. This is especially the case with interactive video disks.

As previously noted, video disks are typically mastered from program material that is first produced on conventional motion picture film or videotape. In some cases, this program material is already in existence and the user simply wants to convert it to the video disk format with little or no modification. In others, material from several existing films or videotapes may be combined to produce a single video disk program. The customized development of video disk programs, however, involves a detailed preproduction analysis of the user's objectives and requirements. Outlines and flowcharts must be created to show the interweaving of a program. When general agreement about the program's format and content is reached, scripts and storyboards are prepared. If the video disk will be computer-controlled, the design and writing of required computer programs must be undertaken concurrently.

Once the video program's script is finalized and the disk layout determined, scenes are filmed or recorded in a studio or on location; required artwork is created; and the text of still frames is prepared. The resulting video and computer programs are then reviewed and revised as required. With nonlinear disks, even small revisions can disrupt the overall program plan. When the program material is finalized, it is sent to the factory for mastering. Taken together, program production and premastering work steps typically require six months or longer to complete. The mastering process itself requires six to twelve weeks. In some cases, an interim check disk is produced for review. The completion of any supporting programs can occur while the disk is being mastered.

Additional Reading

BUSINESS APPLICATIONS

Purcell, C. New picture agency uses video disk systems for instant image selection by clients. *Popular Photography* 89: 50+ (December 1982).

Scott, R. K. GM and the videodisc—Partners in training. *Training and Development Journal* 36: 109–10 (November 1982).

Stewart, S. Videodisc Rx: A survey of health care applications. *Videodisc/Videotex* 3: 115–26 (Spring 1982).

COMPUTER-BASED SYSTEMS

Allen, B. S. The video-computer nexus: Towards an agenda for instructional development. *Journal of Educational Technology Systems* 10: 81–99, 198 (1981).

Bejar, I. I. Videodiscs in education: Integrating the computer and communication technologies. *Byte* 7: 78–104 (June 1982).

Hon, D. The videodisc, microcomputer, and the satellite. *Training and Development Journal* 34: 28–34 (December 1980).

Kadesch, R. R. Interactive video computer learning in physics. *Journal of Educational Technology Systems* 9: 291–301 (1980).

Leveridge, L. L. The interactive videodisc. *Mobius* 3: 68–72 (April 1983).

Leveridge, L. L. A standalone educational/industrial optical video disc player in comparison with computer interfaced players for interactive presentation. *Videodisc News* 2: 10–12 (July 1981).

Negroponte, N. Media room. *Proceedings of the Society for Information Display* 22: 109–13 (1981).

Nugent, G. C., and Stone, C. G. The videodisc meets the microcomputer. *American Annals of the Deaf* 127: 569–72 (1982).

Stone, C. G., and Nugent, G. C. Think it through: An interactive video disc for the hearing impaired. *Johns Hopkins Applied Physics Laboratory Technical Digest* 3: 238–40 (July 1982).

Thorkildsen, R., et al. The interactive videodisc for special education project: Providing CAI for the mentally retarded. *Computing Teacher* 10: 73–6 (April 1983).

Walker, C. L. Computer controlled videodisc/videoplayer systems. *Journal of Educational Technology Systems* 8: 201–6 (1979).

Zollman, D., and Fuller, R. The puzzle of the Tacoma Narrows bridge collapse: An interactive videodisc program for physics instruction. *Creative Computing* 8: 100–9 (October 1982).

EDUCATION AND TRAINING APPLICATIONS

Branson, R., et al. Educational applications research and videodisc technology. *Journal of Educational Technology Systems* 8: 241–62 (1979).

Bunderson, C. V., Olsen, J., and Baillio, B. *Proof of Concept Demonstration and Comparative Evaluation of a Prototype Intelligent Videodisc System*. Orem, Utah: WICAT Learning Design Laboratories, 1981.

Cavanaugh, R. T. Educational-institutional features of optical videodisc system. *SMPTE Journal* 86: 201–9 (1977).

Currier, R. L. Interactive videodisc learning systems. *High Technology* 3: 51–61 (November 1983).

Eastwood, L. Motivations and deterrents to the educational use of intelligent videodisc systems. *Journal of Educational Technology Systems* 7: 303–35 (1978).

Glenn, A. D. Videodiscs and the social studies classroom. *Social Education* 47: 328–30 (1983).

Hiscox, M. D. A summary of the practicality and potential of videodiscs in education. *Videodisc/Videotex* 2: 99–109 (Spring 1982).

Hofmeister, A. M., and Thorkildsen, R. J. Videodisc technology and the preparation of special education teachers. *Teacher Education and Special Education* 4: 34–9 (Summer 1981).

Hon, D. Interactive training in cardiopulmonary resuscitation. *Byte* 7: 108–38 (June 1982).

Kearsley, G. Videodiscs in education and training: The idea becomes reality. *Videodisc/Videotex* 1: 208–20 (Fall 1981).

Kirchner, G. Simon Fraser University videodisc project: Part one—Design and production of an interactive videodisc for elementary school children. *Videodisc/Videotex* 2: 275–87 (Summer 1981).

LeClerq, A. Videodisc technology: Equipment, software, and educational applications. *Library Technology Reports* 17: 293–334 (July-August 1981).

Marx, R. J. Videodisc-based training: Does it make economic sense? *Training* 19: 56–8, 60–1, 65 (March 1982).

Molnar, A. Intelligent videodisc and the learning society. *Journal of Educational Technology Systems* 8: 31–40 (1979).

Otto, S. E. K. Videodisc material retrieval for language teaching. *System* 11: 47–52 (1983).

Propp, G., et al. Videodisc for the hearing impaired. *Volta Review* 83: 321–27 (1981).

Schneider, E. W., and Bennion, J. L. Veni, vidi, vici via videodisc—A simulator for instructional conversations. *System* 11: 41–46 (1983).

Sek, O. Videodisc image retrieval for language teaching. *System* 11: 47–52 (1983).

Wilhelms, F. T. The ABC/NEA Schooldisc program. *Videodisc/Teletext* 1: 6–13 (Winter 1981).

INFORMATION STORAGE AND RETRIEVAL

Fisher, M. Storage and retrieval of planetary photographic images by laser/video disk technology. *Journal of Micrographics* 15: 20–21 (September 1982).

Goldstein, C. M., and Russell, W. D. *The NLM/LHNBC Videodisc Digital Storage Program Status Report*. Bethesda, Maryland: Lister Hill National Center for Biomedical Communications, 1981.

Kenney, G. C. Special purpose applications of the optical videodisc system. *IEEE Transactions on Consumer Electronics* 22: 327–38 (1976).

Meek, G., et al. Videodiscs: A revolution that isn't. *Canadian Library Journal* 39: 357–64 (1982).

Mole, D. The videodisc as a pilot project of the Public Archives of Canada. *Videodisc/Videotex* 3: 154–61 (Summer 1981).

Schipma, P. B. Videodisc for storage of text. *Videodisc/Videotex* 1: 168–72 (Summer 1981).

Schulman, J. L. Video PATSEARCH. *Information Technology and Libraries* 1: 150–56 (1982).

Sonneman, S. S. Videodiscs as a library tool. *Special Libraries* 74: 7–13 (1983).

Sustik, J. M. Art history interactive videodisc for special education project: Providing CAE for the mentally retarded. *Computing Teacher* 10: 73–76 (April 1983).

Winningham, L. New automated storage and retrieval system for large information bases. *Journal of Micrographics* 16: 40–43 (March 1983).

RECREATIONAL APPLICATIONS

Brody, H. Video games enter technology time warp. *High Technology* 3: 36–46 (June 1983).

VIDEO DISK EQUIPMENT

Christopher, T. J., Stone, F. R., and Workman, W. M. Selectavision player. *IEEE Transactions on Consumer Electronics* 27: 340–51 (1981).

Paris, J., and Boss, R. W. Care and maintenance of videodiscs and players. *Videodisc/Videotex* 2: 38–46 (Winter 1981).

Repka, C. P. Stereo audio on CED videodiscs. *IEEE Transactions on Consumer Electronics* 29: 153–67.

VIDEO DISK PRODUCTION

Gordon, W. J. Videodisc testing philosophy and techniques. *RCA Review* 39: 186–97 (1978).

Palermo, P. R., et al. Video disc mastering and replication. *Optics and Laser Technology* 9: 169–74 (August 1977).

Van Raalte, J. A. Videodisc mastering—An overview. *RCA Review* 43: 5–20 (1982).

Weisberg, H. Manufacturing the videodiscs: An overview. *RCA Engineer* 27: 6–10 (January-February 1982).

Winslow, J. S. Mastering and replications of reflective videodiscs. *IEEE Transactions on Consumer Electronics* 22: 318–26 (1976).

VIDEO DISK PROGRAMMING

Crowell, P. Using graphics on videodiscs. *Videodisc/Videotex* 2: 216–21 (Summer 1982).

Lipson, J. Design and development of programs for the videodisc. *Journal of Educational Technology Systems* 9: 277–85 (1980).

National Video Clearinghouse. *The Videotape and Disc Guide to Home Entertainment*. 3d edition. Syossett, New York: National Video Clearinghouse Incorporated, 1982.

Porter, D. Videodiscs, videocassettes, and film study. *Journal of Educational Technology Systems* 11: 83–91 (1982).

Quilliam, P., ed. *The Video Tape and Disc Guide to Home Entertainment—United Kingdom*. Syossett, New York: National Video Clearinghouse Incorporated, 1981.

Sebestyen, I. Videodisc revolution. *Electronic Publishing Review* 2: 41–89 (March 1982).

Shotwell, R. What does videodisc technology offer publishers? *Publishers Weekly* 222: 26–27 (December 3, 1982).

VIDEO DISK TECHNOLOGY

Bayliff, R. W. Teldec videodisc. *International Broadcast Engineer* 86: 34, 36–37 (1972).

Bock, W. Videodisk standards: A software view of the technology. *SMPTE Journal* 92: 571–76 (1983).

Brandinger, J. J. RCA CED videodisc system—An overview. *RCA Review* 42: 333–66 (1981).

Clemens, J. K. Video disks: Three choices. *IEEE Spectrum* 19: 38–42 (March 1982).

Firester, A. H., et al. Optical readout of the RCA videodisc. *RCA Review* 39: 392–426 (1978).

Fox, B. Revolution for video disc. *New Scientist* 96: 150–53 (October 21, 1983).

Heath, T. Alternative videodisc systems. *Videodisc/Videotex* 2: 228–38 (Fall, 1981).

Inoue, T., Hidaka, T., and Roberts, V. The VHD videodisc system. *SMPTE Journal* 91: 1071–76 (1982).

Keizer, E. O., and McCoy, D. S. Evolution of the RCA Selectavision videodisc system—Historical perspective. *RCA Review* 39: 14–32 (1978).

Kybett, H., and Dexnis, P. *Complete Handbook of Home Video Systems*. Reston Virginia: Reston Publishing, 1982.

Lunin, L. F., and Paris, J. Videodisc and optical disk: Technology, research, and applications. *Journal of the American Society for Information Science* 34: 405–40 (1983).

Marsh, F. E. Videodisc technology. *Journal of the American Society for Information Science* 33: 237–44 (1982).

Paulson, C. R., and Doyle, M. J. Videodisc system: A technical report by the SMPTE study group on video disc recording. *SMPTE Journal* 91: 180–85 (1982).

Pettipas, L. A., and Paris, J. Glossary of terms. *Videodisc/Videotex* 1: 173–86 (Summer 1981).

Rice, P., and Dubbe, R. F. Development of the first optical videodisc. *SMPTE Journal* 91: 277–84 (1982).

Sigel, E., et al. *Videodiscs: The Technology, the Applications, and the Future*. White Plains, New York: Knowledge Industries Publications, 1980.

Thorne, K. G., and Bayliff, R. W. Teldec video disc. *Journal of the Royal Television Society* 14: 133–38 (November-December 1972).

CHAPTER 4

TELEVISION SIGNAL DELIVERY SYSTEMS

The preceding chapters have repeatedly referred to "broadcast" video sources—that is, television stations that transmit video signals over the air to television receivers. Such stations can be divided into two broad groups: (1) affiliates of the four national networks (ABC, CBS, NBC, and PBS); and (2) independents who broadcast a combination of syndicated programs, movies, and local programming. Collectively described as "commercial television," these stations are the most pervasive source of video programming and, through the early 1970s, they were the only programming source available in most parts of the United States.

Since the mid-1970s, however, various alternative sources of video programming have gained popularity. Among these, the videocassettes and video disks discussed in the preceding chapters are prerecorded media that provide local input to an appropriately equipped video system. But prerecorded cassettes and disks must be physically transported to a VCR or disk player. This chapter discusses programming services and methodologies that transmit video signals electronically to appropriately equipped receivers. The best known and most firmly established of these is cable television. Other examples include subscription television (STV), satellite master antenna television (SMATV), multipoint distribution television (MDTV), and such emerging broadcasting methods as direct broadcast satellite (DBS) television, low-power television (LPTV), and pay-per-view television. Consumer and institutional viewers even have the option of bypassing intermediate video sources entirely and installing their own satellite earth stations.

Being entertainment oriented, most of the television delivery systems described in this chapter are designed for consumers. A small but growing number of cable services, however, offers news, public affairs, financial, and other information of significance for business applications. Some cable and related video services likewise present cultural and educational programming of interest to schools, community groups, and libraries. In many cases, such programming stimulates an interest in books and other library and educational materials dealing with related subjects. In such instances, video programming can have a direct impact on educational curricula and on library collection development and reference services.

As a part of their franchise agreements, most cable systems make one or more channels available for locally originated programming. At the simplest level, community organizations, church groups, public libraries, and government agencies may provide announcements for video "bulletin board" channels. Such announcements consist of one or more frames of text containing information about local events. Some public libraries have established small studios for the production of lectures, courses, talk shows, and similar programs to be broadcast locally. The low-power television systems described later in this chapter likewise offer opportunities for video programming by local organizations.

Mindful of the diverse interests and information requirements of consumer, business, and library audiences, this chapter surveys the current status of available and emerging alternative video programming services. The chapter begins with a discussion of cable television systems, emphasizing the types of programming currently available to cable subscribers. Later sections deal with other video services.

Cable Television

Overview

Cable television takes its name from the communications medium—coaxial cable—which serves as an alternative to over-the-air broadcasting for the transmission of video signals to television receivers located in homes, institutions, and businesses. The cable itself, which consists of copper wires wound around a common axis, is merely one of four major hardware components in a cable system. The others include an antenna, "head end" equipment, and a converter/receiver. While detailed knowledge of cable television technology is hardly essential to an understanding of the nature and significance of cable services, a brief technical description will help clarify the way in which cable programming is delivered to end users.

Most cable television systems operate in a prescribed geographic area as a franchise awarded by local government in return for fees and other concessions such as the previously mentioned availability of public access channels for locally originated programming. In most cases, exclusive franchises are awarded on the basis of competitive bidding. In others, the franchise award is nonexclusive, but the expense of implementing a cable system in a limited market typically discourages multiple operators. In either case, the system operator erects a master antenna designed to receive broadcast signals. The sources of these signals are discussed later in this chapter. Older cable systems used tower-type microwave antennas, but cable services today rely heavily on satellite-earth stations that permit the reception of programming from a greater diversity of sources. Regardless of the antenna type, the incoming signal is received by "head end" equipment—a group of electronic components that filter, amplify, and modulate it for retransmission over cable lines connected to subscriber locations. Several different types of cable of varying thicknesses are typically used in a given system. Relatively thick and expensive trunk cables serve as the major distribution arteries. Depending on the locality, they may be buried or suspended from telephone poles. Thinner, less expensive feeder cables branch off of the trunk cable to serve individual streets. Inexpensive drop cables are used to connect the feeder cable to converters located in homes, offices, and other subscriber sites.

These converters permit the tuning of cable channels and determine the number of channels the cable system can support. Older cable systems, some of which remain in operation, use the integral tuner of the subscriber's television receiver, thereby limiting the system to just 12 channels. Newer cable systems provide a separate converter box, which replaces the television's tuner. This approach provides significantly greater channel capacity—35 channels being the most common, although the most recently installed cable systems offer 52, 72, 104, or more channels. In a competitive bidding situation, the promise of large channel capacity is often critical to the winning of a cable franchise in a given locality, although critics question whether such channel capacity can be meaningfully used.

Cable systems were introduced in the late 1940s as a means of delivering television signals to remote localities—so-called dead spots that could not be adequately served by conventional broadcast methodologies. The earliest installations were in rural Pennsylvania and Oregon where mountains blocked over-the-air transmission. By the mid-1950s cable systems were operating in rural areas in various parts of the country. These early installations, most of which were operated by local companies, were properly described as community antenna television (CATV) systems because the master antenna was solely designed to provide or greatly improve reception. CATV merely extended the range of conventional television signals. It posed no threat to commercial broadcast television.

From the mid-1960s through the mid-1970s, cable systems spread to rural areas and smaller cities throughout the United States, proving especially popular in localities where only one or two of the commercial television networks could be received by conventionally broadcast signals. At the same time, significant changes were introduced in cable services, which would lay the foundation for future rapid expansion. Going beyond mere signal extension, a growing number of cable operators began offering automated time, weather, and news information on unused channels. The term "cablecasting" was coined to describe such services which, in their simplest form, consisted of a televised set of clocks, thermometers, and barometers. They were the primitive forerunners of the text-oriented cable networks and videotext systems to be discussed later. As a more dramatic supplement to the programming offered by local television stations, some cable operators began importing broadcast signals from other localities, thereby providing viewers with additional channels and establishing a pattern that would subsequently form the basis for the expansion of cable services in urban areas. Signal importation was strongly opposed by conventional broadcasters, however, and a series of court decisions and Federal Communications Commission rulings placed restrictions on the practice.

This same period saw the emergence of the Multiple System Operator (MSO), a company that operates cable systems in several locations. While early cable operators typically consisted of relatively small electronics firms active in their home localities, the MSOs include such large, diversified communications companies as Time Incorporated, Tele-Communications Incorporated, Group W Cable, Cox Cable Communications, Storer Communications, Warner Amex, Times Mirror, and Viacom Cablevision. Their significant capital resources permitted the extension of cable television service to urban and suburban areas during the early 1970s.

In an industry that measures its market potential in terms of the number of homes "passed" by cable, densely populated cities and suburbs offer obvious economic attractions. But while tall buildings—the urban counterpart of the mountains which led to the development of cable television—can obstruct broadcast signals, urban cable subscribers are typically less interested in a clearer picture than in greater programming diversity. To minimize interference when conventional broadcast methods are utilized, a given locality cannot be served by more than seven VHF and five UHF broadcast channels. In metropolitan areas like New York City where all allocatable channels are utilized, cable technology permits a significant expansion of video programming, which would otherwise prove impossible. The implementation of urban cable systems has consequently been accompanied by much analysis and discussion of the purpose and potential of cable television. Recognizing that conventional broadcast television must present programs of mass appeal, cable proponents argue that its large channel capacity permits the development of specialized programming—the implication being that cable television will fulfill the educational and cultural promise of video technology. The term "narrowcasting" is widely used to denote such specialized cable programming.

Education and culture aside, a major change in cable programming resulted from the introduction of satellite transmission technology in the mid-1970s. New companies, variously called cable services or cable networks, began developing programming for broadcast-to-cable systems equipped with satellite earth stations. Rather than merely redistributing programming obtained from local or distant broadcast sources, cable systems can now offer programming not available to viewers of conventional television. In some cases, this programming is offered as part of the basic cable subscription fee. In others, an extra charge is levied. The following sections categorize and describe some of the most important of these cable services. Several factors will, however, influence their availability in particular localities. Some of the services may, for example, impose fees which the cable system operator is reluctant to absorb or pass along to subscribers. With some older 12- or 20-channel cable systems, available channel capacity is fully utilized by conventional broadcast programming and the most popular cable services, making it impossible to introduce interesting services of narrower appeal. As a further constraint, the most widely distributed cable services currently utilize the RCA Satcom IIIR or Satcom IV satellites, and a number of cable systems have installed earth stations designed to receive signals from those satellites. As newer cable services develop, they must broadcast their programming via other satellites, such as Western Union's Westar 4 and Westar 5. Cable system operators may be reluctant to install the additional earth station facilities required to receive signals from those satellites.

Movie Networks

The most widely publicized and popular cable services are designed for the broad consumer market, although much of their programming is of cultural significance. They broadcast feature films approximately three months to one year after their theatrical release. They may also broadcast concerts, stage presentations, sports events, and some original programming, but movies are the staple item, which accounts for their subscriber appeal. The most famous and successful of these services, Home Box Office (HBO), reaches more than 6 million subscribers. Owned by Time Incorporated, it was the first cable television service to utilize satellite transmission, and it established the programming pattern adopted by the other movie networks. Operating 24 hours per day, HBO shows twelve to fifteen different films each month on a rotating schedule that causes films to be repeated at varying times for maximum accessibility. These films are, for the most part, recent Hollywood productions, although some foreign and independent films are shown. Recently, HBO has gone beyond theatrical sources, producing several original motion pictures. Given the limited film production of Hollywood studios and the large number of programming hours which HBO must fill, it is expected that such original motion pictures will become an increasingly important programming resource. As noted above, the HBO programming schedule also includes sports, concerts, comedy presentations, and specials.

Among the other movie networks, Showtime, a joint offering of Viacom International and Teleprompter, has approximately 2 million subscribers. Like HBO, it operates 24 hours a day, and the two services show many of the same movies, although both have expended significant amounts of money to obtain exclusive programming rights to certain films. As a means of enhancing its competitive position, HBO has recently provided production funding for several motion pictures. Over the past several years, Showtime has tried to broaden its audience appeal by expanding its offerings of concerts and stage presentations. It has also produced several mini-series patterned after network television offerings, but with more adult content.

Recognizing the difficulty of competing with HBO, Showtime merged with The Movie Channel, a Warner/Amex cable network, in late 1983, although the two services continued to operate separately at the time this chapter was written. Before the merger, The Movie Channel had slightly over 1 million subscribers. Like the other movie networks, it operates 24 hours a day. As its name implies, its programming consists exclusively of feature films repeated on a schedule conducive to convenient viewing. As noted in chapter 1, it also offers stereo simulcasting via FM radio.

As evidence of the success of HBO, Time Incorporated has introduced a second movie network, Cinemax, which emphasizes films suitable for family viewing. HBO, Showtime, and The Movie Channel—by way of contrast—present many R-rated films not suitable for younger children and which some adult viewers find offensive. Like the other services, Cinemax operates 24 hours per day with films repeated at various times. During daytime hours, Cinemax presents some films presumably designed to appeal to women viewers. Its subscriber base numbers approximately 2.5 million households.

The Home Theater Network (HTN), a cable service offered by Group W Communications, likewise offers films designed for family viewing. It has approximately 250,000 subscribers. Spotlight—a movie network operated by Times Mirror, Cox Cable, and Storer Communications—offers general fare for an estimated 800,000 subscribers. At the time this chapter was written, it faced an uncertain future in this extremely competitive sector of the cable television market.

Several movie networks offer films designed to appeal to specialized audiences. As an example, the Galavision service offered by the Spanish International Network (SIN) features Spanish films and dramatic series, plus sports, comedy, and musical programming. The Escapade service, offered by Cox Cable and Cablevision Systems, emphasizes action and adventure films. As discussed in a later section, the same companies' Bravo network includes many foreign films as part of its cultural programming services. Private Screenings, offered by Satori Productions, features R-rated adult films. Compared to HBO, Showtime, and the other general services, these specialized movie networks operate fewer hours, offer fewer films, are available through fewer cable systems, and have fewer subscribers.

Movie networks are sometimes described as "premium" cable services because the charge for them is not included in the basic cable subscription price. In the simplest approach, the subscriber pays an additional charge for the desired service, but, in recent years, cable system operators have offered special packages in which several movie networks are combined or "tiered" at a price lower than the total cost of the various services operated separately. The best value is typically obtained when the tiered packages complement one another—as is the case with Home Box Office and Cinemax, for example. In some instances, HBO may be tiered with Showtime and/or the Movie Channel in a package characterized by some duplication of programming. Such tiered packages are primarily aimed at affluent suburban households, many of which also have videocassette recorders and/or video disk players.

News and Sports Networks

News programming is the primary form of nonentertainment programming offered by cable networks, and cable news services appeal to consumer, business, and educational audiences. Most of the services are supported by advertising, so access to them is typically included as part of the basic cable subscription fee. Assuming that channel space is available, most cable systems offer one or more of the services described below.

The Cable News Network (CNN), operated by Turner Broadcasting, is the most famous and widely viewed of the cable networks dedicated to news and public affairs programming. Since its introduction in mid-1980, it has offered 24-hour coverage of worldwide news events, supplemented by commentary and special feature stories dealing with a wide range of timely subjects. It is a widely carried cable service that reaches over 20 million subscribers, many of whom are well educated. A related service, the CNN Headline Network (formerly CNN II) provides continuously updated coverage of important news stories, but lacks the depth and features of the full CNN service. It is sometimes carried by broadcast channels in areas not served by cable.

The Satellite News Channel (SNC) began operation in mid-1982 as a joint venture of Group W Communications and ABC Video Enterprises. It discontinued operation in late 1983. During its brief tenure, it provided 24-hour coverage of major news events. As an interesting feature, five minutes of each hour were provided for regional news inserts.

Several cable services offer more specialized news programming. The best known of these, the Cable Satellite Public Affairs Network (C-SPAN), provides complete coverage of the proceedings of the U.S. House of Representatives, congressional hearings, National Press Club luncheons, and other government events. It also presents seminars on government issues intended primarily for high school students. Introduced in early 1979, it operates 24 hours a day and reaches over 14 million cable subscribers. The Financial News Network, which began operating in 1981, emphasizes business news and features a continuous stock ticker. Reaching an estimated 8.5 million households, it operates 12 hours a day and is carried by broadcast stations in some areas not served by cable.

The Weather Channel, introduced in mid-1982 by Landmark Communications, presents around-the-clock coverage of the nation's weather, including weekend and seasonal forecasts plus special weather information for pilots, boaters, and others whose activities are influenced by weather conditions. It reaches an estimated 10 million cable subscribers. Another narrowly focused cable service, the Cable Health Network (CHN), is dedicated to news, discussions, and features dealing with health and fitness. It was operated as an independent service by Viacom International until mid-1983, when it merged with the Daytime cable service discussed in the following section.

The cable news services discussed to this point closely resemble broadcast news programs in combining live announcers with videotaped location segments. Several cable news services use textual page displays. Among these "cabletext" services, Reuters News Views has been in operation since 1971. Available 24 hours a day, it presents general news, financial news, sports reports, and special features rotating in 10-minute cycles. Financial news, presented during weekday business hours only, is based on the Reuter's Financial Report Service used by many banks and brokerage houses. It will consequently prove of interest to such financial institutions and to business libraries affiliated with or serving them. Sports coverage is limited to weekends and evenings. Special features include weather and travel information, movie industry news, horoscopes, and household hints. The UPI Custom Cable, operated by United Press International, is likewise a textual display service that provides news, weather, sports, and financial information. It is offered to cable operators in a satellite version that provides nationwide coverage, and in a newswire version, distributed over leased telephone lines, which includes state and regional news. AP Newscable, a cabletext service operated by the Associated Press, provides news, sports, weather, and financial information to an estimated 5 million subscribers. Dow Jones Cable, a textual service which emphasizes financial and economic news, reaches an estimated 1.5 million subscribers.

For the sports enthusiast, one of the most popular and widely viewed cable services—the Entertainment and Sports Programming Network (ESPN)—presents live and taped coverage of worldwide sports events, major and minor, amateur and professional. Owned by Getty Oil, it was introduced in 1979 and operates 24 hours per day. In 1983, ESPN diversified its programming to include business news from 6 A.M. to 8 A.M., Monday through Friday. Sports programming is also presented by the USA Network discussed in a later section.

Special Interest Programming

As noted above, cable television provides sufficient channel capacity to permit the development of programs intended for specific audiences or special interest groups. To date, the most important examples of such narrowcasting can be divided into four groups: religious programming, minority programming, children's programming, and adult programming.

The history of religious programming dates from the earliest days of television, although, in recent years, the three major networks have generally relegated religious programs to Sunday mornings when viewing is characteristically light. These network programs are typically religious in the broadest sense of the term. Rather than dealing with questions of theology or dogma, they generally emphasize family-oriented material dealing with moral values. While they may be sponsored by particular church organizations, their appeal is often interdenominational. Several cable services by religious organizations feature similar programming. The largest of these, the Christian Broadcasting Network, has been in operation since 1977 and reaches over 23 million cable subscribers. Other examples include the Trinity Broadcasting Network, the National Christian Network, and National Jewish Television. They offer a mixture of inspirational programming, family-oriented films, public affairs discussions, variety shows, and music.

The Eternal Word Network, a Roman Catholic cable service, offers religious and inspirational programming intended primarily for children, the elderly, and the Hispanic community. Started by a group of Franciscan nuns in Birmingham, Alabama, it operates from 8 P.M. to midnight and reaches an estimated 1.5 million subscribers. The Catholic Telecommunications Network of America (CTNA) provides local dioceses and Catholic schools with educational programming, news, photographs, electronic mail, videoconferencing, and other services via satellite. It is not currently being marketed directly to cable subscribers, although some of its programming may be directed to cable or broadcast television outlets by local religious organizations.

While much Catholic, Protestant, and Jewish programming is broadly educational in character, evangelical religious groups have been particularly successful in using television to preach the gospel. Although a number of independent local television stations broadcast such evangelical programs, cable television offers the advantage of 24-hour programming directed to a national audience. The Inspirational Network (formerly the People That Love Network) is the best known of these evangelical religious services. Operated by the Heritage Village Church and Missionary Fellowship, it reaches over 6 million homes with a mixture of preaching, inspirational programming, and religious news.

Turning to nonreligious minority cable services, Black Entertainment Television (BET) offers movies, musical programming, talk shows, and short features of interest to the black community. It operates for six hours nightly and reaches 5 million subscribers. The Spanish International Network (SIN) features Spanish-language films, soap operas, news, sports, music, and variety programs. It operates 24 hours per day and reaches over 3 million homes. As previously noted, SIN also operates Galavision, a premium cable service that offers Spanish films and other entertainment produced largely in Mexico, Latin America, and Spain.

The Daytime cable service, a joint venture of Hearst Publishing and ABC Video Enterprises, is designed specifically for middle and upper middle class women. Operating four hours each weekday afternoon, it emphasizes self-improvement programming in a magazine-type format that draws on such Hearst publications as House Beautiful and Cosmopolitan. It reaches over 9 million cable subscribers, and, as previously noted, it merged with the Cable Health Network in 1983. Scheduled to begin operation in 1984, the Silent Network presents original, captioned video programming for hearing-impaired persons. It will operate one evening per week.

Nickelodeon, developed by Warner Amex Satellite Entertainment Company, is a much publicized and widely viewed cable service for children and adolescents. Operating from 8 A.M. to 9 P.M. daily, it combines much original programming with movies, concerts, and sports events. Much of the early daytime programming is designed for preschool children. Programs in the later hours are intended for older children and adolescents. It reaches over 13 million cable subscribers. The Disney Channel, as the name implies, features new material produced by Walt Disney Studios combined with Disney theatrical films and older television programs.

While the movie networks offer much R-rated material, several cable services feature programming intended specifically for adults. The sexual content of such programming is typically its distinguishing characteristic, although it is far less explicit than the X-rated films routinely available on prerecorded videocassettes. The Playboy Channel is the most widely publicized of these adult cable services. It offers movies, discussion, and short features with content and treatment similar to the material contained in Playboy magazine. It operates from 8 P.M. to 6 A.M. and shares a satellite transponder (which receives and transmits microwave signals) with the National Christian Network. As noted in the previous discussion of movie networks, the Escapade and Private Screenings cable services also offer adult programming.

Cultural and Educational Services

Cultural and educational cable services are generally aimed at well-educated, economically comfortable households who have traditionally avoided conventional television. While programs of artistic or literary interest are offered by the previously discussed movie networks and by the general programming services discussed in the next section, certain cable services are dedicated exclusively to cultural programming. These services interpret culture broadly to include theater, foreign and classic English-language films, documentaries, classical music, jazz, dance, interviews with artists and authors, and even crafts. While some of their programming is obtained from European sources, much of it is developed specifically for the cable audience. Compared to other cable services described in this chapter, the cultural services operate on a restricted schedule and offer no daytime programming.

Two cable services dedicated exclusively to cultural programming—Bravo and Alpha Repertory Television Service (ARTS)—were in operation in 1984. While they offer similar programming, the two services are marketed in different ways. Bravo, mentioned briefly above, is available from 8 P.M. to 6 A.M. and offers a combination of American films, foreign language films, and performing arts programming. Rather than being included in the basic cable package, it is a premium service for which subscribers must pay an extra monthly fee. Strangely, Bravo is marketed as a package with Escapade, the adult movie network. It reaches an estimated 200,000 subscribers. ARTS is supported by advertising revenue and, when offered by a given cable system, is part of the basic cable package. It reaches over 11 million cable subscribers. A joint venture of Hearst publishing and ABC Video Services, ARTS operates from 9 P.M. to midnight.

A third cultural cable service, CBS Cable, discontinued operation in early 1983 despite a very favorable reception by media critics. Its failure has led to renewed speculation about the ultimate compatibility of television and culture. Some observers see the demise of CBS Cable as evidence that cable subscribers simply want greater availability of conventional programming. Others contend that CBS Cable was a victim of cable technology itself, noting that many cable services did not have sufficient available channel space to offer CBS Cable to subscribers. The resulting weak market penetration made it difficult for the service to attract the advertising revenues on which its support was based. As an additional complication noted earlier in this chaper, CBS Cable was offered via the Westar 5 satellite rather than the Satcom IIIR or Satcom IV satellites which most cable systems are equipped to receive.

While many cable services offer some programming that is nominally educational, only the Appalachian Community Service Network (ACSN) Learning Channel is specifically and exclusively educational in character. Developed by the ACSN—a nonprofit organization located in Lexington, Kentucky—it operates from 6 A.M. to 4 P.M. weekdays and 6 A.M. to 1 P.M. on weekends. ACSN programming consists primarily of "telecourses" that can be taken for credit at various participating colleges plus self-improvement and skills-oriented instruction on such diverse topics as cooking, auto repair, speed reading, resume writing, guitar playing, and small business management.

General Programming

The programming patterns and intended audience of some cable services are of a general character, consisting of variety programs, situation comedies, and music that are difficult to distinguish from the standard fare offered by commercial broadcast networks and independent television stations. Such widely diversified programming may have contributed to the demise of the Entertainment Channel, a joint venture of RCA and Rockefeller Center Incorporated. Originally designed as a cultural cable service, a substantial percentage of its schedule consisted of BBC programming, but it also offered movies, comedy, family entertainment, and similar conventional fare. It ceased operation in 1983. Likewise troubled, the USA Network—a joint venture of Time Incorporated, Paramount Pictures, and MCA Incorporated—combines The English Channel, a group of programs produced by Thames Broadcasting; Calliope, a children's program; and extensive coverage of college football and basketball, major league baseball and hockey, professional soccer, and amateur boxing. It operates 24 hours per day, but its daytime schedule is designed to appeal to the programming executives' perception of women's interests; its early evening programs are intended for young people; and its nighttime programming emphasizes sports events for male audiences. The Modern Satellite Network (MSN) operates weekdays only from 10 A.M. to 1 P.M. As might be expected, its programming is intended for housewives and includes consumer news and self-improvement programs. An interesting component of the MSN schedule is the TeleFrance USA network, a package of French programs that includes classic and recent films, dramatic presentations based on literary classics, documentaries, language instruction, and cooking lessons.

Among the general cable services, the most conventional type of television programming is offered by the three so-called superstations—WTBS, a Turner Broadcasting station that originates in Atlanta; WGN, which is owned by the Chicago Tribune Company; and WOR, a New York station operated by RKO General Television. Their collective nickname denotes their widespread availability via satellite rather than the quality of their programming, which consists of the familiar combination of syndicated reruns, movies, and sports events offered by independent television stations. WTBS, which is offered as part of the basic service by most cable systems, reaches over 28 million subscribers, making it the single most pervasive cable service. WGN is available to an estimated 11 million households, while WOR reaches about 5 million cable subscribers.

Music Programming

Preceding chapters have discussed the emerging integration of video and audio technologies as evidenced in the development of television receivers with improved sound systems, the growing interest in stereo television broadcasting, and the introduction of prerecorded stereo videocassettes and video disks. As noted above, movie networks such as Home Box Office and Showtime are increasingly diversifying their programming by offering musical concerts. Classical music and jazz are likewise regular components in the programming offered by cultural cable services. At the time this chapter was written, two cable services specialized in popular music programming. The most innovative and influential of these is Music Television (MTV), produced by Warner Amex Satellite Entertainment Company. Primarily intended for teenagers and young adults, MTV's principal program material consists of short videotaped segments of popular and rock music accompanied by video imagery that depicts the artists or presents a visual interpretation of the musical piece or both. These segments are similar to the prerecorded "Video 45" cassettes described in chapter 2. MTV also presents longer concerts and interviews with musical artists. MTV is available 24 hours per day and reaches an estimated 15 million cable subscribers. Many cable systems offer accompanying stereo sound via FM radio.

The Nashville Network is a more conventional music-oriented cable service offered by Group W Communications. It presents country and western music, comedy, and entertainment industry news. It reaches an estimated 2 million cable subscribers.

Interactive Television

Conventional cable systems—like their broadcast counterparts—are designed for the one-way transmission of video and audio signals to appropriately equipped television receivers. Interactive cable, as the name implies, provides two-way transmission facilities, thereby allowing viewers to send instructions and/or messages to the system operator. While interactive cable systems are straightforward in concept, they can prove complicated and expensive to implement. From the technical standpoint, a specified range of frequencies is allocated for transmission by the cable system operator. A second, narrower range is reserved for transmission by the subscriber. While all coaxial cable is capable of carrying bidirectional signals, the conversion of existing one-way systems to interactive status requires the addition of special amplifiers and related communication equipment. Subscribers' television receivers must also be equipped with a special controller and calculator-style keypad. Newer cable systems are increasingly being installed with such bidirectional facilities in place, although their interactive capabilities may not be utilized by available programming.

Industry analysts, educators, information specialists, and others have been particularly enthusiastic about the characteristics of interactive cable technology, citing its potential advantages in a variety of applications. Unlike conventional television, which relegates the viewer to a passive role, interactive cable permits the development of innovative programming with active viewer involvement. Frequently cited possibilities—utilized by some existing and experimental interactive television systems—include opinion polls, contests, and game shows. New types of comedies or dramatic programs might be developed in which audience decisions, perhaps based on a menu of alternatives, would dictate the subsequent narrative flow. As discussed in the preceding chapter, such programming techniques have been used with interactive video disks. Similarly, the conventional linear structure of television programs might be radically modified so that the viewer is first shown a brief overview segment followed by a menu of alternatives from which more detailed material can be selected. Several experimental systems have utilized this technique for the presentation of more informative commercials.

Interactive cable offers the further potential advantage of receiver addressability, thereby permitting the implementation of pay-per-view systems in which subscribers select the programs they want to see and are charged accordingly. The pay-per-view concept is discussed in greater detail later in this chapter. Interactive cable with its two-way transmission facilities also permits the implementation of various surveillance and control functions, including fire alarms, burglar alarms, remote reading of utility meters, and remote control of appliances. Here, the cable television system serves as the vehicle for services which might also be implemented through the telephone network.

In an application to be described in greater detail in chapter 5, interactive cable can be combined with videotext information services. In such systems, the subscriber's television receiver becomes a terminal linked to computers for purposes of data retrieval, home shopping, remote banking, in-home instruction, home newspaper delivery, electronic mail delivery, teleconferencing, and similar applications. While their consumer appeal is obvious, businesses, libraries, and community groups might participate in such systems as either information providers or information users. In the former capacity, for example, a library might make bibliographic data or service-oriented information available to viewers. At the present time, teletext and videotext systems commonly utilize conventional broadcasting methods or the telephone network, largely because of the widespread availability of those communication facilities. Compared to telephone lines, however, cable offers potential for much faster and economical data transmission, making it an attractive future communication alternative in videotext and teletext applications. The use of cable also frees home telephone lines for voice communications.

The first operational interactive cable system—the famous Qube system developed by Warner Amex—was introduced in Columbus, Ohio, in 1977. Qube systems have since been implemented in Cincinnati, Pittsburgh, St. Louis, Houston, and Dallas. Qube represents the state of the art in interactive cable, and, as such, it has been the subject of much publicity and commentary, most of it based on analysis of the Columbus implementation. It is important to note that interactive capabilities are offered over and above conventional multichannel cable services in areas where Qube holds the cable franchise. Many subscribers receive only conventional cable services, and are not interested in offerings based on interactive capabilities. These offerings can be divided into two major groups: pay-per-view programming and viewer participation programming. A home security service and rudimentary shopping service have also been implemented, but will not be discussed here.

The Qube system operates under the control of a central computer that enables it to address individual receivers. In each Qube location, several channels offer movies, special entertainment, educational presentations, and similar programming on a pay-per-view basis. The most controversial of these channels carries adult films. Subscribers' television receivers are equipped with a special keypad which is used to select desired programming. Unlike conventional premium cable services which are sold on a monthly subscription basis, viewers are only charged for those programs which they actually watch. There is, of course, a monthly subscription charge for the availability of the Qube service itself, and the familiar range of movie networks and other premium services is also available to subscribers.

From the economic standpoint, Qube's pay-per-view capabilities are probably its most significant feature, but its viewer participation programming attracts the most attention. Qube subscribers have used the system's interactive capabilities to render political opinions, score individual rounds in a boxing match, judge beauty contests and talent shows, participate in game shows, and select the cover design for a national magazine. As with pay-per-view programming, viewer participation is based on the Qube keypad/controller, which utilizes specified key sequences to respond to multiple choice questions posed during specially developed television programs. Responses are tabulated immediately by the Qube computer. In a political debate, for example, viewers are informed how the audience as a whole reacted to specific issues discussed. Qube has likewise experimented with an interactive soap opera in which successive scenarios were based on audience decisions.

In addition to Qube, interactive cable systems have been installed by such companies as Cox Cable Communications, Tocom Incorporated, Viacom International, and RKO Cablecom General. As noted earlier in this discussion, many newer cable systems are being installed with two-way transmission potential, although the operator may not initially implement any interactive capabilities. Often, two-way potential is mandated as a condition of the cable franchise award, and the system operator provides it out of necessity rather than interest. To date, interactive cable has involved too few subscribers to permit any meaningful generalizations about its future viability. Despite the attention it has received, much interactive programming is trivial in content. Rather than significantly enriching or otherwise altering subscribers' viewing habits, existing interactive cable services have merely provided them with additional entertainment options.

Inherent programming value aside, serious questions have been raised about the security and privacy implications of interactive cable technology. Of particular concern is the privacy of such subscriber information as viewing preferences, political opinions, financial status, and health status which might be derived from participation in interactive programming. In the absence of government regulations or other restrictions, such personal information might be used to generate mailing lists of subscribers with specific characteristics, sold to third parties interested in particular subscribers, or made available to government agencies for surveillance or evidentiary purposes. Cognizant of the potential for technological abuse, Warner Amex has developed a privacy code for its Qube system operators. Privacy regulations have been enacted in certain localities served by cable systems, and privacy legislation has been introduced in several states and in the U.S. Senate. A bill introduced in New York, for example, establishes the cable subscriber's "expectation of confidentiality" and legal right to access any personal files maintained by the cable system operator. While such efforts are designed to protect the subscriber from breaches of privacy by the cable system operator, additional concern has been expressed about unauthorized electronic access to interactive cable systems or the computers which control them. Vulnerability to such breaches of security is unfortunately inherent in all electronic systems, and various control procedures are at best successful in minimizing their occurrence.

Noncable Alternatives

Subscription Television

While cable television is the most widely publicized and viewed alternative to conventional broadcast video programming, many areas have not been "wired" by cable system operators. Cable service is now available to an estimated 30 percent of American households. Although the original purpose of cable technology was to bring television reception to remote rural areas, the industry's recent expansion efforts have emphasized urban areas and affluent suburbs. As previously noted, the cable television industry measures successful market penetration by the ratio of subscribers to the number of households "passed" during cable installation. Cable system operators are consequently not interested in extending service to sparsely populated areas where subscriber potential is low. Within urban areas, cable system operators are likewise uninterested in wiring low-income neighborhoods. As a result, some cities remain unserved by cable television—the classic example being New York where cable installation has remained limited to a portion of Manhattan, although franchises for the outer boroughs were finally awarded in 1983. As a further constraint, the recent practice of tiering multiple premium services gives cable system operators greater potential for profit from existing installations, thereby diminishing any incentive for geographical expansion.

Just as the limited range of broadcast television signals led to the development of cable systems, the geographic limitations of cable service have spurred the development of alternative delivery systems. Collectively termed "pay television," these alternative delivery systems vary in technology, but share a common emphasis on programming unavailable from conventional broadcast sources. Subscription Television (STV), the oldest and most widely implemented of them, transmits encoded UHF signals to television sets equipped with a special decoder. The signals are received on one of the unused VHF channels—typically, channel 3 or 4. Conventional television service is unaffected. Because they transmit their signals over the air, subscription television systems can be viewed as the broadcast counterparts of "premium" cable services. As with cable systems, the subscriber pays an initial decoder installation fee plus a monthly charge. Programming consists largely of movies supplemented by occasional concerts, stage presentations, and other special programs. Subscription television systems are operated by such companies as Wometco Home Theater, Oak Industries, and SelecTV. They are licensed as broadcast stations serving a given area. Examples include WWHT and WSNL in metropolitan New York and KWHY in Los Angeles.

Multipoint Distribution Television (MDTV)—sometimes termed Multipoint Distribution Service (MDS)—is a variant form of subscription television that broadcasts microwave signals to special antennas mounted on subscribers' rooftops. Programming consists largely of movies and special entertainment. In areas where cable is unavailable, MDTV may provide access to Home Box Office, Showtime, or other premium programming services. Microband Corporation of America, the company that operates the largest number of MDTV franchises, began providing programming to apartment complexes and hotels in the mid-1970s. MDTV was subsequently extended to single-family dwellings in urban and suburban areas. As with subscription television, there is an initial installation charge for the special microwave antenna and related components plus a monthly subscription fee.

STV and MDTV have enjoyed considerable market penetration in areas not served by cable television, but some industry analysts question their long-term viability as cable services expand. Although they provide only a single channel of programming, the monthly STV or MDTV subscription fee typically approaches or exceeds that of cable services, which provide multiple channels. The Federal Communications Commission has recently approved multichannel STV and MDTV broadcasting, but it is too soon to assess the impact of such expansion.

In an interesting variant of subscription television, the ABC Home View Network transmits encoded programming to specially equipped videocassette recorders. The programming consists largely of feature films transmitted between the hours of 2 and 6 A.M. when normal television broadcasting is not operational. The system utilizes special decoders manufactured by Sony. Each decoder has a unique identification code that prohibits replaying tapes on other recorders, thereby preventing the viewing of tapes by nonsubscribers. A similar concept was employed during the 1970s to transmit educational films to videocassette recorders operated by schools. Likewise, some radio stations transmit music at night to audio recorders equipped with special decoder boxes.

Satellites and TVRO Terminals

Compared to cable television, STV and MDTV technologies offer the advantage of rapid implementation, but because their signals are broadcast over the air, they have a limited geographic range. As a result, they typically operate in urban and highly developed suburban areas where population density assures adequate subscriber potential. Since cable system operators are increasingly interested in these same geographic markets, many remote suburban and rural areas—some of which have affluent residents who are well able to afford new technologies—remain unserved by alternative television delivery systems. In some cases, these remote areas cannot even receive clear broadcast signals from network affiliates. A study by the United States Satellite Broadcasting Company, a division of Hubbard Broadcasting, estimates that one million American homes receive no television signals, and another 4.8 million are located in areas served by just one or two stations. A study conducted for Comsat indicates that, at the end of this decade, 30 million homes will remain unserved by cable television. The direct reception of satellite signals offers viewers access to the programming offered by cable services.

As noted in the preceding discussion, satellite transmission has largely replaced telephone lines, terrestrial microwave systems, and other methodologies as a means of distributing programs from television networks, cable services, and syndicated broadcasters to local stations, cable systems, and STV operators. Satellites are essentially relay stations in the sky. They receive microwave signals from earthbound transmitters and relay them to earthbound receivers. Compared to conventional terrestrial microwave transmission methods, satellites offer the substantial advantage of greater geographic range. The specific satellite component that receives and retransmits microwave signals is termed a "transponder." Most satellites have multiple transponders that permit the simultaneous accommodation of several or many signals. In the case of satellites intended for video transmission, each transponder typically carries one color television channel with accompanying sound.

While several hundred satellites are currently orbiting the earth, many are used for voice communications, business data and message transmission, military or maritime purposes, or other applications outside the scope of this discussion. The use of satellites for such video-oriented business applications as video conferencing and facsimile transmission will be treated in later chapters. Satellites used for television transmission are termed "communication" satellites, and their use dates from the early 1960s. The first examples, Echo 1 and Echo 2, were relatively simple, passive devices designed to reflect radio signals without amplification. Telstar I, launched in 1962, set the pattern for all subsequent communication satellites in providing signal amplification. Through the mid-1970s, television applications of communication satellites emphasized the transoceanic transmission of news broadcasts and related programs, the various INTELSTAT satellite systems being used for that purpose. Since the mid-1970s, however, the video industry's attention has been focused on domestic satellite transmission, especially the satellite delivery of cable programming. This section will discuss such domestic satellite facilities and the terminal equipment which enables individual persons or organizations to receive the programs that they transmit.

Domestic communication satellites are positioned in the so-called geosynchronous or geostationary orbit located perpendicular to the equator about 22,300 miles above the earth's surface. In that orbit, the satellites revolve around the earth at the same speed at which the earth revolves around its own axis. They consequently occupy a constant position relative to earthbound antennas, thereby eliminating the need for complex computer tracking mechanisms and permitting continuous reception by a given antenna. By way of contrast, older communication satellites, like Telstar I and II, occupied eliptical orbits which caused them to disappear over the horizon within relatively brief periods of time. The U.S. television industry is currently served by twelve domestic communications satellites: the RCA Satcom F1/F2, Satcom 1R, Satcom F3R, and Satcom F4; the Western Union Westar 2, Westar 3, Westar 4, and Westar 5; the Hughes Galaxy I; and the Comstar D1/D2, Comstar D3, and Comstar D4, which are owned by Comsat and operated by the American Telephone and Telegraph Company. Canadian programming is carried by the Anik D1 and Anik B satellites. Several of these communication satellites are nearing the end of their useful lives, and replacements are to be launched in the near future. Additional launch plans have been announced by RCA (the Satcom 2R and Satcom 6), Hughes Communications (the Galaxy III), Western Union (Westar 6), and other companies.

Communication satellites typically operate as common carriers, leasing transponders to television networks, cable services, and other programming services. Most cable programming is carried by three satellites: Satcom 3R, Satcom 4, and Westar 5. Among these, Satcom 3R is the most extensively utilized. Colloquially termed Cable Net 1, its 24 transponders are fully occupied by the most popular cable services, including Home Box Office, Showtime, The Movie Channel, Cinemax, Cable Network News and CNN Headline News, ESPN, Nickelodeon, MTV, and the WTBS (Atlanta) and WGN (Chicago) superstations. Satcom 3R also carries the ARTS cultural programming service, the Weather Channel, the Reuter News Service, C-SPAN, the Cable Health Network, Daytime, the USA Cable Network, the Home Television Network (HTN), the ACSN educational channel, and such religious programming services as the Inspirational Network, the Christian Broadcasting Network (CBN), the Eternal Word Television Network, the Alternate View Network, and National Jewish Television. Very popular cable services, such as Home Box Office and Showtime, use multiple transponders to provide services to different time zones. Services that do not offer 24-hour programming share transponders. This is the case, for example, with Nickelodeon (which operates daily from 8 A.M. to 9 P.M.) and ARTS (which broadcasts from 9 P.M. until midnight). It is important to note that the cable services carried by a given satellite and/or transponder will vary over time. Several magazines routinely print satellite programming guides that indicate the utilization of transponders for domestic communication satellites.

Among the other communication satellites that provide cable programming, Satcom 4 carries SIN, the Financial News Network, the American Business Network, the American Network, Bravo, the Satellite Program Network, the National Christian Network, the Trinity Broadcasting Network, the Playboy Channel, and Galavision. Westar 5—which recently displaced Satcom 4 as the Cable Net 2 satellite—devotes 15 transponders to cable services, including the Satellite News Channel, the Disney Channel, the Nashville Network, Black Entertainment Television, and the WOR (New York) superstation. Several of these services utilize multiple transponders, so the number of services carried is significantly less than that transmitted by Satcom 3R. Several cable services—including Home Box Office, Spanish International Network, and C-SPAN—have leased transponders on the Galaxy I. With the exception of the defunct CBS Cable cultural programming service, the small number of cable services previously carried by Westar 4 have now switched to other satellites. As discussed earlier in this chapter, the demise of CBS Cable suggests that programming services transmitted by little-used satellites risk being ignored by cable system operators who are understandably reluctant to invest in new receiving equipment. Thus, some cable services may be widely offered simply because they are carried by the Satcom 3R satellite which the vast majority of cable systems are equipped to accept.

While the cable services carried by communication satellites are specifically intended for cable system operators who will retransmit them to subscribers, they can be received at any site equipped with an appropriate earth station. Unlike more complex satellite earth stations that can both transmit and receive microwave signals, earth stations used for the reception of programming carried by communication satellites are described as TVRO (for Television Receive-Only) terminals. The typical installation consists of three groups of interconnected components: an antenna, a low noise amplifier, and a receiver.

The dish-shaped antenna is the most visible and familiar of these components. Its most prominent feature is a parabolic or spherical reflector, which directs the incoming signal to a less conspicuous but equally important assembly called a "feed horn," which, in turn, transmits it to the low noise amplifier. TVRO reflectors designed for institutional or home installations range from 4 to 20 feet in diameter.

In general, performance and cost vary directly with reflector size, although increased satellite signal strength has combined with improvements in earth station component design to permit the effective use of progressively smaller antennas. Most installations require at least a 10-foot antenna to obtain viewable images, although 8-foot antennas can be successfully utilized in some locations. The performance of 4- to 6-foot antennas, while currently marginal, is expected to improve significantly over the next several years, and the TVRO industry is projecting the eventual use of 2- to 3-foot antennas.

Regardless of size, the simplest antennas are installed on fixed mounts and are positioned at the time of installation to receive signals from a single satellite only. More flexible antennas can be repositioned to receive signals from more than one satellite. The most primitive movable mounts are manually operated. More complex and convenient devices feature motorized transports. Several companies offer computerized tracking units that facilitate the location of various satellites.

Communication satellites transmit at relatively low power. Older satellites operate at a maximum power of just 5 watts per channel, while newer satellites transmit at 8.5 watts. By the time these low power signals reach a user's TVRO antenna, they are relatively weak. The low noise amplifier (LNA), as its name implies, amplifies the incoming signal, ideally introducing minimal noise in the process (figure 25). The amplified satellite signal is then passed to a device called a "downconverter," which converts it to a lower frequency compatible with television display. With most earth stations, the downconverter is built into the receiver. Some newer models combine the low noise amplifier and downconverter in a single

FIGURE 25

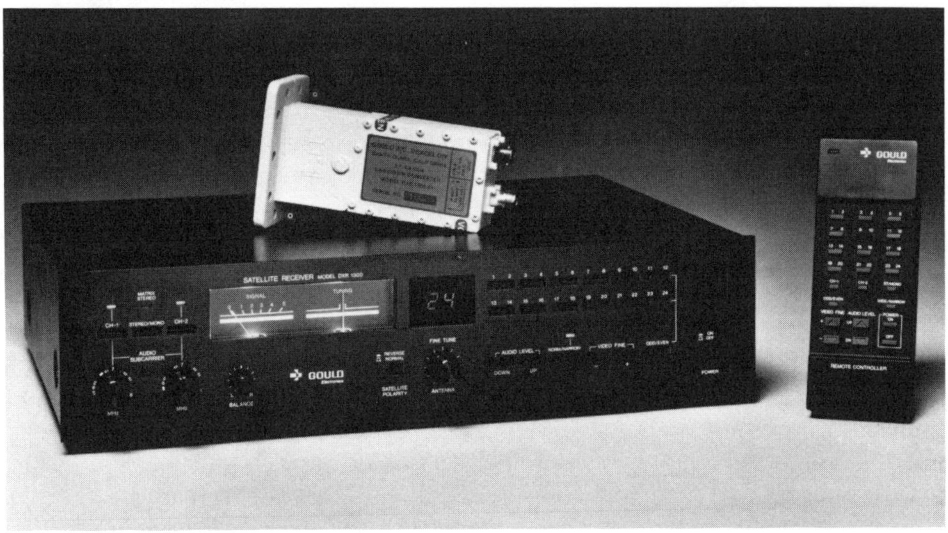

Used to select transponders, this satellite receiver and low noise amplifier features electronic tuning, stereo capability, and full-function remote controller. (Courtesy: Dexcel Division, Gould Electronics)

device called a "low noise converter" (LNC). This arrangement simplifies the electrical connections between the antenna and LNA, which are located outdoors, and the receiver, which is located indoors. The receiver itself is connected to a television set or video monitor. The newest models feature controls that permit satellite selection, transponder selection, and audio adjustments. For convenience, some models include a remote control unit.

TVRO earth stations are an increasingly common fixture on the rooftops of apartment buildings, condominium complexes, and hotels. As planned communities, such facilities are routinely wired with master antenna systems designed to ensure good reception in apartments or residences. Many of these conventional antennas have been supplemented by TVRO terminals that can provide satellite programming to guests or residents on a subscription or fee basis. Such satellite master antenna television (SMATV) systems offer programming comparable to cable systems, but are not subject to the franchise fees and restrictions associated with cable television.

Since the late 1970s, when a Neiman-Marcus Christmas catalog featured a TVRO earth station for $36,000, prices have decreased steadily and significantly. In 1984, TVRO terminals suitable for office or home use could be installed for less than $3,000, although a budget of $5,000 to $7,000 will provide much greater flexibility in equipment selection. As prices have declined, TVRO terminals have been installed by many businesses and institutions, as well as by an increasing number of affluent homeowners in remote suburban and rural areas not served by cable television. Academic and special libraries may have access to TVRO facilities operated by the universities, corporations, government agencies, or other organizations with which they are affiliated. In 1982, the Lake County Public Library in Merrillville, Indiana, became the first such institution to install its own TVRO terminal.

The proliferation of TVRO terminals has raised questions about the legality of intercepting communication satellite signals intended for reception and eventual retransmission by cable systems, STV operators, and other intermediaries. There is no law against the installation of a TVRO earth station, but Section 605 of the Communications Act of 1934 prohibits the unauthorized interception or use of radio communications—of which satellite communications are an example—by persons other than their intended recipients. Exceptions are made for broadcast television and radio signals and for amateur radio transmission, but businesses, schools, libraries, or other groups wishing to receive programming from communication satellites must obtain a license or other written permission from the source of programming—that is, from the individual cable services. Failure to do so is a federal offense.

Some cable services—such as Home Box Office, Showtime, and other premium channels—have strongly opposed the operation of TVRO terminals and routinely refuse such permission. A few cable services charge TVRO owners a small fee for permission to view their programming. With other services—notably, the Inspirational Network and other religious programming services which are interested in the widest possible audience—permission is readily given. To legitimize their installations and avoid possible prosecution, some TVRO owners obtain written permission to receive one or more of the religious programming services. In the privacy of their homes or offices, however, they may use their equipment to receive other, unauthorized programming services. The premium cable services naturally oppose this practice and—in the manner of the Sony Betamax case discussed in chapter 2—have threatened various legal actions, claiming violations of the previously noted Communications Act of 1934 and of the Copyright Act of 1976. To date, however, no legal suits have been brought against individual TVRO owners.

On the opposite side, the Society for Private and Commercial Earth Stations (SPACE) was formed in 1980 to protect the rights and interests of TVRO terminal owners and manufacturers. Contending that the Communications Act of 1934 is inappropriately applied to TVRO technology, SPACE maintains that the right to view satellite programming is grounded in the principle of freedom of access to information, and that any prohibition of such viewing denies important information services to persons located in areas not served by cable television. SPACE was instrumental in the preparation of the Satellite Viewing Rights Act (S. 2437 and H.R. 5176), which clarifies provisions of the Communications Act of 1934 pertaining to television programming transmitted by satellite. Signed by President Reagan on October 30, 1984, the Act permits the reception of such programming by TVRO earth stations operated by individuals. It does not address such reception by schools, libraries, or other organizations.

Direct Broadcast Satellite

As discussed in the preceding section, the video programming carried by communication satellites is intended for transmission to cable system operators and other specified receivers rather than to the general public. This programming may be intercepted by TVRO terminals operated by persons or organizations other than the designated recipients, but such interception is not intended by the programming source. Direct Broadcast Satellite (DBS) service, which was announced but not operational at the time this chapter was written, is a new television delivery system that will transmit signals to anyone equipped to receive them. Initially approved by the Federal Communications Commission in 1979, DBS systems will broadcast television programming to earth station receivers located in the backyards or on the rooftops of homes and office buildings.

Compared to STV, MDTV, or other systems that utilize terrestrial broadcasting methods, the use of satellites greatly extends the range of the television signal, enabling DBS systems to serve very large geographic regions. Unlike existing communications satellites that operate in the so-called C-Band portion of the electromagnetic spectrum at frequencies ranging from 4 to 7 Gigahertz, systems will transmit at the Ku-Band frequencies of 10 to 12 Gigahertz. In addition, DBS systems will transmit signals that are significantly stronger than those transmitted by communication satellites.

This combination of higher broadcast frequencies and greater signal strength will permit the use of smaller, less expensive earth station receivers. As discussed in the preceding section, most TVRO antennas measure 10 feet or larger in diameter, require considerable installation space, and cost upwards of $3,000. DBS earth stations will consist of "mini dishes" measuring about 2 feet in diameter. They will be easily installed on a rooftop, and are expected to be priced from several hundred to

$1,000. As with cable systems, STV, and TVRO terminals, the DBS subscriber's television receiver must also be equipped with a converter box that performs amplification, channel selection, and any required signal decoding.

Because of the widespread use of satellites for various governmental, business, and entertainment purposes, DBS systems are of international interest. Spectrum allocations, orbital slots, and technical standards for the western hemisphere were established in mid-1983 at a conference held in Geneva. The United States sought and received eight orbital slots, each capable of delivering 32 channels. At the time of this writing, the FCC had received DBS service applications from a number of companies, including RCA, CBS, Satellite Television Corporation (STC), DBS Corporation, Satellite Syndicated Systems, and Hubbard Broadcasting. The proposal submitted by STC, a division of Comsat, indicates the type of programming that DBS systems will provide. STC plans to launch four satellites to provide three channels of programming to the continental United States, Alaska, and Hawaii. The three channels will offer programming that closely resembles that currently available from cable services. In the manner of the previously discussed movie networks, Channel A will feature major motion pictures plus concerts, theatrical presentations, and other special programs. Channel B will offer classic films, children's programming, variety shows, and general entertainment. Channel C will feature adult education programs, sports events, and news programming. As with cable and STV systems, subscribers will pay an initial fee for the installation of the earth station and converter box, plus a monthly charge estimated at less than $20 per month.

Among other DBS applicants, CBS has proposed the implementation of high definition (HDTV) service. As discussed in chapter 1, HDTV will depart from prevailing 525-line NTSC resolution in utilizing television signals containing over 1,100 horizontal scan lines per frame. The television aspect ratio will likewise be changed to 5:3 from the present 4:3. The resulting images will be of significantly greater clarity and will have a theater-like appearance. Present telecommunication facilities—whether based on terrestrial or satellite technologies—do not permit the implementation of high definition television systems, with their greater bandwidth requirements. HDTV systems might be implemented within the context of a direct satellite broadcasting, but opponents are concerned that it will use the major portion of the broadcast spectrum allocated to DBS systems, leaving little scope for other services. At the time this chapter was written, the FCC had indicated its intention to allocate selected DBS frequencies for experimentation with HDTV broadcasting.

Because the implementation of DBS systems involves considerable planning, preparation, and expense—an estimated $625 million dollars in the case of Satellite Television Corporation—operational systems are not expected before the mid-1980s. Several companies are in the process of implementing a direct broadcast satellite service to begin in 1985 or 1986. One such service, to be operated by United Satellite Television, will provide four channels of programming—consisting of movies, sports, news, and special events—to the northeastern United States. It will utilize the Canadian Anik-C3, but, unlike the DBS systems described above, it will transmit a relatively weak, lower frequency signal that will require a somewhat larger earth station than those planned for high frequency DBS services. A similar service has been successfully used to transmit television programming to areas of northern Canada, which are beyond the range of conventional broadcasting. Other early implementations of DBS service have been announced by Comsat and Skyband.

Low-Power Television Systems

Conventional VHF and UHF television stations broadcast high power signals that permit clear reception over large geographical areas, but can interfere with the signals of other stations in nearby locations. To avoid such interference, stations broadcasting over the same channel must be at least 170 miles apart. Low-power television (LPTV) systems, as the name indicates, operate at lower wattage and have a broadcast range limited to about 15 miles in any given direction. They operate over channels that may be in use in a nearby area, but their low power signals do not cause interference.

While LPTV service received initial FCC approval in 1981, the LPTV concept is an outgrowth of the several thousand "translator" stations that have long operated in rural areas of the United States. Like the earliest cable television systems, these translator stations receive signals from distant stations and rebroadcast them to local residents over different channels, thereby extending the service area of the original station. They serve mountainous or remote areas that would otherwise remain beyond the reach of conventional television broadcasting. LPTV systems resemble these translator stations in technology, but, rather than merely relaying signals originated by other stations, they can originate programming. While they may supplement or replace translator stations in rural areas, LPTV stations will operate in urban areas as well.

Estimated costs to implement LPTV broadcasting capability range from $30,000 to over $150,000, depending on the types of services to be offered and the amount and nature of any local program production to be undertaken. These costs are very modest when compared to those associated with the implementation of a conventional VHF or UHF station, and LPTV operators are generally free of regulations that prescribe percentages of news and local programming or limit the amount of broadcast time devoted to commercials. Since approving the service, the FCC has received thousands of applications from persons and organizations attracted by the economic or other potential of LPTV. Several large companies—including ABC; Turner Broadcasting; the Neighborhood TV Company, which is partly owned by the Allstate subsidiary of Sears; and Golden West Broadcasters, owned by Gene Autry—have applied for multiple licenses, possibly with the intention of establishing a kind of "fourth network" of LPTV stations carrying common programming. The FCC considers LPTV to be an entrepreneurial activity, however, and has indicated that applications submitted by minorities and small businesses will receive preferential consideration.

At the time this chapter was written, only a few LPTV stations were in operation, but FCC license applications indicate a variety of programming plans. The most sophisticated LPTV stations will produce their own programs, emphasizing coverage of local news or sports events. In the manner of the local origination programming associated with cable systems, some library or educational programming might likewise be included. Some LPTV stations will engage in narrowcasting for special audiences. A number of minority groups, religious organizations, labor unions, and community groups have applied for LPTV licenses for this purpose. Other LPTV stations will resemble independent television stations in emphasizing syndicated programming and reruns. Still others will operate as subscription television systems, receiving movie networks or other programming services via satellite for encoded retransmission to paying customers. In some cases, a combination of these programming methods will be used.

Some of these services overlap with those offered by cable television systems, and questions have been raised about the economic viability of LPTV in areas served by cable. Current FCC regulations do not mandate that cable systems carry LPTV stations that operate in a given locality, and, given the diversity of services competing for the limited number of channels supported by most cable systems, it is unlikely that many cable operators will voluntarily carry LPTV programming. Homes wired for cable will consequently be unable to receive LPTV signals. LPTV stations operating over a given channel may likewise face competition from conventional television stations which may be licensed to operate over that channel in the future. In such situations, LPTV stations have secondary priority and, should interference prove to be a problem, they must either reduce their signal power or discontinue operation.

Pay-Per-View Television

Premium cable channels, subscription television, and other forms of pay television levy a charge for the availability of programming whether or not it is actually viewed. In pay-per-view (PPV) television, however, the viewer pays for individual programs as they are viewed. Pay-per-view is not designed as a replacement for other forms of pay television. It is instead intended for special programming events not covered by existing services. The two PPV applications most often cited are major sports events, such as championship boxing matches, which are now televised on a closed circuit basis, and motion pictures, which might be made available on a pay-per-view basis at the same time as or shortly after their theatrical release. In 1982, for example, MCA and Universal Studios offered a PPV showing, via cable, of *The Pirates of Penzance* on the same night as its New York City premiere.

The PPV concept is compatible with conventional broadcasting, cable operations, subscription television, direct satellite broadcasting, or low-power television. Two implementation methods are possible. The simplest of these—and the one that is applicable to both broadcast and cable delivery systems—involves the use of a small, disposable decoder designed to receive scrambled signals representing the PPV program. The decoder must be purchased in advance of the event from designated retail outlets or from cable or broadcast system operators. While the decoder itself is a simple and inexpensive device, its cost reflects the price of the PPV program and may vary from event to event. A technologically more sophisticated approach utilizes "receiver addressability" to transmit particular PPV programs only to those persons who have indicated an interest in them. The most advanced variant of this approach is implemented in the context of an interactive cable system in which the viewer enters designated command sequences in order to initiate viewing of PPV events. The PPV program is transmitted to the indicated receiver, and a billing is automatically generated. Some noninteractive cable or STV systems are likewise equipped with addressable converter boxes. In such installations, subscribers must preorder the transmission of PPV programs by telephone or mail. The PPV charge is typically added to the monthly cable bill.

Additional Readings

GENERAL SURVEYS

Frost, J. *World Radio TV Handbook*. New York: Watson Guptill, 1984.

Gross, L. S. *The New Television Technology*. Dubuque, Iowa: William C. Brown, 1983.

Mahoney, S., ed. *Keeping Pace with the New Television—Public Television and Changing Technology*. Washington: National Association of Educational Broadcasters, 1980.

Remley, F. M. *Tomorrow's Television*. Scarsdale, New York: Society of Motion Picture and Television Engineers, 1982.

Tuomola, O., ed. *International TV and Video Guide*. New York: New York Zeotrope, 1983.

CABLE PROGRAMMING

Bagamery, A. SIN, the original. *Forbes* 130: 96–99 (November 22, 1982).

Beck, K. *Cultivating the Wasteland: Can Cable Put the Vision Back in TV?* New York: American Council on the Arts, 1983.

Blakely, R. J. *To Serve the Public Interest: Educational Broadcasting in the United States*. Syracuse: Syracuse University Press, 1979.

Charren, P., and Sandler, M. W. *Changing Channels*. Reading, Massachusetts: Addison-Wesley, 1983.

Collins, R. J. *A Voice from Afar: The History of Telecommunications in Canada*. Toronto: McGraw-Hill Ryerson, 1977.

Eissler, C. O. Tiered services delivery and control. *IEEE Transactions on Consumer Electronics* 26: 24–31 (1980).

Hadden, J. K., and Swann, C. E. *Prime Time Preachers: The Rise of Televangelism*. Reading, Massachusetts: Addison-Wesley, 1981.

Holden, S. When puberty hits them, MTV is waiting. *The Dial* 4: 37–38 (June 1983).

Jehoram, H., ed. *Cable Television: Media and Copyright Law Aspects*. Hingham, Massachusetts: Kluwer Academic, 1983.

Kanner, B. Can't stop the music channel. *New York Magazine* 15: 18–21 (October 11, 1982).

Litman, B. R. Emerging oligopoly of pay-TV in the U.S.A. *Telecommunications Policy* 5: 121–35.

Roman, J. W. *Cablemania: The Cable Television Sourcebook*. Englewood Cliffs, New Jersey: Prentice-Hall, 1983.

Sloan, A., and Bagamery, A. The electronic pulpit. *Forbes* 126: 116–24 (July 7, 1980).

Sloan Commission on Cable Communications. *On the Cable: The Television of Abundance*. New York: McGraw-Hill, 1971.

CABLE TECHNOLOGY

Akgun, M. B. Comparison of technology and capital costs for new home services. *IEEE Transactions on Cable Television* 5: 124–38 (1980).

Baldwin, T. F., and McVoy, D. S. *Cable Communications*. Englewood Cliffs, New Jersey: Prentice-Hall, 1983.

Bivins, K. T. Cable television in the United States and Europe. *Electronic Publishing Review* 3: 131–43 (June 1983).

Dagen, C. L. Playcable: A technological alternative for information services. *IEEE Transactions on Consumer Electronics* 26: 402–6 (1980).

Ernst, M. L. Cable's economic impacts. *Technology Review* 8: 52–55 (January 1983).

Hollowell, M. L. *The Cable-Broadband Communications Book*. White Plains, New York: Knowledge Industries Publications, 1983.

Lewis, P. M. *Community Television and Cable in Britain*. New York: New York Zeotrope, 1978.

Phillips, M. A. M. *CATV: A History of Community Antenna Television*. Evanston, Illinois: Northwestern University Press, 1971.

Smith, R. L. *The Wired Nation*. New York: Harper and Row, 1972.

Varley, P. Cities as operators. *Technology Review* 86: 57–60 (January 1983).

INTERACTIVE CABLE SYSTEMS

Baldwin, T. F., Muth, T. A., and Saxton, J. E. Public policy in two-way cable: Difficult issues for a developing technology. *Telecommunications Policy* 3: 126–33 (1979).

Baldwin, T. F., et al. Cognitive and affective outcomes of a telecommunication interactive system: The MSU/Rockford two-way cable project. *Journal of Communications* 28: 180–94 (1978).

Bushman, F. A., and Robinson, R. Two-way television: A tool for new product research. *Business Horizons* 42: 69–75 (July-August 1981).

Ellis, M. L., et al. Indax: An operational interactive cabletext system. *IEEE Journal on Selected Areas in Communications* 1: 285–94 (1983).

Finley, M. R. Design considerations for second generation Hi-Ovis. In *Proceedings of FOC '79: Fiber Optics and Communications*, pp. 202–7. Brookline, Massachusetts: Information Gatekeepers, 1979.

Wolf, S., and Latane, B. If laboratory research doesn't square with you, then Qube it: The potential of interactive TV for social psychological research. *Personal and Social Psychology Bulletin* 7: 344–52 (1981).

Wright, J. B., Block, M. P., and McVoy, D. S. An evolutionary approach to the development of two-way cable communication technology. *IEEE Transactions on Cable Television* 2: 52–61 (1977).

LIBRARY APPLICATIONS

Burk, L. C., and Esteves, R., eds. *Video and Cable Guidelines*. Chicago: American Library Association, 1980.

Diebler, M. The library superstation: A library guide to satellite earth stations. *Information Technology and Libraries* 1: 231–37 (1982).

Donaldson, M. F. First public library satellite receiver system. *Information Technology and Libraries* 1: 327–30 (1982).

Sturken, M. Video systems for libraries: An EFLA workshop. *Sightlines* 16: 16–18 (Spring, 1983).

LOW-POWER TELEVISION

Jacobs, G. Low power television. *IEEE Spectrum* 19: 54–59 (June 1982).

Wyche, M.C., and Stamler, D. The local promise of low power TV. *Satellite Communications* 7: 30–33 (April 1983).

PAY-PER-VIEW TV

Perr, C. D. Security and addressability for pay-TV. *Electronic Technology* 17: 55–57 (March 3, 1983).

Thompson, G. B. Pay television—Some new possibilities. *Telesis* 8: 20–25 (January 1981).

SATELLITE SYSTEMS

Bargellini, P. L. Commercial U.S. satellites. *IEEE Spectrum* 16: 30–37 (October 1979).

Blonstein, L. Direct broadcasting by satellite in Europe: System characteristics of direct broadcasting. *Aeronautical Journal* 86: 123–26 (April 1982).

Easton, A. T. *The Home Satellite TV Book: How to Put the World in Your Yard.* New York: Putnam Publishing Group, 1981.

Eustace, P. DBS: A question of standards. *Engineer* 255: 32–33 (December 2, 1983).

Fawcette, J. Direct satellite TV: The 12-GHz challenge. *High Technology* 2: 42–51 (January-February 1982).

Fox, B. Satellite TV starts the ultimate craze. *New Scientist* 95: 680–83 (1982).

Freedman, K. G. Direct broadcast satellite receivers. *Radio and Electronics Engineer* 52: 127–33 (March 1982).

Freeling, M. R., and Schiff, L. Technical standards for direct broadcast satellite systems. *RCA Review* 42: 408–23 (1981).

Goldberg, J. *Satellite Reception: A Personal User's Guide.* Englewood Cliffs, New Jersey: Prentice-Hall, 1984.

Goodman, D. Direct broadcast satellite television. *Radio-Electronics* 53: 55–58 (December 1982).

Martin, J. *Communications Satellite Systems.* Englewood Cliffs, New Jersey: Prentice-Hall, 1978.

Pritchard, W. L., and Kase, C. A. Getting set for direct broadcast satellites. *IEEE Spectrum* 18: 22–28 (August 1981).

TELEVISION BROADCASTING

Ducey, R. V. Predicting the adoption of broadcasting innovations by relating technical attributes to user needs: Implications for system designs. *IEEE Transactions on Broadcasting* 29: 52–59 (1983).

Emery, W. B. *National and International Systems of Broadcasting: Their History, Operation, and Control.* East Lansing: Michigan State University Press, 1969.

Gieseler, P. B. UHF television: A review and update. *Proceedings of the IEEE* 70: 1254–63 (1982).

Head, S. W., and Sterling, C. H. *Broadcasting in America: A Survey of Television, Radio, and New Technologies.* 4th edition. Boston: Houghton Mifflin, 1982.

Herrndorf, P. Canadian broadcasting—The challenge for the eighties. *SMPTE Journal* 90: 1051–53 (1981).

Hufford, G. A., and Murray, J. P. Television coverage in the coterminous United States: Methodology and results. *Proceedings of the IEEE* 70: 1263–68 (1982).

Kahn, F. J., ed. *Documents of American Broadcasting.* 4th edition. Englewood Cliffs, New Jersey: Prentice-Hall, 1984.

Litman, B. R. U.S. TV networks' response to new technology. *Telecommunications Policy* 7: 163–77 (June 1983).

Litman, B. R. *Vertical Structure of the Television Broadcasting Industry*. East Lansing: Michigan State University, 1979.

Sidey, P., et al. History of British television. *SMPTE Journal* 90: 1165–72 (1981).

Strauss, L. *Home Video and Broadcasting: The Fight for Position, 1981–86*. White Plains, New York: Knowledge Industries Publications, 1981.

CHAPTER 5

VIDEOTEXT AND RELATED SYSTEMS

The preceding chapters have dealt with video systems that are primarily designed to display information in the form of graphic images derived from broadcast, cable, or local sources. While such information may contain occasional text segments, such text typically operates in the service of visual material. This is the case, for example, with the textual frames of interactive video disk programs that solicit viewer responses to direct the subsequent presentation of graphic images. The notable exceptions are those cable services, such as Reuters News View and Dow Jones Cable News, that continuously display textual information. Some local cable systems also operate community bulletin boards that function in a similar manner. Such "cabletext" services might be considered primitive variants of the videotext systems to be discussed in this chapter, but they differ from true videotext technology in at least one important respect: the sequence and speed of information display is entirely controlled by the originator. With videotext systems, by way of contrast, the viewer selects desired information and controls the speed and sequence in which it is displayed.

The term "videotext" is widely and loosely used to denote information processing activities ranging from online information retrieval to the electronic dissemination of microcomputer software, and any discussion of videotext systems must first deal with the problem of terminology. As used in this book, "videotext" is a generic designation for systems that disseminate combinations of textual and graphic information to modified television receivers or other relatively inexpensive terminals. Unlike the video systems discussed to this point, the textual information is of primary significance, and graphics play a complementary or, in some cases, decorative role. While animation is possible, videotext information typically consists of preformatted still frames dealing with specific topics.

Since their inception in the early 1970s, videotext systems have been divided into two broad groups on the basis of the dissemination methodology utilized:

1. Teletext systems, sometimes called "broadcast videotext," utilize a portion of the conventional television signal to transmit information over the air or through cable operators.

2. Viewdata, or "interactive videotext," uses telephone lines and operates in much the same manner as conventional timeshared computing services.

Recently, however, trade publications, vendor announcements, and some technical literature have begun using the term "videotext" as an alternative to viewdata, distinguishing it from teletext. The Comité Consultatif International Téléphonique et Télégraphique (CCITT), the international body responsible for the development of telecommunications standards, has endorsed this usage, recommending that the generic term "videotext" be discontinued. Others have suggested the use of different, presumably more meaningful terms such as "videoprint" for all video-based systems that are textual in orientation. Terminology is far from being standardized, and various combinations of the foregoing terms are used interchangeably and, often, erroneously. Following the usage most firmly established in professional literature, this book retains videotext as the generic designation and maintains the customary distinction between its teletext and viewdata variants.

Videotext originated as a consumer-oriented service designed to deliver information to home television receivers. While this remains its primary focus, videotext services commonly provide news and economic information of considerable interest to business, government agencies, and other organizations. In addition, special interest videotext systems have been developed specifically for business audiences. Equally important, videotext offers excellent commercial opportunities for businesses and other organizations through both advertisement and the fee-based provision of information.

As with the cable services discussed in the preceding chapter, the library implications of videotext systems are rooted in combinations of interest, cooperation, and competition. As will be discussed in later sections of this chapter, much of the information provided by videotext systems duplicates or supplements the contents of reference books and other printed materials. Videotext systems can consequently be viewed as a potentially valuable resource to be made available to the library's clientele. In this respect, they closely resemble the more conventional online search services offered by such companies as the Dialog Information Service, System Development Corporation, and Bibliographic Retrieval Services. Libraries might also serve as videotext information providers, using these services as the vehicle for announcing new acquisitions and journal subscriptions, providing remote access to the card catalog or other holdings information, or permitting electronic reservation of items. Examples of such applications are discussed in a later section. Finally, and ominously, the direct delivery capabilities of videotext systems represent a possible long-term threat to libraries that act as intermediaries between information providers and users. Although several of the more aggressive American vendors have described their videotext services as possible models for an electronic library of the future, the scope of videotext systems is presently far narrower than that of library services, and there is little competition between the two modes of information delivery. If anything, the abbreviated information offered by videotext systems may stimulate an interest in the more detailed reference materials offered by libraries.

This chapter begins with a discussion of videotext technology, emphasizing fundamental concepts of significance for consumers, businesses, libraries, and other users and providers of videotext information services. Subsequent sections describe the types of available information and discuss examples of operational and experimental systems. The chapter closes with a brief description of some interesting information services that are related to, and often confused with, videotext.

Videotext Technology

Teletext vs. Viewdata

As discussed above, videotext systems are traditionally divided into two broad variants: teletext and viewdata. Teletext is a broadcast method that uses an otherwise unused portion of the conventional television signal called the vertical blanking interval (VBI) to transmit textual and simple graphic information composed as a series of still frames. This information, which is encoded as digital data, is displayed by television receivers equipped with a special decoder. It is ignored by unmodified receivers. Most existing teletext systems utilize the vertical blanking interval to transmit 2 lines of data. One teletext frame, composed of 24 lines, is transmitted in a sequence of 12 vertical blanking intervals. In the European PAL and SECAM video systems where teletext originated, vertical blanking intervals occur at a rate of 50 per second, yielding a teletext broadcast rate of 4 frames per second.

Borrowing terminology from the publishing industry, teletext information is usually formatted as a "magazine" consisting of a predetermined number of pages or frames continuously broadcast on a recirculating basis. As will be described in greater detail in a later section, one or more pages serve as an index. After consulting the index, the viewer enters the number of a desired page. This page is captured by the teletext decoder as it is rebroadcast, and is stored in its internal memory for screen display. The number of pages in the magazine determines the retrieval time, and the need for reasonable access time constrains magazine size. Most teletext magazines consist of about 100 frames which, at a rate of 4 frames per second, provides a worst case access time of 25 seconds and an average access time of 13.5 seconds. A 200-frame magazine would double the amount of available information with a corresponding doubling of access time, as individual frames are rebroadcast at longer intervals. Similarly, any reduction in the number of frames would yield faster access times. The magazine's size could be increased, and reasonable access times maintained, if a larger portion of each vertical blanking interval were utilized for teletext information. Alternatively, an entire channel might be dedicated exclusively to teletext, thereby permitting very rapid access to several thousand pages. Unfortunately, unused VHF or UHF channels are rarely available in the urban areas where the teletext market is broadest, but full-channel teletext service might be provided by some high capacity cable systems.

Viewdata systems, like their teletext counterparts, present information formatted in pages or frames consisting of text and graphics. But rather than being continuously rebroadcast in a magazine format, viewdata pages are maintained as a computerized data base on magnetic disks or other direct access storage devices, awaiting retrieval commands issued from a user terminal. The size of the data base is determined by the amount of available online storage, and systems offering several hundred thousand pages have been implemented. The specific computer and data base configuration varies from implementation to implementation. In the simplest approach—employed by some business viewdata systems and in short-term viewdata experiments—a single computer is used, although this configuration is vulnerable to equipment downtime. In the British Prestel system, discussed later in this chapter, the data base is replicated on multiple computer systems in different geographic locations. Although it requires considerable online storage facilities, the replicated approach offers good protection against the failure of any single computer, and geographic scattering reduces telecommunication charges for most users. As an extension of this approach, individual data bases may combine a common core of general information with some pages of local appeal. Alternatively, the most frequently requested pages might be maintained by local computer facilities, with the remainder of the data base stored in one master center. Such combinations of local and remote data bases are utilized by the West German Bildschirmtext system. As yet another possibility, multiple computer systems, might specialize in particular types of information, with retrieval requests being automatically routed to the appropriate site. In the French Teletel plan, viewdata computers serve as nodes in a data communications network that provides access to data bases maintained by many different computers.

As with teletext, viewdata systems transmit digital data to modified television receivers or low cost terminals equipped with special decoders. But unlike teletext, which broadcasts this data over the air, viewdata terminals are typically connected to remote computers via telephone lines that permit two-way communication. As is the case with all timesharing computer systems, the telephone network offers the substantial advantages of extensive geographic coverage and reasonable telecommunication costs. Its disadvantage is a limited transmission rate—usually 1200 bits per second—which forces system designers to reduce the amount of information contained in a given page in order to achieve a reasonable transmission time. This is typically accomplished by eliminating detail and simplifying graphics. Coaxial cable and microwave transmission, either of which would permit the faster transmission of more complex images, have been discussed as possible alternatives to telephone lines. In both the United States and Europe, these alternative telecommunications facilities suffer the disadvantage of limited availability. As discussed in the preceding chapter, cable television is available to less than 30 percent of American homes, and cable penetration in European countries ranges from 2 to 15 percent. With about 60 percent of its households wired for cable television, Canada is in the best position to implement higher speed viewdata communications. Two-way cable facilities remain uncommon in all countries, although hybrid systems have been suggested in which telephone lines are used to transmit the terminal user's retrieval requests to the viewdata computer system, and cable is used to transmit the desired frames back to the terminal.

Compared to viewdata technology, teletext systems require no special telecommunications or computer facilities and are consequently simpler and faster to implement. But their interactive facilities are limited to the selection of desired pages from a recirculating magazine, and constraints on magazine size restrict opportunities for the information providers on whom the commercial success of videotext systems depends. In most teletext systems, the available page capacity must be rationed among participating information providers. Viewdata systems, on the other hand, require greater implementation effort, more elaborate computer systems with large amounts of online storage facilities, and somewhat more expensive user terminals. As significant advantages over teletext, however, they can provide highly interactive access to a much greater number of pages. This, in turn, enhances their subscriber appeal and offers greater commercial opportunity to prospective information providers, each of whom can contribute a greater number of pages.

As a further advantage, the computer-like nature of viewdata systems allows them to address a broader range of information processing applications. They can, for example, be expanded to offer conventional computing services, electronic message capabilities, home banking, and home shopping. Such expansion is not possible with teletext, and prevailing opinion strongly affirms the greater long-term potential of viewdata systems. The two technologies do not necessarily compete with one another, however, and teletext might serve as a simpler precursor to viewdata in areas where videotext services are being introduced. Alternatively, the two services might coexist, teletext being used for news headlines or other rapidly changing information and viewdata for more varied and detailed retrieval requirements.

Videotext Terminals

As noted above, both teletext and viewdata systems transmit encoded digital data to specially designed receivers. These receivers are called "user terminals" to distinguish them from the "editing terminals" used by information providers. Most observers agree that the widespread availability of inexpensive user terminals is critical to the successful implementation of videotext systems. The simplest configuration is a modified color television receiver equipped with a decoder, memory circuitry, a keyboard, and—for use in viewdata systems—a modem. The decoder is a microprocessor that accepts incoming videotext signals, distinguishes control codes from data, and transfers them to memory circuits from which they are continuously displayed on the television screen. Ideally, a given decoder should be useful for both teletext and viewdata signals. Most videotext terminals currently store a single page of data, although, as memory prices drop, multipage memories should become increasingly common.

The videotext terminal's keypad is used for frame selection and other system interaction. Teletext systems usually feature simple, calculator-style numeric keypads that are sufficient to enter page numbers and other simple commands. Viewdata systems, with their greater capabilities and complexity, typically utilize alphanumeric keyboards similar to those of the conventional computer terminals described in chapter 8. Regardless of layout, videotext terminal keyboards are lightweight and are designed for tabletop or lap use (figure 26). To keep size and cost to a minimum, conventional typewriter-style keycaps are rarely used. Instead, most models feature flat membrane keyboards or calculator-style key buttons. Since videotext retrieval operations, as described in a later section, rarely necessitate the high speed typing associated with terminal or microcomputer applications, such keyboards pose little inconvenience.

Modems, as noted above, are required in viewdata applications, where they permit the transmission and reception of data via telephone lines. Most viewdata terminals are equipped with a Bell 212A or equivalent modem for data communication at 1,200 bits per second. The nature and function of modems will be discussed more fully in chapter 8. Because they receive broadcast signals, teletext terminals do not require modems.

FIGURE 26

The least expensive videotext adapters are simple keyboards designed for attachment to customer-owned television receivers. (Courtesy: Quazon)

In addition to these essential components, some videotext terminals can be equipped with cassette recorders, disk drives, printers, or other peripheral attachments. Some models offer special convenience features such as the automatic dialing of prestored telephone numbers, support for the call waiting feature if provided by the telephone in use, and security and encryption capabilities that permit home banking and related services.

In Great Britain, new color television sets can be purchased with integral videotext decoders, keyboards, and modems. Such sets provide the highest quality reception and feature a simplified styling that results from the elimination of separate components. Such videotext-ready televisions are currently priced about $200 to $250 higher than conventional color television receivers, although the price differential should be gradually reduced with the decreasing cost of electronic components.

In Europe, where a substantial percentage of television sets are rented, videotext subscribers can usually exchange their conventional receivers for newer models compatible with videotext reception, paying only the extra monthly charge associated with the more complex equipment. But in countries such as the United States where television sets are typically owned, prospective videotext subscribers are understandably reluctant to purchase special television receivers. All videotext system operators consequently offer add-on decoders and related components designed for attachment to customer-owned television sets. These add-on decoders offer a psychological advantage, since the prospective subscriber sees only the relatively small purchase or monthly rental charge for the decoder, not the much higher cost of a replacement television receiver.

Like cable converters, videocassette recorders, video disk players, and other peripheral video devices, videotext decoder boxes are attached to the receiver's antenna poles. The inevitable result, as previously noted, is some signal degradation. The displayed information is typically quite legible, but colors and images are not as bright and sharp as those displayed by receivers with integral videotext decoders. As discussed in chapter 1, this signal degradation is minimized with video monitors or component television systems that can accept direct input from the videotext decoder. In France, where the nationwide implementation of videotext is planned, all newly manufactured television receivers must be equipped with input jacks for the direct connection of decoders and other video peripheral devices.

In addition to modified television receivers, videotext terminals have been developed for special applications. Of particular significance for this discussion are public access videotext terminals designed for installation in libraries, community centers, shopping malls, government buildings, and similar locations where they will be available to uninstructed users on a walk-up basis. These public access terminals are actually protective enclosures for a video monitor and videotext decoder. Typically, a keyboard and accompanying instructions are located on the front panel. If desired, the terminal can be configured for coin operation.

As an alternative to conventional television sets, some videotext systems employ dedicated terminals that closely resemble conventional computer terminals (figure 27). In France, for example, such terminals have been distributed to participants in an electronic directory assistance project that will eventually be implemented on a nationwide basis. In other countries, they are often used in viewdata systems developed for business applications. Designed for compactness and economy, these special videotext terminals make extensive use of microprocessors and integrated memory circuits. Unlike more expensive terminals, they often utilize calculator-style keybuttons instead of typewriter keycaps. To simplify operation and minimize the memorization of commands, dedicated keys are provided for the most important

FIGURE 27

Some videotext systems employ special terminals which closely resemble microcomputers. (Courtesy: Electrohome)

videotext functions. At 9 inches (diagonal), their screens are smaller than those of most video display terminals, and, to further reduce costs, they often substitute shades of gray for the full color display capabilities provided by modified television receivers. For maximum versatility, some models are designed for either videotext operations or conventional computer communications. In a variant of this approach, several companies offer software packages that will enable the most popular microcomputer systems to function as videotext terminals.

Display Capabilities

As briefly indicated in the preceding sections, videotext systems format information into pages containing combinations of text and graphics. A videotext page is the equivalent of one television frame, and the page format is largely determined by the resolution characteristics of the television receivers that are most often used as videotext terminals. Following the procedure employed by British and French videotext systems, individual pages are divided into a grid of rectangular cells, each of which is used to store a textual character or graphic symbol. In Europe, where videotext systems originated and where operating experience is most extensive, the grid format consists of 24 to 26 horizontal lines of data, each containing 40 characters. In North America, where NTSC resolution standards provide fewer scan lines than their PAL or SECAM counterparts, videotext page formats are typically composed of 15 to 20 lines of data, each containing 32 to 40 characters. In this context, it is important to maintain the distinction between horizontal scan lines and videotext data lines. As discussed in chapter 1, horizontal lines consist of successive picture elements that are selectively illuminated to form the video image. Videotext data lines are composed of multiple scan lines and picture elements. As a further point of clarification, both the European and North American videotext page formats differ markedly from conventional computer display formats, which typically provide 24 lines of 80 or 132 characters each.

Like the video display terminals to be discussed in chapter 8, videotext systems transmit data as sequences of 7- or 8-bit codes that are converted by the decoder into displayable characters. The typical videotext typographic repertoire, and the set of prerecorded cells used to create the alphamosaics that will be described below, includes the upper- and lowercase alphabet (including diacritical marks and accented characters in European applications outside of the United Kingdom), numeric digits, punctuation marks, and other symbols commonly found in printed text. As noted above, each character occupies a single cell and, in the manner of conventional computer display terminals, is formed by altering the luminance of picture elements in a predetermined pattern or matrix. Prevailing matrix sizes range from 6 by 10 picture elements in the British Prestel system to 8 by 10 picture elements in the French Antiope system. To enhance legibility, lowercase characters such as the *p*, *q*, and *y* are displayed with descending stems, and one to three blank picture elements are left between individual characters and data lines. Character rounding techniques are used to eliminate the jagged edges resulting from matrix composition (figure 28).

To avoid an intimidating and potentially confusing format, most videotext pages are limited to about 100 words, the remaining space being occupied by graphics that highlight or complement the text. While this reliance on graphics is a common feature of all videotext systems, there have been significant and much publicized variations in the method by which graphic displays are created. Three methods are currently available: alphamosaic, alphageometric, and alphaphotographic. In the alphamosaic method—used in the United Kingdom, France, and other European countries that have adopted British and French videotext technology—individual cells are divided into a 6-part matrix comprised of 3 rows and 2 columns. Picture elements in each part of the matrix can be represented as either light or dark shades. In conventional alphamosaic systems, the repertoire of reproduceable mosaic symbols is built into the videotext terminal and cannot be varied. The 64 possible light and dark combinations form a set of mosaics that can be assembled to create graphic images. Each mosaic symbol is represented by a 7- or 8-bit data code that is easily transmitted and consumes little memory space in the videotext decoder. As a significant advantage, alphamosaic systems can use simple, inexpensive terminals with relatively small memories. On the negative side, alphamosaic graphics are often criticized for their ragged appearance. They can represent relatively simple shapes, but are unsuitable for line drawings or more complex presentations.

The number of preprogrammed alphamosaic cells is limited, but it can be expanded by a technique called "dynamically redefinable character sets" (DRCS) which allows additional, special purpose character sets—such as musical symbols or non-Roman alphabets—to be loaded into the videotext terminal at the time they are to be displayed. These character sets are electronically transmitted by the videotext operator as required. A somewhat more complex terminal with a larger memory is required, but display versatility is significantly improved.

The alphageometric approach, developed by the Canadian Department of Communications for use in its Telidon videotext system, offers much more extensive graphic display capabilities. Rather than transmitting codes that represent the mosaic characters to be combined in a given graphic presentation, the alphageometric approach transmits coded commands, called "picture description instructions" (PDIs), that indicate the type of geometric figure to be displayed (such as a line, an arc, a rectangle, or a polygon) and its starting and ending locations within the display area. The structure of these picture description instructions resembles the command languages employed in computer-aided design systems and in programming languages such as BASIC, LOGO, and PILOT, which have graphic extensions. Operating under the control of stored programs, the alphageometric terminal interprets the incoming instructions and draws the indicated figures.

Conceived as a second generation videotext system, alphageometric graphics are of noticeably higher quality and greater variety than those produced by the alphamosaic approach. As a further advantage, PDIs use an abstract notation that is independent of the resolution capabilities of any particular terminal. Should higher resolution video displays become widespread, alphageometric systems will be able to use them. The often cited disadvantage of alphageometric systems is the requirement for a more complex terminal with a relatively large internal memory. These terminals are currently several hundred dollars more expensive than alphamosaic models, but anticipated reductions in the cost of electronic circuitry are expected to reduce that differential significantly, making the alphageometric approach increasingly attractive.

While they offer a noticeable improvement over alphamosaic displays, alphageometric graphics do not approach the quality and detail associated with video images originating from broadcast sources, cable systems, videocassette recorders, or video disk players (figure 29). As noted above, videotext images, whether based on alphamosaic or alphageometric concepts, are intentionally simplified to reduce their information content and, consequently, the required transmission time.

By way of contrast, the alphaphotographic method of representing videotext graphics provides quality and detail equivalent to that of conventional video images. It accomplishes this by significantly increasing the amount of information transmitted about individual pages. In effect, several hundred thousand picture elements are individually encoded using multiple bit patterns to represent various colors. The resulting signal may consist of several million bits of data which, in turn, requires a videotext terminal with a very large internal memory. A further problem resulting from the limitations of telephone network transmission at 1,200 bits per second is the impractically long transmission times—on the order of 10 to 60 minutes per frame, even with data compression techniques. No operational videotext systems are currently using alphaphotographic coding although several systems have demonstrated alphaphotographic capabilities on an experimental basis. In the Picture Prestel demonstration, for example, alphaphotographic encoding was utilized to produce a small, high quality inset within a videotext frame encoded by alphamosaic methods. Such limitation of image area reduces the terminal's memory requirement and permits transmission times of approximately one minute.

Regardless of the graphic encoding method used, videotext systems rely heavily

FIGURE 28

With alphamosaic systems, conventional text is readable, but block characters have jagged edges and graphics are primitive. (Courtesy: Oracle Teletext Limited)

FIGURE 29

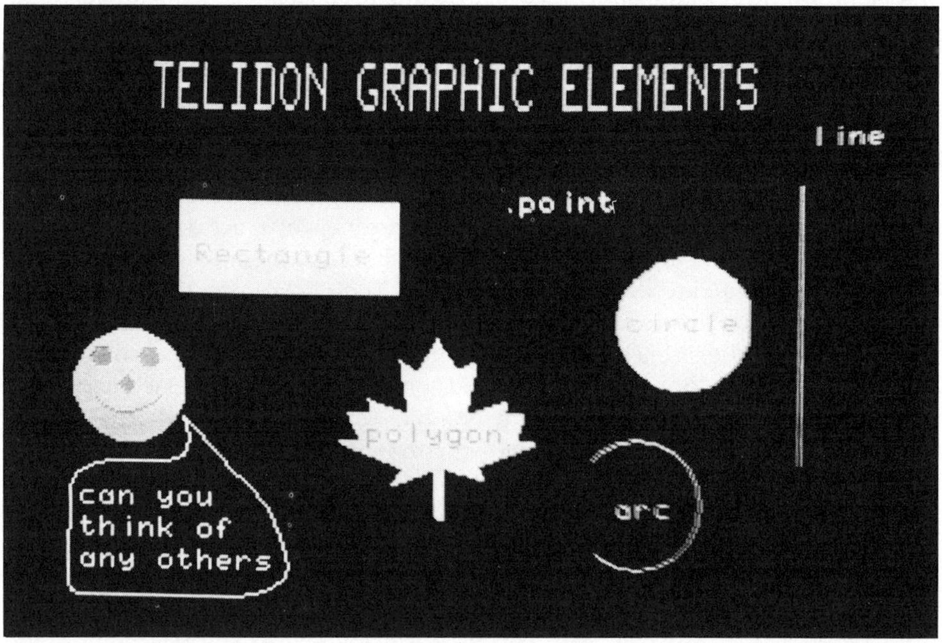

Alphageometric display offers higher graphic quality than alphamosaic. (Courtesy: Govt. of Canada, Dept. of Communications)

on color to highlight textual information and enhance the appearance of graphics. In this respect, videotext systems depart sharply from display patterns employed by conventional computer systems, most of which rely exclusively on monochrome displays. In addition to black-and-white, most videotext systems use six colors: yellow, cyan, green, magenta, red, and blue, all of which can be displayed in various hues. Color changes are commonly used instead of line breaks to separate text segments and to demarcate screens. For maximum clarity, no more than three colors are typically used at one time.

To further enhance the appearance and variety of videotext pages, characters can be displayed in various sizes, in reduced intensity, or in reverse video (dark on a light background, rather than the opposite which is common with conventional computer displays). Blinking and underlining can be used to further highlight particular text segments.

Standardization

As noted in the preceding section, there is considerable variation—and, in fact, rivalry—in the prevalent methods of displaying graphic images used by existing videotext systems. The distinction between alphamosaic and alphageometric graphic coding is the most obvious area of incompatibility, but—as a further complication—there is some variation within the alphamosaic approach. Videotext systems transmit signals that consist of combinations of data and control characters. The latter are used to initiate color changes, intensity changes, blinking, or other special display attributes. Although they both use alphamosaic graphics, British and French videotext systems differ in their handling of these control characters.

The British Prestel, CEEFAX, and ORACLE systems use a synchronous, fixed format method of alphamosaic presentation in which each line of transmitted data corresponds to a given row on the display screen. Each alphanumeric character or graphic symbol occupies one display cell and is stored in a corresponding location in the receiver's internal memory. Control characters, which are embedded in the incoming data stream, are processed serially and occupy memory cells that would otherwise be devoted to displayable characters. Their corresponding screen locations are either displayed as a repetition of the adjacent color or as a blank space. By way of contrast, the French ANTIOPE system uses an asynchronous method of alphamosaic presentation in which data and control codes are processed in parallel fashion. Alphanumeric characters and graphic symbols are stored in a display memory, and control codes are stored in corresponding locations in a separate memory.

While the videotext user may perceive little difference in the two approaches, the French method requires a slightly more complex decoder, but permits somewhat more varied graphic displays, since colors and other visual attributes can be changed on a character-by-character basis without sacrificing display space. In the British approach, control characters consume available space in display memory and on the video screen. As a further point of variation, British videotext systems can use a 7-bit character coding scheme, while the French system, which must display accented characters and diacritical marks, requires the greater number of combinations offered by 8-bit character codes. There are likewise differences in the specific codes used to represent particular characters.

Claims for the superiority of a given method of presentation go beyond national pride. Countries like Great Britain and France have made substantial investments in videotext technology which they hope to license to other countries or to private firms. From the user's standpoint, however, standardization is preferable to competition. Such standardization would presumably eliminate much wasteful duplication of technical research; offer a broader, more lucrative market for information providers; facilitate the transportability of information from one system to another; lead to economies of scale in the manufacturing of videotext transmission and reception equipment; and permit the design of universal decoders.

To date, however, videotext standardization efforts have been less concerned with the reconciliation of incompatible methodologies than with the codification of prevailing practices. This is the case, for example, with the CCITT S.100 recommendation entitled "International Information Exchange for Interactive Videotext." Approved by the Comité Consultatif International Téléphonique et Télégraphique in late 1980, it merely recognizes the existence of three different approaches—the British Prestel, French ANTIOPE, and Canadian Telidon systems—as subsets of a videotext standard. In 1981, the Conference Européenne des Postes et Télécommunications (CEPT) formulated a unified alphamosaic system based on both the British and French models. Termed the European Unified Standard (EUS), it will permit the design of decoders and data bases suitable for use in many countries.

Perhaps the most widely publicized of videotext standardization efforts, the North American Presentation Level Protocol System (NAPLPS) was jointly formulated by the American National Standards Institute (ANSI) and the Canadian Standards Association (CSA) in 1982. Relying heavily on a videotext protocol developed by the American Telephone and Telegraph Company, NAPLPS combines elements of alphamosaic and alphageometric systems, emphasizing the latter, but going beyond the Telidon system in its provision of PDI. A number of companies are manufacturing NAPLPS terminals. Although this discussion emphasizes videotext applications, NAPLPS is a general purpose standard for the formatting and display of graphic information. As such, it can also be used by conventional computer systems to encode pictures to be reproduced by graphic terminals, printers, plotters, typesetters, and related equipment.

Videotext Installations and Experiments

The European Experience

In marked contrast to other innovations in video technology, most of which have originated in the United States or Japan, videotext is primarily a European development, and the existing body of knowledge and assumptions about videotext is largely based on experience derived from systems operating in European countries. Of these, Great Britain has the most extensive videotext experience and the greatest number of operational systems.

British experiments with teletext technology date from the early 1970s and grew out of British Broadcasting Corporation's interest in closed captioning systems, both for their use by persons with hearing impairments and their potential significance for language minorities within the United Kingdom, South Africa, and Canada. After several years of technical testing and pilot programs, commercial teletext service was introduced in 1976, and Great Britain is now served by two teletext systems: CEEFAX, a British Broadcasting Corporation service that operates on BBC-1 and BBC-2; and ORACLE, which is operated by the Independent Broadcasting Authority (IBA) and is broadcast over the two commercial television channels, Independent Television (ITV) and Channel 4.

From its inception, British teletext has been viewed as a logical extension of normal broadcast activities—a kind of "printed radio"—and the early planning and operation of CEEFAX services were dominated by journalists. British teletext does not seek new applications. It merely provides an alternative treatment of topics covered by other broadcasting services. Compared to radio and television broadcasting, however, teletext offers two potentially significant advantages:

1. Teletext systems respond quickly to content changes. Rather than waiting for broadcasts at regularly scheduled intervals, news bulletins, sports results, weather changes, and other significant developments can be reported immediately.

2. As an advantage of convenience rather than content, teletext viewers can select items of interest to them. Teletext pages can be examined at the viewer's leisure in any sequence.

Although they share this news orientation, the two CEEFAX operations differ in purpose and content. The BBC-1 service resembles a daily newspaper or evening news broadcast in emphasizing news headlines, sports results, current weather, and financial reports. The BBC-2 service, which features more detailed background information and in-depth reporting, is analogous to a weekly news magazine. Both services offer several hundred pages in the magazine format that is characteristic of teletext systems.

User acceptance of British teletext reflects a pattern characteristic of much technological innovation. A disappointing early reception has been followed by steadily increasing popularity. As a broadcast methodology, teletext service is free to viewers equipped with appropriately modified television receivers. CEEFAX operating costs are covered by the obligatory licensing fees paid by British television owners. ORACLE costs are covered by advertising revenues. Teletext acceptance is further encouraged by the extent and nature of British television installations. An estimated 97 percent of British households have at least one color television set, and about half of them are rented. At a cost of several additional dollars per month, these conventional rented sets can be exchanged for teletext-compatible models. As previously noted, existing receivers can be equipped with teletext decoders, and new color television sets can be purchased with integral teletext decoders for the highest quality reception.

While British teletext service can build on the excellent market penetration of television receivers, viewdata services are at an understandable disadvantage in a country where only 60 percent of the homes have telephones. Prestel, the famous viewdata service operated by the British Post Office (BPO), became publicly available in 1979. Its underlying concepts date from 1970 and were an outgrowth of BPO experiments with Viewphone, the British counterpart of Picturephone—a telephone system that permitted visual as well as audio communication. The Prestel data base is computer-maintained and is replicated at multiple service centers that are accessed via the telephone network, using specially modified television receivers. British teletext and viewdata standards are based on the same alphamosaic display concepts, and Prestel signals are compatible with CEEFAX and ORACLE decoders.

Conceived as a vehicle for stimulating telephone usage during nonbusiness hours, Prestel was originally developed as a domestic service. But, unlike teletext, Prestel was never considered a public utility and—like other videotext systems—it imposes charges for services utilized. These charges proved too high to attract a substantial base of home subscribers, and Prestel's emphasis soon shifted to business customers who are presumably willing to pay for information of perceived value. The BPO has not abandoned the concept of domestic information services, however, and hopes that public acceptance will produce one million subscribers by the late 1980s. That subscriber volume is considered essential if Prestel rates are to be reduced to affordable levels. In this respect, however, Prestel finds itself in a dilemma characteristic of most videotext services: economies of scale essential to reasonable rates and low cost decoders can be achieved if the number of subscribers reaches a specified level, but the currently high rate structure and decoder prices discourages such subscriber growth.

Like Britain, France has experimented with videotext technology since the early 1970s, most of the research work being done by the Centre Commun d'Études de Télévision et Télécommunication (CCETT). Historically, French telecommunications services have been considered among the worst in Europe. Telephone service, which is state operated, has low household penetration and is widely criticized. French interest in videotext is part of an ambitious national plan to improve and expand telecommunications services. Initiated in the late 1970s by the administration of Giscard d'Estaing, the plan is based on an influential 1978 report by Simon Nora and Alain Minc, which recommended substantial government investment in integrated information systems and technologically oriented manufacturing activities.

Nora and Minc coined the term "télématique" to denote the combination of computer and telecommunications technology, which they considered the basis for future economic expansion and social progress. The development of videotext technology is but one facet of the telematique concept. Others include the design and manufacturing of compact low cost computer terminals and facsimile equipment, and the development of the so-called smart card, a plastic card with integral memory chips being widely promoted for various retailing, credit, and governmental applications. Intelmatique, an organization established by the French Telecommunications Administration, is responsible for the worldwide marketing of telematique concepts and products.

The aggressive promotion of telematique products and the considerable notoriety gained by French videotext technology contrasts sharply with its surprisingly limited application within France itself. The overall videotext concept is well articulated. It provides for a single standard for teletext and viewdata, but specific technologies and services have undergone a series of confusing name changes. ANTIOPE (Acquisition Numérique et Télévisualisation d'Images Organisées en Pages d'Écriture) is the current name for the French videotext standard. As previously noted, it is an alphamosaic system that differs from its British counterpart in several respects, including its handling of control codes and in its specific display capabilities. The ANTIOPE standard forms the basis for French teletext services that have been operational since the late 1970s. Designed for both domestic and business users, they provide the customary mixture of news, sports, weather, travel, and financial information.

Télétel is the current name for the French viewdata system based on the ANTIOPE videotext standard. Two earlier viewdata systems, Tictac and TITAN, were implemented on an experimental basis in the mid- to late 1970s. Teletel is especially notable for its computer network configuration and its approach to information storage. Unlike the Prestel computer system, which actually maintains the data bases containing videotext information, Télétel computers serve as gateways that perform network access, protocol conversion, and similar operations. The actual videotext data bases are maintained by external computers operated by information providers. Teletel uses TRANSPAC, the French data communications network, to route information requests to and from appropriate computers and terminals.

Télétel's capabilities were recently tested in two interesting projects. In the much publicized 3V trial, selected households in the affluent Paris suburbs of Velizy, Versailles, and Val-De-Bieure were given access to a broad range of videotext information and transaction services. In the Electronic Directory Assistance Project in Ille-et-Vilaine, the original intention was to install terminals in 275,000 locations, thereby replacing printed telephone directories. The project was designed as part of an ambitious program to install 30 million such terminals by 1992. The presumed direct benefit would be a significant cost reduction resulting from the nationwide elimination of printed directories and a significant reduction in the 6,000 person workforce dedicated to directory assistance operations. As secondary benefits, the project would promote the mass production of low priced terminals, which might be sold to other countries, and French homes would be equipped to utilize other videotext services. But, in a demonstration of the close relationship of videotext and politics in European countries, the Electronic Directory Assistance Project—the embodiment of the telematique concept so strongly advocated by former president d'Estaing—has been drastically modified by the Mitterand government, which made participation voluntary rather than mandatory. Critics question whether a project of such reduced scope can yield the economies of scale essential to the manufacturing of sufficiently low cost terminals.

Rather than developing their own videotext technologies, other western European countries have implemented systems based on British or French models. West Germany, with a substantial body of installed television receivers and a modern telephone system, has experimented with teletext systems since the late 1970s and has implemented one of Europe's most impressive viewdata systems. Both the teletext and viewdata implementations are based on British alphamosaic concepts. The viewdata system, called Bildschirmtext, is operated by the Bundespost, the federal postal and telecommunications agency. It strongly emphasizes gateway access to a network of data bases maintained by external computers. Many of its services are transactional rather than informational, a distinction that will be discussed more fully in a later section of this chapter. To encourage user acceptance, the Bundespost subsidizes decoders and charges very low subscriber fees.

Among other countries, Austria likewise has a teletext system based on British technology. With an estimated 125,000 viewers in a television population of 2 million homes, it enjoys perhaps the greatest penetration of any videotext system. (Great Britain, by way of contrast, has about 500,000 teletext viewers in a television population of 20 million homes.) Austria is reportedly planning a viewdata system similar in concept to the German Bildschirmtext. Holland, which has both a large base of installed television sets and an efficient telephone system, has experimented with a CEEFAX-type teletext system. Its Viditel pilot viewdata system was inaugurated in 1982. In Sweden, where the societal implications of information processing technology are strongly emphasized, the teletext system is an outgrowth of closed captioning programs designed to provide subtitling for both deaf persons and southern European immigrants. The system, called Text-TV, has been operated by the Swedish Broadcasting Corporation since 1980, and most television sets are expected to be teletext-compatible by 1985. Teledata, the Norwegian viewdata system, was implemented on a trial basis in late 1980. Denmark has had a teletext system, which provides both general information and subtitling, since 1977. Finland's Telset viewdata system, the only European videotext system to be implemented by private sector rather than government initiatives, entered field trials in 1978. Finland also has a teletext system operated by Finnish Radio. All four Scandinavian countries have adopted British videotext standards.

Videotext demonstrations and field trials have likewise been implemented in Italy, Hungary, Spain, Switzerland, and Greece. Of these, only Greece plans a system based on ANTIOPE technology. The others will utilize the British videotext standard. Belgium, which has implemented a CEEFAX-type teletext system for its Flemish-speaking population, has demonstrated an ANTIOPE-based system for its French-speaking population.

Videotext in Other Countries

While videotext concepts developed in Europe, experimental and operational teletext and viewdata systems have been implemented in other parts of the world. In Australia, for example, commercial channels have experimented with British CEEFAX technology for teletext broadcasting, but the Australian Broadcasting Commission has selected the French ANTIOPE system for its teletext field trials.

In Japan, Nippon Hoso Kyokai (NHK), the Japanese broadcasting corporation, proposed teletext services as early as 1976, and an experimental service—termed the Character Information Broadcasting Station (CIBS)—was implemented in 1978. Similarly, the Telescan teletext system, developed by Asahi Broadcasting, features text superimposed on television images. With respect to viewdata, Japanese developments are especially noteworthy for their use of innovative graphic formation techniques and alternative transmission technologies. As noted above, European videotext systems utilize 8-bit coding schemes to provide the 256 different combinations required for the transmission of alphabetic characters, accent and diacritical marks, numeric digits, punctuation marks, and other symbols commonly encountered in written text. Representation of the several thousand different characters used in Japan's various written languages, however, exceeds the capabilities of conventional coding schemes. In addition, the legible reproduction of ideographic characters requires high quality graphics capabilities which exceed those of alphamosaic and alphageometric systems.

In the Character and Pattern Telephone Access Information Network (CAPTAIN), developed by Nippon Telegraph and Telephone, these problems are resolved by using alphaphotographic techniques for high quality graphic display. As previously discussed, alphaphotographic techniques employ predetermined combinations of bits to successively encode and transmit individual picture elements, thereby providing much greater detail than is possible with alphamosaic and alphageometric methodologies. A similar technique is used by the facsimile transmission systems discussed in the next chapter. Because CAPTAIN graphics are transmitted in dot pattern form, they are significantly sharper, more complex, and more varied than those provided by western videotext systems. Alphaphotographic techniques have also been used in the Data and Video Information Network System (DAVINS), an extended version of CAPTAIN developed by Fujitsu.

As a major problem, the greater detail provided by alphaphotographic techniques requires a larger terminal memory and much greater transmission capacity. Because more information is being transmitted, the time required to display individual frames will prove noticeably longer than it is in conventional Prestel, ANTIOPE, or Telidon systems. Even at maximum permissible transmission speeds, frame formation can require several minutes when ordinary telephone lines are used as the communication medium. To minimize this problem, the CAPTAIN system uses data compression techniques to reduce the amount of information to be transmitted without sacrificing image complexity. Transmission time is correspondingly reduced to less than 30 seconds per frame, but that time is still much longer than the several seconds required for alphamosaic or alphageometric image formation. As an emerging alternative, several Japanese videotext experiments have utilized interactive cable technology to provide the greater telecommunications capacity required for high-speed transmission. Because it offers greater communication capacity than ordinary telephone lines, coaxial cable can transmit complex videotext frames in a matter of seconds. Coaxial cable facilities are used for videotext transmission in the experimental Video Response System (VRS), implemented by Nippon Telegraph and Telephone, and in the Coaxial Cable Information Service (CCIS) and Hi-OVIS systems, where it is used to transmit videotext images stored on microfiche.

As the developer of Telidon, the alphageometric method of graphics formation, Canada is often ranked with Great Britain and France as a videotext pioneer. But Telidon is a technology, not an operational videotext system. While it was developed by the Canadian Department of Communications, it has been used in videotext systems implemented in Venezuela, Switzerland, and other countries. Worldwide acceptance of Telidon technology has been significantly enhanced by its incorporation in the standard developed by American Telephone and Telegraph (AT&T). The AT&T protocol, in turn, had a significant impact on the development of the North American Presentation Level Protocol (NAPLPS) discussed earlier in this chapter.

Within Canada itself, the first Telidon field trial was conducted by the Ontario Educational Communications Authority in early 1980. It provided teletext services via satellite broadcasting and viewdata transmission via telephone lines. Since that time, many Canadian manufacturing and consulting firms have become involved in the design and production of Telidon equipment, and a number of interesting Telidon-based videotext experiments and operational systems have been implemented by both the public and private sector. In Toronto, Montreal, and Ottawa, for example, participants in Bell Canada's Project VISTA field trial utilize residential and public terminals to access 20,000 English-language and 10,000 French-language pages of information. In Toronto, Infomart implemented the Teleguide, an experimental videotext system using public terminals to provide access to a data base of tourist information. Project Grassroots, the first commercial Telidon system, was implemented in 1981 by Infomart and the Manitoba Telephone System. An outgrowth of Project Ida, an unsuccessful videotext system that used coaxial cable transmission, Project Grassroots provides 20,000 pages of information aimed primarily at the agribusiness market in the provinces of Manitoba, Alberta, Saskatchewan, and Ontario. Videotext experiments and field trials of varying scope have likewise been conducted by Alberta Government Telephone, British Columbia Telephone, Maritime Telephone and Telegraph, New Brunswick Telephone, Saskatchewan Telecommunications, the Canadian Broadcasting Corporation, the Cable Telecommunication Research Institute, and various cable system operators.

Videotext in the United States

As videotext systems establish themselves in Europe and, increasingly, in other countries, worldwide industry attention has focused on the large and potentially lucrative American market. At first glance, the United States appears more than ready for videotext technology, and most of the ingredients that are considered essential to successful system implementation are already in place. The United States has, for example, a modern, efficient, nationwide telephone system. A very high percentage of American households are equipped with at least one color television, and there is growing acceptance of alternative video technology in the form of videocassette recorders, video disk players, and video games. In many cases, the American communities that represent the best candidates for the implementation of videotext systems are already served by conventional or interactive cable television systems that might serve as a delivery vehicle for videotext services. These communities are largely suburban with high household incomes. A substantial percentage of their residents are college graduates under 45 years of age. Overall, the American population is entertainment-oriented and increasingly aware of the importance of information in daily life. Many Americans have routine exposure to computer technology at work or school, and personal computers are an increasingly common household item. These computers are often attached to television sets, reinforcing the connection between video technology and information display.

But, despite this impressive technological and demographic infrastructure, the widespread implementation of American videotext systems has been impeded by important differences in the organization of European and American telecommunication activities. In European countries, telecommunications and broadcasting services are largely nationalized. Videotext research is subsidized by European governments, and, with the previously noted exception of Finland, government plays a very active role in the implementation of teletext and viewdata systems. In some cases, as with the British Prestel system, videotext is viewed as a means of stimulating telephone installations and off-hours usage, which will correspondingly increase governmental revenues. In others, videotext and other information processing technologies are implemented as public utilities apart from any concern for profitability. This is the case, for example, in the Scandinavian countries where videotext systems are implemented in the context of social democratic policies designed to stimulate education and culture, assist minorities and handicapped persons, and generally provide beneficial services that cannot be profitably offered by the private sector. As yet another motive, government sponsorship of videotext may be designed to stimulate the development of exportable technology and related products and services. As previously discussed, France provides the most notable example of this motivation.

In analyzing the potential market for new products and services, economists recognize the impact of both demand and availability. Some critics of European videotext systems contend that government subsidies have produced services for which there is little demonstrable demand. While the availability of free teletext services may attract some viewers, they point to the British Prestel system's failure to attract a substantial number of paying subscribers as evidence that videotext is actually a technology in search of a market. They further question the viability of such supply-driven services in the United States, where government has shown little interest in either the economic or policy implications of videotext technology.

Unlike European countries, American telecommunication and broadcasting activities operate in the private sector, apart from government subsidies, but under government regulation. The Federal Communications Commission, which is authorized to regulate the use of the vertical blanking interval employed for teletext broadcasting, has so far exerted little regulatory control over teletext activities. Because they utilize telephone transmission rather than broadcast signals, viewdata systems are not subject to FCC regulations. With the exception of a few publicly funded teletext and viewdata demonstrations, American videotext activities are the result of private sector initiatives. American broadcasters, telecommunications companies, publishers, and other organizations are unquestionably interested in the economic potential of videotext, but they are equally concerned about market demand. A decade of European experience has clearly demonstrated the technical viability of videotext services. Since the late 1970s, American experiments and field trials have attempted to establish their economic viability.

As in European countries, American interest in teletext technology is partly an outgrowth of research on closed captioning systems for hearing impaired persons. In the late 1970s, the National Captioning Institute and the Public Broadcasting Service implemented closed captioned telecasts, using special decoders manufactured and sold by Sears. The first general purpose American teletext experiment, however, dates from 1978 when KSL-TV, a Salt Lake City television station operated by Bonneville International Corporation, implemented an experimental service based on CEEFAX technology. In the following year, CBS—the most innovative of the three major networks in its receptivity to alternative video technologies—experimented with both CEEFAX and ANTIOPE teletext transmission through station KMOX-TV in St. Louis. These experiments were subsequently extended to KNXT-TV and KPIX-TV, the CBS affiliate stations in Los Angeles and San Francisco, respectively. The Los Angeles teletext tests were coordinated with KNBC-TV, the NBC affiliate station, and KCET-TV, the Los Angeles public television station. In 1981, the Corporation for Public Broadcasting, the National Science Foundation, the U.S. Department of Education, and the New York University Alternate Media Center implemented a publicly funded teletext experiment utilizing WETA-TV, the public television station in Washington, D.C. Based on Telidon technology, the experiment placed decoders in selected households and public locations.

Following the European example, these American teletext experiments offered the customary mixture of news, weather, sports, and financial information, accompanied by some lighter feature stories. They typically involved a relatively small data base, a limited geographic area, and a small number of households selected for their receptivity and affluence, the latter factor being important for the advertiser appeal on which commercial teletext services must depend. In the early 1980s, several organizations announced more comprehensive, commercial teletext services to be made available on a nationwide basis. Examples include the CBS ExtraVision and NBC Teletext services. Both began transmission in early 1983, although the unavailability of sufficient quantities of decoders delayed their actual implementation. Using its WKRC-TV station in Cincinnati, Taft Broadcasting implemented its Electra teletext service in mid-1983, using decoders manufactured by Zenith.

In the spring of 1981, WFLD-TV in Chicago began transmitting the KEYFAX teletext service produced by Field Electronic Publishing, a subsidiary of Field Enterprises that owns WFLD and is also the publisher of the World Book Encyclopedia. In late 1981, WFLD introduced its NITE-OWL service, a decoderless version of KEYFAX broadcasted between midnight and 6 A.M. as a magazine of 60 frames continuously transmitted on a 20-minute cycle. In 1982, Field Electronic Publishing established KEYCOM, a joint venture with Honeywell Incorporated and Centel Corporation to distribute KEYFAX via the WTBS Superstation satellite service, which is available to an estimated 25 million American homes served by cable television systems. KEYFAX service is made available to cable system operators for retransmission to households equipped with special keypad decoders that lease for about $10 per month. Because KEYFAX uses the WTBS vertical blanking interval, it does not require additional channel capacity. It should consequently prove attractive to operators of older, limited capacity cable systems who would like to offer additional services without an expensive upgrading of their transmission facilities. In late 1982, Time Incorporated also announced a teletext service to be distributed via satellite to cable system operators, although the service was cancelled in 1983 prior to commercial availability. Interestingly, Time planned to utilize a full cable channel rather than the vertical blanking interval of an existing programming service. As discussed earlier in this chapter, the use of a full channel permits a teletext magazine of 4,000 to 5,000 pages without a significant degradation of frame access time.

The Electronics Industries Association established a teletext standards committee in 1979, and the recent proliferation of American teletext services has been accompanied by renewed concern for standardization that will permit economies of scale in decoder manufacturing and the use of a single decoder for multiple systems broadcasting in a given area. At the time of this writing, however, most American teletext services were utilizing one of two incompatible broadcasting techniques:

1. The so-called World System broadcast teletext standard is based on British CEEFAX technology adapted to worldwide broadcasting requirements. As noted earlier in this chapter, the British alphamosaic display method produces relatively simple graphic presentations, but offers the advantage of relatively simple, inexpensive decoders. Internationally, it is the most widely used teletext broadcasting method.

2. The North American Broadcast Teletext Specification (NABTS) combines features of the French ANTIOPE and Canadian Telidon systems. In the United States, its strongest advocate has been CBS. Compared to the World System, NABTS offers superior graphics display capabilities, but the required decoders are more complex and expensive.

Both the World System and NABTS were examined by the Federal Communications Commission as proposed U.S. teletext standards, but the FCC declined to select either of them. As a further complication, some American teletext systems use broadcasting techniques based on proprietary modifications of CEEFAX or Telidon technologies. These proprietary systems are necessarily incompatible with one another and with the World System and NABTS teletext protocols.

American viewdata experiments date from 1979 when the U.S. Department of Agriculture implemented its Project Green Thumb, an information system serving the Kentucky farm community. In the same year, American Telephone and Telegraph tested an Electronic Information Service designed to provide selected residents of Albany, New York, with online access to the telephone directory. A second trial scheduled for Austin, Texas, was cancelled when local newspapers protested, fearing an eventual loss of advertising revenues should the electronic service prove popular. Several viewdata field trials of more ambitious scope were implemented in 1980. In a videotext experiment of special interest to libraries, the Channel 2000 project—jointly sponsored by the Online Computer Library Center (OCLC) and Bank One—served 200 households in Columbus, Ohio. Channel 2000 emphasized reference and educational information rather than the combination of news, commercial, and recreational material, which have become a staple item of subsequent viewdata systems. Channel 2000 users could access any of seven data bases, including the catalog of the Public Library of Columbus and Franklin County, together with an electronic circulation service similar to the commercial ordering services discussed later in this chapter. Other available information included a video encyclopedia, consisting of the full text of the 21-volume *Academic American Encyclopedia*; a public information service pertaining to such matters as employment, taxes, voting eligibility, human services, and recreation; a community calendar compiled by the local chamber of commerce; reading and math programs prepared by Ohio State University; and a home banking service that enabled participants to determine account balances, review transactions, and pay bills electronically.

Despite its educational focus, the Channel 2000 Project received only a fraction of the publicity accorded the Viewtron field trial begun in mid-1980 in Coral Gables, Florida. Conducted by Viewdata Corporation of America—a subsidiary of Knight Ridder Newspapers, the nation's largest newspaper chain (as measured by daily circulation)—in a joint venture with American Telephone and Telegraph, Viewtron provided over 200 selected households with interactive access to various informational, transactional, and recreational services using British Prestel technology. On the basis of its early tests, Knight Ridder has implemented a commercial Viewtron offering with a major expansion of service that will eventually reach 18 American cities.

In another well-publicized field trial begun in early 1982, the Times Mirror Company—a publisher with diversified interests in television stations and cable systems—tested a viewdata service in 350 households in Orange County, California. The system's 30,000 pages of information included material from such Times Mirror publications as the *Los Angeles Times* and *Popular Science*. The service utilized Telidon technology, and, during the field trial, Times Mirror joined with Infomart, the Canadian company responsible for the Grassroots and Teleguide systems discussed in the previous section, to form Videotext America. As with Knight Ridder's Viewtron service, Videotext America expects to inaugurate and significantly expand commercial viewdata services over the next several years.

In late 1982, CBS and American Telephone and Telegraph implemented their Venture One viewdata field trial in Ridgewood, New Jersey. It reached 200 homes with a combination of informational and transactional services. Some of the informational pages incorporated material from such CBS publications as *Woman's Day* and *Mechanix Illustrated*. Transmission methodologies conform to the ATT Presentation Level Protocol that formed the basis for the North American Presentation Level Protocol (NAPLPS) standard discussed in an earlier section.

Among other viewdata experiments of the early 1980s, Continental Telephone used ANTIOPE technology in its ConTelVision field trial in Manassas, Virginia. ANTIOPE was likewise selected by First Bank Systems for a transaction-oriented viewdata field trial in Minnesota. While most viewdata experiments used the telephone network as the communications link, interactive cable technology has been used as a videotext transmission medium by the Warner Amex QUBE system in Columbus, Ohio; by Cox Communications' Indax system in San Diego and Omaha; and in the BISON viewdata experiment conducted by Belo Corporation in Dallas.

Videotext as an Information Service

The Information Providers

As discussed here, videotext is essentially a household information service that provides access to information of general interest and utility. While its viewdata variant permits the online retrieval of specific frames maintained by computers, videotext systems are not designed to compete with the specialized bibliographic search services and other online information retrieval systems—such as DIALOG, ORBIT, BRS, Lexis, Nexis, Westlaw, or MEDLINE—which are widely used by libraries, businesses, and other organizations to support research in specialized fields. As will be discussed later in this chapter, some videotext systems are designed primarily or exclusively for business users or special groups, and several of the specialized information retrieval services listed have recently entered the household market. This discussion, however, will delineate the types of information provided by the general-purpose teletext and viewdata systems described in the preceding sections.

As noted earlier, teletext system operators often regard the service as an extension, or variant version, of television news broadcasting, and this view is reflected in teletext's characteristic emphasis on news, weather, sports, and financial information. The last of these includes stock market activity reports, commodities pricing, and business and industry news. In the manner of televised news, these staple items are supplemented by feature reports on important developments in such fields as science, health, education, and entertainment. Additional information content will vary from system to system, but typically include reports of traffic congestion, airline, and rail delays; announcements of available jobs; useful consumer information, such as grocery prices, recipes, postal rates, and personal financial advice; schedules for movies, theaters, concerts, art exhibits, and local tourist attractions; and other items ranging from horoscopes to gardening tips.

With most teletext services, this information is prepared by an in-house staff of journalists, and little, if any, use is made of outside information providers. The journalistic approach is evident in the packaging of teletext services as a magazine consisting of a predetermined number of pages, and in the use of combinations of headline and detail frames to report news stories. Compared to conventional print or broadcast journalism, however, teletext offers the advantage of real-time reporting of events. Rather than waiting for the next edition of a newspaper or a regularly scheduled broadcast, teletext frames can be created or modified at any time. On the negative side, reasonable access time requirements typically limit the teletext magazine's capacity to about 200 pages (unless a full channel is used). Teletext frames themselves can only contain about 100 words, and their graphics display capabilities are much cruder than those associated with print publications or conventional television images.

Where broadcasting services are nationalized, teletext operating costs are covered by government subsidies. Commercial teletext systems, however, depend on advertising as a source of revenue, since, apart from decoder charges, teletext is a free service. Teletext advertising can take either of two forms:

1. Entire frames can be devoted to advertisements. The effectiveness of this approach is questionable, since, unlike ordinary television viewing where exposure to commercial messages is unavoidable, teletext frames are not displayed sequentially and users can simply decline to view advertisements.

2. In frame sponsorship, a brief advertiser's logo or message appears in the top or bottom margin of a frame that contains news or other information. Thus, in the manner of conventional television, a brewery may sponsor frames containing sports reports or a pharmaceuticals company may sponsor frames containing health news.

Compared to teletext, viewdata systems resemble computer-based information retrieval systems more than broadcasting services, and they can support much larger data bases offering more diverse information. Both videotext variants provide news information, but the greater frame capacity of viewdata systems permits more extensive news coverage and greater depth of reporting. In addition to the customary headlines and brief stories, viewdata news frames may contain various combinations of statistical data, such as economic indicators, consumer price indexes, productivity reports, employment data, and sports records; news coverage of individual states or countries; newsletter-type reports on specific subjects, such as health or science, or for specific audiences, such as farmers; and detailed meterological reports which present technical information not suitable for general weather forecasts. As discussed in the preceding sections, American viewdata systems such as Viewtron and Videotex America are operated by publishing companies that derive this information from their newspapers, magazines, or other printed sources. Alternatively, news frames may contain wire service information. Some detailed statistical information may be prepared by or derived from government agencies.

Compared to teletext, viewdata systems can provide much more personal service information. Typical examples include consumer information, including food prices and buying guides, financial planning and tax advice, energy conservation advice, and product reviews; community service information, including descriptions of community or social service agencies and lists of courses offered by local schools and colleges; information about hobbies, such as stamp and coin collecting; and entertainment information, including television listings, movie and theater schedules and reviews, and book reviews. To attract younger viewers, most viewdata frames feature games, contests, quizzes, and children's stories.

Compared to teletext services, the larger frame capacity of viewdata systems both permits and encourages the significantly greater involvement of outside information providers—the so-called IPs. Viewdata information is variously provided by government agencies, local institutions, nonprofit organizations, or commercial firms. Libraries and library-related organizations provide information to several viewdata systems. The participation of OCLC and the Columbus and Franklin County Public Library in the Channel 2000 videotext experiment was discussed in the preceding section. Several British and Canadian libraries have contributed information to viewdata systems, and the American Library Association is an information provider to several American videotext services. For the Viewtron system, for example, ALA provides selected reviews from *Booklist* and *Openers*, their purpose being to encourage reading and library usage.

While government agencies and nonprofit organizations may be motivated by the expanded service opportunities offered by viewdata systems, commercial information providers are attracted by their economic potential. This potential can be realized in two ways: (1) through additional advertising exposure, either through page sponsorship or dedicated advertising frames; and (2) through usage revenues. In addition to decoder rental or purchase fees, viewdata subscribers are typically charged for each frame that they access. These frame charges are nominal (usually, a few cents each) and are clearly indicated in index frames and in the data frames themselves. A percentage of these charges is deducted by the viewdata system operator. The remainder is paid to the information provider. Given its relative newness, viewdata usage is currently low, and page revenues are correspondingly modest. As usage increases, however, income is potentially significant.

Among commercial information providers, publishing companies are heavily represented in both European and American viewdata systems. Since information is their product, publishers are strongly interested in page charge revenues. Viewdata offers them an alternative packaging for information presented in their conventional printed media, together with the prospect of reaching new audiences that have traditionally ignored books, magazines, and newspapers. Of these three types of publications, "electronic editions" of newspapers have received the greatest attention, although initial reception of this concept has proven less than enthusiastic. Despite the advantages of timeliness and online access, viewdata display is presently an expensive and inconvenient way to read the daily newspaper. Accumulated page charges can far exceed the cost of the printed product, and page layout is limited in both its typography and graphic display capabilities.

Similar limitations apply to magazine and book publishing via videotext, although some interesting applications have been developed. Magazine publishers, such as CBS, who operate viewdata systems typically include frames derived from their printed editions. Several viewdata services offer special versions of encyclopedias and other reference books. For the Viewtron experiment in Coral Gables, for example, *Congressional Quarterly* provided biographies of Florida congressmen, together with their addresses and voting records on major bills. While their current impact appears negligible, such videotext services may pose a long-term threat to conventional publications. As discussed in the preceding section, newspaper publishers' protests forced AT&T to cancel its announced field trial of a viewdata telephone directory. On the positive side, the inclusion of information extracted from newspapers, magazines, and books in viewdata systems can stimulate an interest in the fuller printed publications. Such wider exposure for printed publications is of obvious significance to libraries.

Even more than publishing, the banking industry has participated actively in the development of viewdata systems, both as information providers and, in the case of several American viewdata experiments, as operators. As information providers, banks have emphasized three types of services:

1. General information about the availability of savings accounts, checking accounts, investment instruments, loans, and other financial services. Such information can be offered through both teletext and viewdata systems.

2. Balance inquiries and other access to information about specific savings, checking, and loan accounts. Such services require the interactive capabilities associated with viewdata systems.

3. Transaction processing, in which viewdata users can pay bills and transfer funds between accounts.

In most cases, balance inquiry and transaction processing capabilities are implemented in a gateway configuration in which the viewdata system provides access to information maintained by external computers. As previously discussed, the gateway concept has been implemented in France and West Germany, and it is planned for several American viewdata systems.

Like banking, the travel and tourism industry utilizes viewdata services for a combination of information and transactional services. Airlines, hotels, rental car companies, and individual travel agencies are well represented as commercial information providers in European viewdata systems. They offer information about tourist attractions, special fares or hotel rates, and package tours, as well as airline and rail schedules. Viewdata's transactional capabilities permit automatic ticketing, a service also provided for concerts, theatrical presentations, and other events.

Among other commercial information providers, real estate companies use both viewdata and teletext systems to provide residential and business property listings consisting of textual descriptions supplemented by graphic depictions of floor plans. They also offer general information about home buying, mortgage availability, and interest rates. In a conceptually similar application, employment agencies use videotext systems for job listings. Viewdata systems are likewise used by various types of retail sales organizations, including automobile dealers, caterers, clothing stores, florists, grocery stores, and restaurants—the last of these making their menus electronically available to prospective diners. In addition to providing general information about available products and services, retail organizations are attracted by the transactional processing capabilities of viewdata. While viewdata's textual and graphics display capabilities are much more primitive than those permitted by printed advertising, electronic ordering is well suited to catalog sales or discounted sales operations where the consumer is aware of the attributes of specific products and simply wants to purchase a given item at the lowest possible price. For the consumer, electronic ordering offers rapid response. For the sales organization, it offers the significant advantage of reduced administration and paperwork.

Information Creation and Retrieval

Whether it is provided by commercial enterprises or nonprofit groups, videotext information is stored by computers as a series of preformatted pages containing combinations of text and graphics. As with all computer-stored data, the content of videotext pages must be converted to computer-processible form. In the Japanese CAPTAIN system, this conversion is accomplished by scanning documents containing images of desired page layouts, but European and North American videotext systems use special editing terminals for the entry and formatting of textual and graphic information. These terminals are the videotext counterpart of the page makeup devices in conventional publishing operations. They may be operated by the information providers themselves or by any of the growing number of consulting firms and service bureaus that specialize in videotext systems design.

The most primitive editing terminals are essentially enhanced versions of user terminals. They consist of a color television receiver with a special keyboard designed for the entry and manipulation of textual information and graphic symbols (figure 30). The keyboard contains a typewriter-like alphanumeric section plus special color control and function keys. In alphamosaic systems, a graphics generator keypad contains the basic mosaic symbols from which graphic images are composed. In alphageometric systems, dedicated keys may be provided for individual picture definition instructions. Like user terminals, editing terminals are designed to operate with specific videotext protocols, although several vendors now offer multi-protocol devices.

Regardless of protocol, software for editing terminals provides word processing facilities for the entry and manipulation of text, supplemented by page makeup capabilities for the creation and integration of graphics. The simplest editing terminals are designed exclusively for online operation and depend on a remote computer for both software and storage. Page layouts are entered directly into the videotext computer system from which they can subsequently be recalled for editing. Many new editing terminals, however, are microcomputer-controlled devices that contain integral software and storage for standalone entry and editing operations. With these terminals, all work is performed offline, and page formats are not transmitted to the videotext computer system until they are finalized. Dedicated videotext editing terminals have been developed by such companies as American Bell, Bell Northern Research, and Norpak. Alternatively, several companies offer videotext editing software that runs on the most popular brands of microcomputers.

FIGURE 30

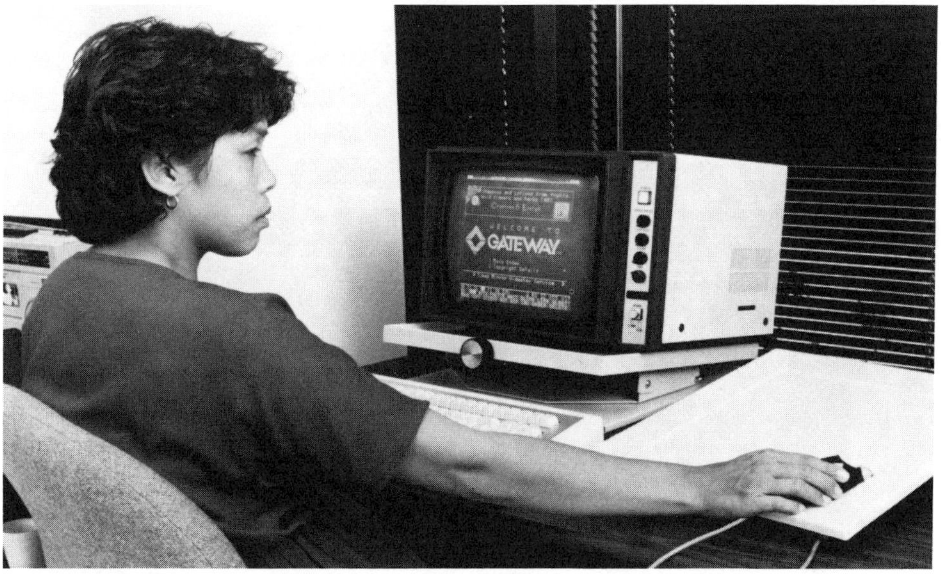

Editing terminals with keyboards and graphics tablets are used to create videotext frames. (Courtesy: Times Mirror)

The typical videotext user terminal is a straightforward device that consists of a color television receiver equipped with decoder circuitry and a numeric keypad or an alphanumeric keyboard for the entry of command sequences. From their inception, videotext systems have been designed for use by untrained persons. They emphasize obvious retrieval procedures and simplicity of operation, even at the cost of efficiency, speed, and convenience. Although keyword searching, logical coordination of search parameters, and other sophisticated operations characteristic of information retrieval systems developed primarily for library applications are supported on a limited basis by Teletel, CAPTAIN, and other videotext systems, most system designers rely on the menu-oriented approach and hierarchical page organization scheme introduced by British teletext and viewdata systems.

The basic unit of information in videotext systems is a page that consists of one or more preformatted frames containing a combination of text and graphics. Unlike conventional data base structures that typically separate data and its associated indexes, most videotext data bases consist of a combination of index and information pages (figure 31). Each index page represents an entry node that leads to a series of hierarchically arranged offspring pages. Page numbers reflect these hierarchical relationships, so that an index page numbered 195 would refer the user to information pages numbered 1951, 1952, 1953, and so on. Pages that elaborate on the information content of those pages would be numbered 19511, 19512, 19513, 19521, 19522, and so forth. Continuation frames for a given page include an alphabetic suffix

FIGURE 31

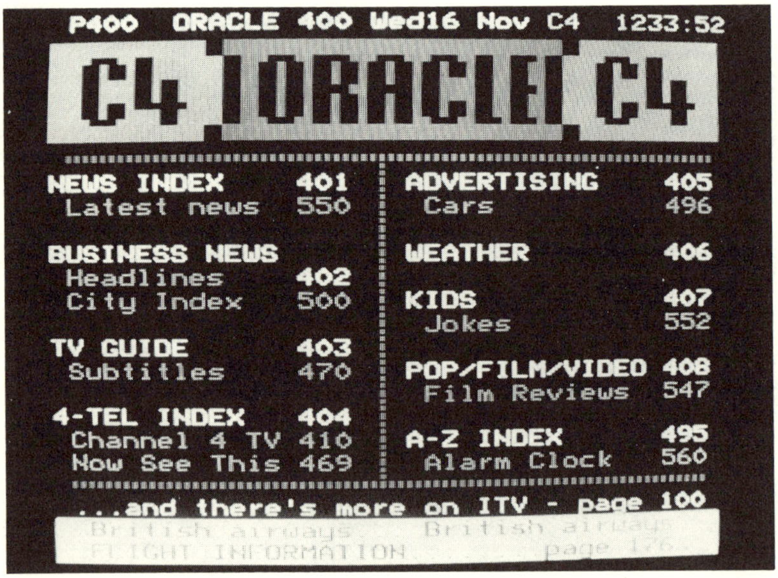

Videotext systems make extensive use of indexes to direct users to desired frames. (Courtesy: Oracle Teletext Limited)

as part of the page number. In some videotext systems, blocks of page numbers are reserved for specific information providers.

If a given frame's number is known, it can be entered directly at the videotext terminal's keypad, and that frame will be displayed. Usually, however, the user must first consult one of the index frames to determine the numbers of desired data frames. As is characteristic with menu-oriented retrieval systems, a given index frame may lead to additional, progressively more detailed index frames, which must be sequentially examined in order to reach a relevant information page. Once an information page is reached, however, it often contains cross-references to related pages, thereby providing alternative routes that allow the user to partly circumvent the system's menu structure and speed up retrieval. Given these cross-references, the typical videotext system is properly characterized as having a network rather than a tree-like data structure. To assist the user further in navigating through a videotext data base, control sequences entered at the videotext terminal's keypad will redisplay a previous frame, redisplay the last menu, display previously viewed frames in reverse sequence, and perform similar operations.

Special Videotext Services

As discussed in a preceding section, the gateway concept expands the scope of viewdata services by allowing access to external computers. At the present time, such gateway access emphasizes home banking, home shopping, and related transactional services, but some viewdata systems offer access to computational facilities and electronic messaging services. In the latter case, messages typed at a videotext terminal are stored by a remote computer pending receipt by a specified videotext user. Such electronic message systems are increasingly common in business applications where they are implemented in the context of conventional computer and data communication systems. Their availability as a videotext service is recent.

Related to transactional services, a remote monitoring service provides burglar and fire facilities as part of a videotext system. Such capabilities are frequently cited as desirable by prospective videotext users, although they raise troublesome questions about the potential for invasion of privacy inherent in new technologies. Telesoftware, another innovative videotext service, has likewise received much recent attention. As implemented in either teletext or viewdata systems, telesoftware involves the electronic delivery of computer programs to videotext terminals for local execution. The videotext terminal used in a telesoftware application must be a microcomputer capable of standalone operation, and the information is transmitted in character-coded form rather than as video images.

While videotext was originally conceived as a consumer-oriented technology providing information of broad appeal, there has been considerable recent interest in specialized videotext services for business, government, and institutional users. As discussed above, the British Prestel service has switched its marketing emphasis from household to business applications where page charges and related costs can be more easily justified. American videotext services, most of which operate for profit rather than under government subsidies, are likewise interested in the economic potential of the business market. From the standpoint of business users accustomed to computerized information systems, the combination of text and graphics characteristic of videotext is well suited to applications requiring simple, economical computer-generated color displays. Videotext systems can be used by corporations, universities, hotels, convention centers, banks, libraries, and other organizations to display such information as news bulletins, weather reports, daily activities listings, community events schedules, telephone directories, and carpool and mass transit schedules. With their menu-oriented retrieval approach, videotext systems can also prove easier to use and require less elaborate training and documentation than conventional computer-based information systems.

In an approach employed by some European systems, specialized business-oriented videotext services can be implemented for a closed user group (CUG) within a general purpose, public videotext system. While such specialized data is maintained by remote videotext computers, access to it is restricted by passwords or other techniques to specific users or specific terminals. Alternatively, business-oriented videotext systems can be implemented on a private, in-house basis. Companies such as IBM, Digital Equipment, Aregon, Genesys Group, MODCOMP, and Shuttle Corporation market special videotext software or complete turnkey videotext systems incorporating micro-, mini-, or full-size computers.

Finally, a growing number of companies have developed home information services with conventional computer terminals, data storage techniques, and communication protocols. Although such systems are technically not video-based and consequently fall outside the intent of this book, they are described here briefly because they resemble videotext systems in scope and content and are intended for much the same market. They are often misleadingly characterized as videotext systems in journal articles, trade publications, and advertisements, but they are patterned after conventional timeshared computer systems. While specially equipped color television receivers may be used to access such services, color and graphics—the distinguishing features of true videotext systems—play little, if any, role in information display. More often, a microcomputer equipped with a modem and telecommunications software package serves as the access device, and some features of these services are specifically designed to appeal to computer enthusiasts.

These information services have proven especially popular in the United States, where microcomputers are an increasingly common household item and conventional videotext systems have been slow to develop. The best known examples include the Source, developed by the Telecomputing Corporation of America, which is now a subsidiary of Reader's Digest; CompuServe, a subsidiary of H&R Block; and the Dow Jones Information Service. Like other computer timesharing services, they are accessed through the telephone network on a dial-up basis. Their information retrieval offerings closely resemble those associated with viewdata systems. Emphasis is placed on such consumer-oriented information as airline schedules, restaurant guides, movie reviews, product reports, personal financial advice, and horoscopes. Of greater interest to business and libraries are news wire releases, electronic editions of selected newspapers, a surprisingly extensive range of financial information services, and online encyclopedias and other reference books.

Because they do not store this data as preformatted pages, the Source, CompuServe, and the Dow Jones Information Service can provide access to more information and can support more varied search techniques than do videotext services. In addition to information retrieval capabilities, such services also offer various combinations of electronic shopping, electronic banking, and other transactional services; computational capabilities, including access to systems and application software that run on the services' own computers; telesoftware capabilities for the downloading of software to microcomputers for local execution; electronic message services; and various educational and recreational services that use the interactive capabilities of online computer systems.

Of particular significance for this discussion are those home information services offered by companies that have traditionally marketed their services to libraries and related research organizations. Examples include the DIALOG Knowledge Index and the Bibliographic Retrieval Services (BRS) After Dark services, both of which offer online bibliographic retrieval capabilities to individuals equipped with terminals or microcomputers. Both companies operate major library-oriented retrieval services and offer their home information services during a limited number of evening and weekend hours. Access is further limited to a selected group of data bases of presumably broad appeal, and online search and printing capabilities are more limited than those provided with the companies' full services. Rates vary between the two services and with the particular retrieval operations performed, but they are significantly lower than those charged for full daytime access to the DIALOG or BRS retrieval services.

Additional Readings

CONSUMER APPLICATIONS

Biehal, G. Implications of consumer information processing research for the design of consumer information systems. *Journal of Consumer Affairs* 17: 107–22 (Summer 1983).

Durand, P. The public service potential of videotex and teletext. *Telecommunications Policy* 7: 149–62 (June 1983).

Elton, M., and Carey, J. Computerizing information: Consumer reactions to teletext. *Journal of Communications* 33: 162–73 (1983).

Jones, M. G. The challenge of the new information technologies: The need to respond to citizens' information needs. *Information Society* 2: 145–56 (1983).

Kerr, S. T. Videotex at the street level: Public acceptance of viewdata services in Great Britain. *Videodisc/Videotex* 3: 196–205 (Summer 1983).

Mecca, R. G. Newspapers and home information systems: The present, the promise, and the peril. *Videodisc/Teletext* 1: 18–29 (Winter 1981).

Tydeman, J. Videotex: Ushering in the electronic household. *The Futurist* 16: 54–61 (February 1982).

LIBRARY APPLICATIONS

Adams, J., and Adams, R. Videotex and teletext: New role for libraries. *Wilson Library Bulletin* 57: 206–11 (November 1982).

Carr, R. Prestel in the test trial—An academic library user looks back. *Journal of Librarianship* 12: 145–58 (1980).

Cawkell, A. E. Will information flow to the citizen be improved with videotex systems? *ASLIB Proceedings* 32: 264–69 (1980).

Cherry, S. S. Telereference: The new TV information systems. *American Libraries* 11: 94–110 (February 1980).

Criner, K., and Johnson-Hall, M. Videotex: Threat or opportunity. *Special Libraries* 71: 379–85 (1980).

Gothberg, H. J. M. Vid/telreference: The new frontier. *Reference Librarian* 5: 1–14 (Fall-Winter 1982).

Hayden, V. Conflicting perceptions of viewdata and its benefits. *Library Management* 2: 1–60 (1981).

Kennan, S. Teletext and viewdata services in British public libraries. *Library Journal* 107: 1285–89 (1982).

Martyn, J. Prestel and public libraries: An LA/ASLIB experiment. *ASLIB Proceedings* 31: 216–36 (1979).

Nash, M. Videotex versus online bibliographic databases: A Canadian perspective. *On-Line Review* 6: 291–96 (1982).

Nash, M. M., and Periera, M. J. Telidon and library applications. *Canadian Library Journal* 39: 249–54 (August 1982).

Phillips, R. A public access videotex library service. *Online* 6: 34–39 (September 1982).

Rice, J. Telereference service: The potential for libraries. *Library Journal* 108: 1839–43 (October 1, 1983).

Sweeney, R. T. Remote electronic delivery of information through libraries. *Drexel Library Quarterly* 17: 18–35 (Fall 1981).

Tenne-Sens, A. Telidon graphics and library applications. *Information Technology and Libraries* 1: 98–110 (1982).

Tenopir, C. Dialog's Knowledge Index and BRS After Dark: Data base searching on personal computers. *Library Journal* 108: 471–74 (1983).

Toombs, Y. M. A Telidon user survey. *Canadian Library Journal* 40: 21–25 (February 1983).

Toombs, Y. M., and Wilson, B. The Calgary libraries Telidon trial. *Information Technology and Libraries* 1: 331–36 (1982).

Yeates, R. *Prestel in the Public Library*. London: British Library, 1982.

PUBLIC POLICY IMPLICATIONS

Martin, J. *The Wired Society—A Challenge for Tomorrow*. Englewood Cliffs, New Jersey: Prentice-Hall, 1978.

Nora, S., and Minc, A. *The Computerization of Society*. Cambridge: MIT Press, 1980.

Peyton, D. Videotex policy issues in the United States. *Electronic Publishing Review* 1: 251–62 (December 1981).

Tydeman, J., and Lipinski, H. *Teletext and Videotext in the United States: Market Potential, Technology, and Public Policy Issues*. New York: McGraw-Hill, 1982.

PUBLISHING APPLICATIONS

Bendig, M. W. Encyclopedia online: Channel 2000 and the Academic American Encyclopedia. *Reference Service Review* 10: 25–26 (Summer 1982).

Greenagel, F. L. ARETE—A 3000-year-old word for the latest in electronic publishing. *Electronic Publishing Review* 1: 177–82 (September 1981).

Neustadt, R. M. *The Birth of Electronic Publishing: Legal and Economic Issues in Telephone, Cable, and Over-the-Air Teletext and Videotext*. White Plains, New York: Knowledge Industries Publications, 1982.

Neustadt, R. M. Electronic publishing: Which pathway to the home? *Electronic Publishing Review* 3: 49–53 (March 1983).

Smith, A. *Goodbye Gutenberg: The Newspaper Revolution of the 1980s*. Oxford: Oxford University Press, 1980.

Tyler, M. Videotex, Prestel, and teletext—The economics and politics of some electronic publishing media. *Telecommunications Policy* 3: 37–51 (1979).

Weaver, D. H. *Videotex Journalism: Teletext, Viewdata, and the News*. Hillsdale, New Jersey: Larence Erlbaum Associates, 1983.

TELETEXT TECHNOLOGY

Blatt, J. Teletext: a new television service for home information and captioning. *Volta Review* 84: 209–17 (1982).

Blatt, J., Rosch, G., and Osterer, C. Promise of teletext for hearing impaired audiences. *IEEE Transactions on Consumer Electronics* 26: 717–22 (1980).

Edwards, K. Broadcast teletext: The next mass medium? *The Futurist* 16: 21–24 (October 1982).

Hedger, J., Raggett, M., and Warburton, A. Telesoftware—Value added teletext. *IEEE Transactions on Consumer Electronics* 26: 555–67 (1980).

Mothersole, P. L. Teletext and viewdata: New information systems using the domestic television receiver. *Proceedings of the IEE* 126: 1350–54 (1979).

VIDEOTEXT IMPLEMENTATIONS

Harashima, S., et al. Japanese videotex system CAPTAIN: Experimental service and user reactions outline. *IEEE Transactions on Communications* 29: 1959–67 (1981).

Hlynka, D., and Hurly, P. Project Ida: Manitoba's telecommunications experiment. *Videodisc/Teletext* 1: 86–93 (Spring 1981).

Hoke, P. Germany's Bildschirmtext: The catalog-videotex connection. *Direct Marketing* 46: 108–14 (July 1983).

Jaakola, P., Hirvonnen, M., and Baerlund, O. Telset, the Finnish viewdata. *Computer Communications* 2: 69–73 (April 1979).

Kvarnefalk, G. Datavision and Text TV in Sweden. *Computer Communications* 2: 74–75 (April 1979).

Leduc, N. F. Teletext and videotex in North America: The Canadian perspective. *Telecommunications Policy* 4: 9–16 (1980).

Money, S. A. *Teletext and Viewdata*. London: Butterworth, 1979.

Morise, R. C. Videotex in America: The birth of electronic newspapers. *Editor and Publisher* 115: 41–47 (June 1982).

Nakajima, H., and Watanabe, T. Advanced CAPTAIN system and an approach to commercial service. *IEEE Journal on Selected Areas of Communication* 1: 278–85 (1983).

Noll, A. M. Teletext and videotext in North America: Service and system implications. *Telecommunications Policy* 4: 17–24 (1980).

O'Brien, C. D., and Bown, H. G. Perspective on the development of videotex in North America. *IEEE Journal on Selected Areas of Communication* 1: 260–66 (1983).

Pierce, W. D., Reid, S. J., and Peterson, W. M. A low cost terminal for the 1980s: Project Green Thumb. *IEEE Transactions on Consumer Electronics* 26: 487–505 (August 1980).

Rice, R. E., and Paisley, W. The Green Thumb videotex experiment: Evaluation and policy implications. *Telecommunications Policy* 6: 223–35 (September 1982).

Rose, F. E. Telidon and Canadian government information. *Government Publications Review* 9: 345–50 (1982).

Sigel, E., et al. *The Future of Videotext: Worldwide Prospects for Home-Office Electronic Information Services.* White Plains, New York: Knowledge Industries Publications, 1983.

Sigel, E., ed. *Videotext: The Coming Revolution in Home-Office Information Retrieval.* White Plains, New York: Knowledge Industries Publications, 1979.

Truxal, C. Americanizing videotext. *IEEE Spectrum* 19: 52–56 (November 1982).

Von Vignau, R. A. Bildschirmtext and the CEPT videotex system. *IEEE Journal on Selected Areas of Communication* 1: 254–59 (1983).

Winsbury, R., ed. *Viewdata in Action: A Comparative Study of Prestel.* New York: McGraw-Hill, 1981.

Wood, J. Corporate videotex systems and cost effectiveness. *Computer Communications* 6: 90–93 (April 1983).

Woolfe, R. *Videotex: The New Television/Telephone Information Services.* London: Heyden Books, 1980.

VIDEOTEXT STANDARDS

Childs, G. European videotex standard. *Computer Communications* 5: 226–33 (October 1982).

Schmid, P., and Maurer, C. Presentation level protocol for national videotex services. *Computer Communications* 4: 267–72 (December 1981).

Wetherington, J. D. Story of PLP. *IEEE Journal on Selected Areas of Communication* 1: 267–77 (1983).

VIDEOTEXT SYSTEMS DESIGN

Borgman, C. L. The videotex user interface: Design considerations and feature analysis. *Videodisc/Videotex* 2: 115–31 (September 1982).

Campbell, J. A., and Thomas, H. B. The videotex marketplace: A theory of evolution. *Telecommunications Policy* 5: 111–20 (June 1981).

Chitnis, A. M., and Costs, J. M. Videotex services: Network and terminal alternatives. *IEEE Transactions on Consumer Electronics* 25: 269–77 (1979).

Foster, J. J., and Bruce, M. Looking for entries in videotext tables: A comparison of four color formats. *Journal of Applied Psychology* 67: 611–15 (1982).

Gecsei, J. *The Architecture of Videotex Systems.* Englewood Cliffs, New Jersey: Prentice-Hall, 1983.

Godfrey, D., and Chang, E. *The Telidon Book.* Toronto: Press Porcepic, 1981.

Maurer, H. A., Rausch, W., and Sebestyen, I. Alphabetic searching in videotex systems. *Electronic Publishing Review* 1: 217–23 (September 1981).

Muter, P., et al. Extended reading of continuous text on television screens. *Human Factors* 24: 501–8 (1982).

Rorvig, M. E. Videotex shopping systems: Techniques for the presentation of information. *Electronic Publishing Review* 3: 39–48 (March 1983).

Tompa, F. W., Gecsei, J., and Bochmann, G. Data structuring facilities for interactive videotex systems. *Computer* 14: 72–81 (August 1981).

White, T. A. Transmission of alphanumerics by television displays. *Displays* 2: 295–99 (July 1981).

VIEWDATA TECHNOLOGY

Chorafas, D. M. *Interactive Videotext*. New York: Petrocelli Books, 1981.

Cicora, W. S., Sprignoli, G., and Thomas, W. An introduction to teletext and viewdata with comments on compatibility. *IEEE Transactions on Consumer Electronics* 25: 235–45 (1979).

Fedida, S. Viewdata gateways: Commercial significance and economic criteria. *Computer Communications* 5: 181–85 (August 1982).

Fedida, S., and Malik, R. *The Viewdata Revolution*. New York: Wiley, 1979.

Martin, J. *Viewdata and the Information Society*. Englewood Cliffs, New Jersey: Prentice-Hall, 1982.

Maurer, H. A., Rausch, W., and Sebestyen, I. Videotex message systems. *Electronic Publishing Review* 1: 267–96 (December 1981).

Mayne, A. J. *The Videotex Revolution*. Dallas: October Press, 1982.

CHAPTER 6

DOCUMENT-ORIENTED VIDEO SYSTEMS

While textual information is an important component in the videotext, cabletext, and video disk systems discussed in preceding chapters, prevailing 525-line NTSC and 625-line PAL and SECAM television standards do not provide sufficient resolution for the legible display of typewritten or printed text. Where text is to be displayed, video frames must be specially formatted with large characters to ensure legibility. By way of contrast, this chapter discusses systems that use video technology for the transmission, storage, and retrieval of ordinary documents. Like the video-based information systems described in preceding chapters, they represent information as a series of horizontal scan lines, each composed of a series of individual picture elements. They operate at significantly higher resolutions, however, and utilize special components rather than conventional television receivers. They are primarily designed for business, not consumer, applications, and they have considerable potential for library operations.

Available document-oriented, video-based information systems can be divided into three broad groups:

1. Facsimile—variously called "telefacsimile" or, simply, "fax"—is the best known and most widely utilized example. It is a telecommunications technology that uses video scanning to transmit document images electronically from one location to another. At the receiving location, the image is usually reconstructed as a paper copy or facsimile of the original document. A facsimile device can consequently be viewed as either a remote copier or, more appropriate to this discussion, as a video system that prints still pictures on paper rather than displaying moving images on a screen.

2. A variant form of facsimile technology, called "microfacsimile," transmits images from centralized microfilm, microfiche, or other microform files to remote printers, microfilm recorders, or display devices.

3. Continuing a discussion begun in chapter 3, the newest form of document-oriented, video-based information system scans documents for recording as video images on magnetic or optical disks. These document-oriented video disk systems became commercially available in late 1983 and are expected to play a significant role in information storage and retrieval.

This chapter begins with an introduction to facsimile technology, followed by a discussion of the performance characteristics of available equipment and its potential for business and library applications. Later sections provide a similar treatment of microfacsimile and document-oriented video disk systems.

Facsimile Transmission

Facsimile Technology

Like all information transmission devices, a facsimile system consists of an integrated configuration of equipment and communication facilities designed to transmit information-bearing signals from one point to another. The transmission itself originates at a source terminal—a transmitter or scanner—and it terminates at the receiver. Most vendors combine transmission and reception capabilities in a single terminal called a "transceiver." Full duplex transceivers can transmit and receive documents simultaneously. Most transceivers, however, are half duplex devices capable of either transmission or reception, but not at the same time. As will be discussed later in this section, the facsimile signal is conveyed by a telephone line or other communication facility.

The function of the facsimile transmitter is to scan a document, called the "subject copy," using an optical assembly and a light source to convert the document's tonal variations into electrical signals suitable for transmission over the intended communications medium. In terms of physical appearance, the transmitter may be either a desktop or floor-standing device. Most available units resemble a photocopier or computer printer in appearance (figure 32).

The document insertion mechanism determines the types and sizes of subject copy that can be scanned by a given transmitter. In the oldest and formerly most prevalent method, the subject copy is wrapped around a cylinder that rotates at high speed while a scanning mechanism moves slowly down its long axis. While a number of rotating cylinder scanners remain in use, most newer models feature flat-bed scanning in which the subject copy is inserted into a slot and automatically transported past a stationary scanning mechanism. Cylinder-type scanners are typically limited to subject copies measuring 8.5 by 14 inches or smaller. Flat-bed scanners can often accept larger documents. Many flat-bed models place no practical limitations on document length, although their width is typically limited by the dimensions of the input slot.

As a constraint of significance for library applications, both the cylinder-type and the flat-bed scanner place limitations on the thickness of the subject copy, and neither can accept bound volumes. As a result, journal articles and similar documents must either be unbound or copied onto sheets of paper prior to scanning. Copier-like scanners with glass platens have been developed, but they are not readily available in the United States. Several companies—including Terminal Data Corporation, Eikonix, and Datacopy—offer overhead scanners that can accept bound volumes positioned face-up on a flat exposure surface. Like the newer facsimile transmitters discussed later in this chapter, these devices use digital encoding

FIGURE 32

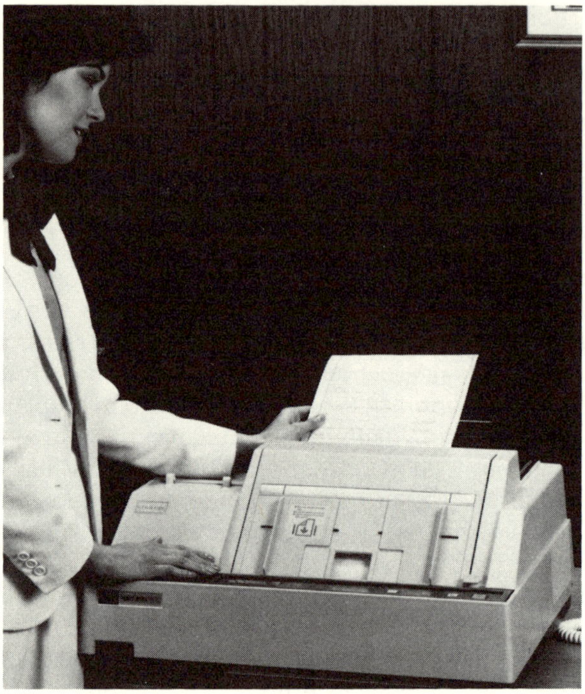

Styled like desktop copiers, facsimile transceivers utilize video technology to send and receive document images. (Courtesy: 3M Company)

techniques. Unlike conventional facsimile products, however, they are typically sold as components to be integrated with computers, video terminals, and facsimile receivers in customized systems. In an older variant of this approach, slow-scan television (SSTV) systems utilize video cameras to transmit document images as an analog signal to remote display devices or printers. Best suited to graphic materials, slow-scan television systems continue to be used in the videoconferencing applications discussed in chapter 7.

Like other video-based transmission and recording systems, the facsimile scanner divides the subject copy into a grid or raster of picture elements or pixels. Facsimile scanning resolution, as discussed later in this chapter, varies from system to system, but it invariably provides more pixels than are encountered with conventional broadcast television, videocassette, and consumer-oriented video disk systems. Older scanners, many of which remain in use, use mechanical illumination techniques with spot or flood lights. Newer models feature solid state charge-coupled device (CCD) arrays, photodiode arrays, fiber optics, lasers, or other electronic scanning mechanisms.

Regardless of design and illumination method, a facsimile scanner is essentially a densitometer. Light reflected from individual picture elements is measured by a photocell and converted to an electrical signal, the nature of which varies with the intensity of the reflected light. Being dark, the text areas of a typical business or library document absorb light while the white background areas reflect it. The resulting electrical signal may represent, or encode, these light intensity variations in either analog or digital form:

1. In the analog approach—the oldest facsimile encoding technique—the transmitter generates a continually varying electrical signal that represents the subject copy as a serial stream of light intensity variations. Depending on the transmitter's sensitivity, varying intensity levels may be used to encode eight or more shades of gray. Analog encoding is thus well suited to the transmission of magazine articles, mug shots, real estate descriptions, and other documents containing photographs or continuous tone illustrations.
2. Digital facsimile transmitters are image digitizers designed specifically for document transmission applications. Rather than utilizing continually varying electrical signals, an image digitizer represents dark and light picture elements as a series of discrete on/off electrical pulses. The digital transmitter measures the light reflectance value of each pixel, determining whether it exceeds some preestablished threshold amount. If it does, the pixel is encoded as white. If it does not, it is encoded as black. While custom-developed digital facsimile systems can encode gray scale information, commercially available models transmit gray areas as either black or white pixels, depending on their light reflectance values. They are consequently poorly suited to the transmission of photographs. But, as will be discussed in the next section, digital transmitters do permit the use of signal compression techniques that can significantly reduce transmission time. In addition, as will be described below, the digital facsimile signal can be transmitted to a computer for storage or processing. As a result, they are the current focus of industry attention and are likely to dominate facsimile equipment design in the coming years.

In most facsimile applications, the communications medium is a telephone line, and the ability to interconnect with the public telephone network has contributed significantly to the growth of facsimile technology. Most available facsimile equipment is designed to work with ordinary switched telephone lines. Leased lines can also be used, but are not required. In the manner of terminal-to-computer communications, the transmitter operator simply dials the telephone number associated with the desired receiver to complete the connection. In most cases, equipment synchronization is automatic, and transmission can begin immediately. In the typical business or library application, operator attention will be required during approximately one-third of the transmission time. During the remaining two-thirds, the operator can perform light clerical chores in the vicinity of the transmitter.

Several automated accessories can further reduce the amount of operator involvement. Automatic feeding permits the rapid mounting or insertion of successive subject copies. An optional feature with some inexpensive analog transmitters, it is virtually required for the efficient use of high-speed digital transmitters. Automatic answering eliminates operator involvement in the establishment and maintenance of telephone contact at the receiver. Automatic dialers capable of storing 100 or more telephone numbers are an increasingly common option with newer equipment. With the public telephone network, full weekday long distance rates are reduced substantially during evening hours. Automatic dialers permit transmission after normal business hours when an operator is not in attendance. It can prove especially useful in transmissions between offices in different time zones. Where offices in both the transmitting and receiving sites are closed, automatic dialing can be used in conjunction with unattended reception. Polling is a variant form of automatic dialing in which a transmitter calls another transceiver to determine whether it has been preloaded with documents to be sent on signal. Polling allows the receiving device to control the time of transmission.

High-speed facsimile transmitters that use terrestrial microwave or satellite transmission have been demonstrated. While commercial models are planned for the near future, they were not available at the time this chapter was written. In recent years, several companies have developed telecommunications networks specifically designed for the transmission of facsimile signals. Examples include Graphnet, a service of Graphic Scanning Corporation, and Speedfax, a facsimile network developed by SPC Communications. Patterned after the so-called value added computer communications networks like Telenet and Tymnet, these facsimile networks serve as an economical alternative to the conventional telephone network. Their charges are lower than comparable long distance charges and are based on elapsed transmission time without regard to distance.

Like computer terminals, facsimile devices emit an electrical signal—termed a "baseband signal"—that cannot be directly transmitted over telephone lines intended for voice communications. The public telephone network consists of analog communication facilities that are designed to respond to the range of frequencies most commonly represented in the human voice. While many facsimile transmitters—as discussed above—use analog encoding techniques, a substantial portion of their baseband signals fall outside of the frequency range supported by the telephone network. These analog baseband signals must consequently be transformed or "modulated" before transmission. Most analog facsimile devices feature an integral modem or acoustic coupler for this purpose. In the absence of purely digital telecommunications facilities, digital facsimile signals must likewise be converted to an appropriate analog form for transmission over the telephone network. This digital-to-analog conversion is likewise accomplished by an integral modem that is typically supplied with the facsimile equipment.

Facsimile receivers also feature integral modems that decode incoming signals, interpreting their intensity variations and recording them as a pattern of light and dark areas that form a paper facsimile of the subject copy. As a general operating principle, the receiver makes dark marks in areas corresponding to dark pixels in the subject copy, thereby reconstructing the document image. Any of several recording processes may be used:

1. Most facsimile receivers employ the electrofax or direct electrostatic process, which uses a coated, photoconductive paper. The paper is charged in darkness and exposed to a light source capable of displaying a pattern of light intensity variations corresponding to the various picture elements in the subject copy. The resulting image is developed through the application of a charged toner. The electrofax process is both reliable and economical. It is also used by many photocopiers and microfilm reader/printers and will prove acceptable for a broad range of business applications.

2. In the electrosensitive or electrothermal process, a special recording paper features a dark carbon underlayer covered with an opaque white coating. An electric current, passed from a stylus through the paper, decomposes the coating in areas corresponding to dark portions of the subject copy, revealing the dark underlayer. A similar process is used by some computer terminals.

3. Several facsimile receivers produce plain paper output, using either xerographic or ink-jet printing technology. The latter approach, in which microscopic ink pellets are sprayed on paper, is also used by computer and word processing printers. The xerographic or direct electrostatic process uses lasers or other light sources to produce latent images on an intermediate, photoconductive surface. These images are then developed by an electrically charged toner that is transferred to ordinary paper. With both the ink-jet and xerographic processes, the provision of plain paper copies encourages user acceptance.

4. Some older facsimile receivers follow the electrolytic process in which varying electrical voltages, passed through a stylus, are used to discolor a conductive paper in areas corresponding to dark portions of the subject copy.

5. Special purpose facsimile receivers designed for the transmission of newspictures, fingerprints, or similar documents employ silver gelatin, dry silver, or other recording technologies. Such receivers are rarely encountered in ordinary business applications.

Like photocopiers, facsimile receivers may be loaded with rolls or sheets of paper, and output sizes vary with the type of paper stock utilized. Most sheet-fed receivers will copy onto legal size (8.5 by 14 inches) or smaller paper, although a few available models can produce copies measuring ledger size (14 by 17 inches). Such machines are of particular interest to libraries that must transmit large journal pages or newspapers. As an alternative method of accommodating larger documents, some facsimile receivers will reduce such images to letter size (8.5 by 11 inches). Roll-fed receivers typically offer considerable flexibility in producing copies that measure either 8.5 or 11 inches wide by any practical length. Roll-fed devices offer the additional advantage of cutting copies to size, thereby minimizing paper consumption where smaller documents or portions of documents are transmitted.

While facsimile receivers have customarily produced paper output, facsimile signals can also be displayed on a video screen. As will be described more fully in chapter 8, several vendors offer special video monitors and terminals designed for this purpose. They typically feature letter-size screens with high resolution capabilities suited to the display of document images and computer-generated graphics. As discussed in later sections, they are most widely employed in microfacsimile systems or where facsimile transmitters interface with video disk storage systems.

Historically, facsimile devices have been used for direct point-to-point communication between a given transmitter and receiver. In several of the facsimile communication networks discussed above, however, computers are used as intermediary repositories for transmitted facsimile signals. In some cases, the computer reprocesses the facsimile signal, converting it to a form suitable for transmission to an otherwise incompatible receiver. Alternatively, the computer may hold the facsimile signal for retransmission at a later time, typically in the evening when telephone rates are lower. Such store-and-forward operation may also be used for automatic retransmission when the telephone line to the intended receiver is busy, thereby freeing the facsimile transmitter for other uses.

History and Applications

Basic facsimile concepts date from the nineteenth century, although practical applications did not develop until the 1920s. From that time until the present, facsimile has been widely and sucessfully utilized by newspaper publishers, police departments, meteorological stations, and military installations to transmit document images ranging from fingerprints to maps. These applications generally have complex input and quality requirements that can only be met by specially designed, relatively expensive equipment developed by companies like the Datalog Division of Litton Industries, the Alden Electronic and Impulse Recording Equipment Company, Muirhead Corporation, Stewart-Warner Datafax Corporation, and Harris Corporation. Perhaps the most familiar of these specialized facsimile applications involves the transmission of photographs for printing by newspapers. The requirements of most business and library applications are typically less complicated, and simpler, general-purpose facsimile systems began appearing in the late 1950s.

Developed by Xerox Corporation, 3M Company, Graphic Sciences, and other office products vendors, the earliest general-purpose facsimile systems were marketed as office machines rather than specialized scientific instruments. From the business standpoint, facsimile has always been considered a technology with an obvious market—the rapid transmission of time-sensitive documents. As a message transmission technology, it coexists with TWX, telex, communicating word processors, and other devices that transmit information as a sequence of individually encoded characters rather than as a signal representing the light reflectance properties of successive picture elements in a preexisting subject copy. But while character-oriented transmission methodologies require the retyping of document content by trained operators working at special terminals, facsimile systems require little operator training and can accept existing documents containing combinations of text and graphics. As a further advantage in certain business and library applications, facsimile can transmit foreign language documents that may not be readily representable in character-coded form. Compared to electronic message systems that encode individual characters rather than document images, facsimile technology is also more resistant to transmission impairments. Such impairments typically result in minor distortions that rarely impair the utility of facsimile copies.

Despite these significant advantages, business-oriented facsimile systems suffered more than a decade of very limited acceptance. Unlike special facsimile systems that are tailored to the requirements of particular applications, the earliest general-purpose facsimile equipment proved unreliable, slow, incapable of consistently satisfactory output quality, and unpredictably expensive. While a number of corporations, government agencies, and nonprofit institutions acquired facsimile transmission devices during the 1960s and early 1970s, they were too often considered a barely acceptable last resort to be used in emergency situations only.

During the same period, a number of libraries likewise experimented with facsimile. As in business, facsimile's potential for libraries proved obvious, and the earliest and most widely discussed applications involved the high-speed transmission of journal articles in response to interlibrary loan requests. But, reflecting the general business experience discussed above, the results of these experiments proved disappointing. Available equipment was judged too unreliable and output quality too inconsistent to support routine use. While facsimile proved unquestionably faster than conventional postal delivery, the transmission of lengthy journal articles could require several hours with an operator in attendance during the entire time. Libraries also found operating costs difficult to predict, and both costs and transmission times were often aggravated by the necessity of retransmission due to equipment failure or telecommunication impairments. As complicating factors for which the prevailing state of technology cannot be blamed, some of these facsimile experiments were of insufficient duration to permit the successful integration of the new service into existing interlibrary loan operations. In addition, users who requested facsimile transmission for rapid document delivery too often indicated their indifference to the service by failing to pick up requested materials for hours or days after it was received and printed.

Beginning in the mid-1970s, however, facsimile experienced a significant revival of business interest that was largely attributable to two factors: (1) the very strong interest in electronic mail and message systems that characterized office automation activities in the mid- to late 1970s; and (2) continuing developments in facsimile technology that resulted in significant improvements in equipment reliability, copy quality, transmission speed, and equipment compatibility. By the early 1980s, existing facsimile vendors had completely revamped their product lines. Attracted by rising sales, companies like Exxon Office Systems, Rapicom, Panafax, Canon, Sharp, NEC Information Systems, and Pitney Bowes entered the field. As with the video-based information systems discussed in preceding chapters, Japanese and European innovations played a critical role in facsimile's resurgence, and most of the equipment sold by American companies is actually manufactured in Japan or France.

Today, most medium to large businesses and government agencies are equipped with one or more facsimile transceivers. Library administrators, however, seem less aware of these developments than their business counterparts. Although many corporate and government libraries have access to facsimile transmission facilities, and several public and academic libraries have recently implemented facsimile networks utilizing newer equipment, facsimile remains an underutilized technology in libraries. It is likely, however, that the demand for high-speed document delivery will intensify as users of online bibliographic searching and other forms of automation require expanded and improved interlibrary loans.

Performance Characteristics and Costs

Like other video-based information systems, facsimile images are composed of a grid or raster of picture elements arranged in horizontal scan lines. But unlike display-oriented video systems which measure resolution in terms of the number of scan lines contained in an entire screen, facsimile resolutions are expressed in lines per inch (or, in European applications, lines per millimeter) of subject copy. Facsimile resolution is measured both horizontally and vertically. The horizontal measurement indicates the number of scan lines. The vertical measurement indicates the number of picture elements per line. The greater the number of scan lines and picture elements, the sharper the transitions from light to dark areas will appear in the facsimile copy. The determination of adequate resolution for a given facsimile application is typically based on a combination of user requirements and the physical and typographic characteristics of the subject copy to be transmitted. Such determination is complicated by the interrelationship of resolution, transmission time, and transmission cost. The higher the resolution, the greater the detail that must be transmitted for a given image and the longer the required transmission time. Telecommunication charges, an important component in facsimile transmission costs, will rise as well. In order to achieve an acceptable transmission time and cost, resolution must often be compromised.

Unrealistic user requirements and expectations can pose significant problems for systems analysts and others responsible for the implementation of facsimile systems. Unlike other reprographic technologies—such as photocopying or microfilming—in which the highest attainable output quality is invariably desired, most facsimile systems are simply designed to produce useful—that is, legible—output. Two levels of legibility are typically distinguished: (1) character legibility, in which each individual character in a facsimile copy is readily identifiable (figure 33A); and (2) word legibility, in which some characters may be obscured, but individual words can be conclusively identified from their surrounding context (figure 33B). Resolution requirements for character legibility are obviously greater, and—while character legibility is required for the accurate interpretation of numerical data, labelled graphs, and tables—word legibility suffices for most narrative text.

Since the 1960s, most analog facsimile systems have provided horizontal and vertical resolution of approximately 100 lines per inch (4 lines per millimeter). A letter size (8.5 by 11 inch) page will consequently be represented by approximately 935,000 picture elements. Such resolution typically provides character legibility in

FIGURE 33

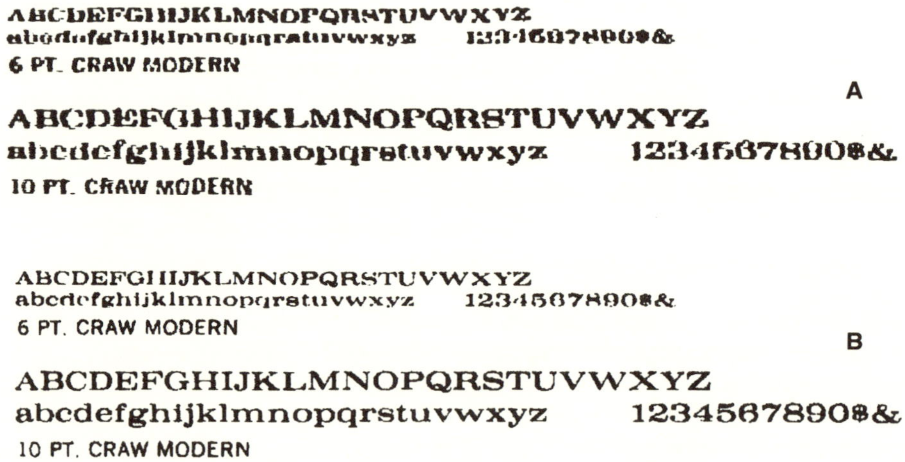

In word-legible transmission (A), some characters might be confused if they were not viewed in the context of the alphabet, for example, i, j, and 1; c and o; p and n. In character-legible transmission (B), these characters are distinct in their own right. (Source: *Library Technology Reports*, September-October 1978).

the transmission of technical reports, office correspondence, and other typewritten documents. It is also adequate for printed materials set in 8-point or larger type sizes. Unfortunately, many journal articles, monographs, reference books, and other library materials contain footnotes, labelled graphs, photograph captions, and other text segments set in 6-point or even 4-point type. Such small type sizes cannot be transmitted with predictable character legibility at 100 lines per inch, although word legibility is usually attainable. As an operator-selectable feature, most analog facsimile systems permit a one-third reduction in transmission time by degrading vertical resolution to approximately 50 picture elements per line. The resulting facsimile copy consists of approximately 465,000 picture elements and typically provides word legibility for typewritten text or printed documents set in larger typefaces.

Prospects for character legibility at a given resolution can usually be increased by optimizing the subject copy for facsimile transmission. For best results, documents should be created in large typefaces on high opacity white paper, using a good typewriter or comparable device equipped with a carbon ribbon. But, while such techniques can be applied to correspondence, standardized forms, and other ordinary business documents, few librarians have control over the typography and physical appearance of the bibliographic materials in their collections. As is the case with both microfilming and photocopying, the diverse and often unpredictable characteristics of library materials impose resolution requirements that are rarely encountered in ordinary business facsimile applications. Special facsimile systems designed for the transmission of newspictures, fingerprints, weather maps, and similar documents have long provided high resolution capabilities. Such special equipment can be purchased by libraries, but it is very expensive. During the 1970s, several vendors of analog facsimile systems offered models operating at horizontal resolutions exceeding 200 lines per inch, with a comparable number of picture elements per line. The resulting output quality approached that commonly associated with photocopiers. Designed for applications where output quality was more important than speed and economy, these high resolution systems operated slowly. Transmitting twice the number of picture elements generated by conventional business facsimile devices, each transaction took twice as long and telephone charges were consequently doubled. In the mid-1970s, however, digital facsimile systems began offering higher resolution while actually reducing transmission time. While analog systems remain important, digital facsimile—as previously noted—is the current focus of most vendors' product development and marketing efforts.

The operating speed of all facsimile equipment is expressed in terms of the time required to transmit a letter-size page. With analog facsimile systems, as described above, the light reflectance values of successively encountered picture elements are represented by a continually varying electrical signal. From their introduction in the 1960s through the mid-1970s, most analog facsimile systems required six minutes to transmit the 935,000 picture elements that constitute a letter-size subject copy at an approximate resolution of 100 horizontal and vertical lines per inch. Some of these devices remain in use, and, as noted in the preceding discussion, their required transmission time can be reduced to four minutes by degrading resolution to 50 picture elements per line. In the late 1970s, most vendors began replacing their six-minute analog systems with newer models capable of transmitting a letter-size page in just three minutes at a resolution of 100 horizontal and vertical lines per inch.

With degraded resolution, transmission time can be reduced to two minutes. Some analog systems employ special techniques—such as white space skipping, in which the transmitter skips over any scan lines that consist exclusively of white picture elements—to further reduce transmission time, but analog encoding methodologies offer only limited prospects for future development.

Digital encoding techniques offer considerably greater flexibility and opportunities for improved performance. As previously discussed, the digital facsimile signal consists of a computer-like stream of discrete on/off pulses or bits that represent the dark and light picture elements in the subject copy. Unlike analog systems that transmit the facsimile signal directly from the scanner, digital transmitters feature an integral microcomputer that analyzes and compresses the signal, reducing the amount of information that must be transmitted. While various approaches have been developed, the most widely used data compression methodology is run-length encoding—so called because it results in a coded message indicating the number of successively encountered picture elements of a given type. Rather than consisting of frequently alternating black-and-white picture elements, the typical subject copy contains relatively long stretches of light or dark areas within a given scan line. Instead, for example, of transmitting 512 pulses to represent an equivalent string of black or white picture elements, run-length encoding transmits only the line position of the first picture element plus the 9-bit binary code for 512. The actual advantage will vary with the characteristics of the subject copy, but simple horizontal run-length encoding schemes can yield compression ratios of approximately 6:1. More complex two-dimensional methods, which employ both horizontal and vertical analysis, offer compression ratios of approximately 8:1. Experimental data compression methods, which use complicated symbol matching techniques, suggest that future digital facsimile systems may offer compression ratios ranging from 40:1 to 150:1.

Once compressed, the digital facsimile signal is converted to analog form for transmission over ordinary telephone lines. The typical digital facsimile system employing one-dimensional run-length encoding can transmit a letter-size page in approximately one minute at a resolution of 200 horizontal and vertical lines per inch. They consequently offer a significant performance advantage in terms of both quality and speed when compared to the analog systems discussed above. Transmission time can be reduced to approximately 30 seconds by degrading resolution along either the horizontal or vertical dimension. An increasing number of systems use two-dimensional encoding techniques to reduce the required transmission time to as little as 20 seconds per letter-size page. Regardless of the particular method used, the digital facsimile receiver is itself equipped with a microcomputer that converts the compressed signal into a form suitable for reproduction as a facsimile copy.

Whether digital or analog devices are used, facsimile costs consist of a combination of interrelated elements, including equipment purchase or rental, supply consumption, long distance telephone or other telecommunications charges, and labor. Largely due to the fear of obsolescence, most facsimile equipment is rented rather than purchased. As might be expected, digital facsimile devices are significantly more expensive to rent or purchase than their slower, less complex analog counterparts. Analog facsimile transceivers capable of three-minute operation can currently be rented for as little as $100 per month or purchased for less than $2,500. Monthly rental charges for digital facsimile transceivers range from about $200 to over $400, with purchase prices beginning at about $5,500 and ranging upward to $15,000. Unlike photocopiers with rental charges based on volume of activity, facsimile equipment rental is typically a fixed monthly cost that includes maintenance. If equipment is purchased, maintenance must be purchased separately.

Equipment rental or purchase represents the only fixed cost in a facsimile system. Supplies, labor, and telecommunications charges are variable cost items that will rise or fall with the volume of facsimile transactions. Supply costs depend on the recording process used, but will rarely exceed ten cents per copy. In terms of labor, facsimile machines are designed to be operated by clerical employees rather than specially trained technical personnel. As previously discussed, unattended answering, automatic dialing, and other special features can significantly reduce labor requirements. In most facsimile applications, long distance telephone charges will prove the most significant variable cost. This is especially the case with lower speed analog transceivers. In high volume applications, the accumulated savings in long distance telephone charges associated with high-speed digital systems can outweigh their higher equipment costs, resulting in a lower unit cost per transmission. The actual break-even point will necessarily vary from application to application, but may prove as low as several hundred pages per month if one of the least expensive digital transceivers is selected. On the other hand, organizations that intend to make only occasional use of facsimile transmission are best served by low-cost, low-speed analog systems.

Businesses, government agencies, and other organizations interested in the establishment of facsimile networks to link several offices must be concerned with the selection of compatible equipment. As used in this context, compatibility denotes the ability of a given facsimile transmitter and receiver, or two transceivers, to communicate with one another. As discussed above, facsimile technology has changed considerably since its commercial introduction, and, by the late 1970s, three classes of facsimile equipment were widely available: (1) older analog systems designed for six-minute operation with the ability to transmit a letter-size page in four minutes with degraded resolution; (2) newer analog devices capable of three- or two-minute transmission, depending on the desired resolution; and (3) digital systems capable of transmitting a letter-size page in one minute or less. As might be expected, analog and digital devices are incompatible with one another, and, until recently, there has been no assurance of compatibility among the analog or digital devices of different manufacturers, even when the same encoding methodologies and transmission speeds are utilized. Older analog machines, for example, utilized several different and incompatible modulation techniques. In some cases, the equipment of different vendors proved compatible when operating at six minutes, but incompatible when transmitting at four. To meet the broadest range of communication requirements, several vendors introduced complicated, multi-purpose machines capable of either digital or analog transmission at various speeds.

Since the 1970s, however, the Comité Consultatif International Téléphonique et Télégraphique (CCITT), the group responsible for the development of international telecommunication standards, has developed standards designed to promote compatibility among the facsimile equipment of different manufacturers. These standards specify operating characteristics for three groups of facsimile devices, categorized by encoding methodology and transmission speed:

1. CCITT Group I consists of six-minute analog units offering a horizontal and vertical resolution of 96 lines per inch. Since the Group I standard was formulated after the development of the product group itself, its appearance merely recognizes the existence of this type of device rather than influencing its operating characteristics. As a further constraint, the Group I standard does not address the four-minute, lower resolution mode supported by many six-minute machines. While some vendors still offer Group I machines and many such devices are still encountered in low volume installations, they no longer represent a viable equipment alternative for most businesses and libraries.

2. CCITT Group II, the first standard to have a direct impact on facsimile equipment design, consists of three-minute analog units operating at a horizontal resolution of 100 lines per inch with 100 picture elements per line. As of this writing, Group II machines represent the most effective and economical alternative for organizations anticipating low to medium volume facsimile transmission activity. As previously discussed, some three-minute devices offer the additional capability of two-minute transmission with degraded resolution, but the Group II standard does not address those operating characteristics, and there is no guarantee of compatibility among the Group II machines of different manufacturers when operating in the two-minute mode. As a further point of complication, some vendors have developed three-minute analog devices that do not conform to CCITT Group II specifications. Typically, these are older machines introduced before the formulation of the Group II standard.

3. CCITT Group III consists of digital facsimile systems that use data compression methods for high-speed transmission. All CCITT Group III devices use the modified Huffman code, a one-dimensional data compression technique that yields signal compaction ratios ranging from 4:1 to 8:1. As an option, the Group III standard permits the use of the two-dimensional modified relative element address designate (READ) code, which provides compression ratios ranging from 6:1 to 12:1. Group III facsimile systems are nominally designed for transmission of a letter-size document in one minute or less. The actual transmission time will vary with the density of the subject copy, the data transmission rate, and the desired resolution. At 9,600 bits per second, for example, a typical letter-size page will be transmitted in about 30 seconds at a nominal resolution of 200 horizontal by 100 vertical lines per inch or in about 60 seconds at a nominal resolution of 200 horizontal and vertical lines per inch. In many cases, however, ordinary telephone lines will not support reliable transmission at such high data rates. In such situations, the transmission time must be reduced to 4,800 or even 2,400 bits per second, and the required transmission time will be correspondingly increased. Some Group III machines are equipped with "step down" modems that sample line conditions and automatically adjust the transmission rate between 9,600 and 2,400 bits per second as required. While all newer digital facsimile devices offer Group III compatibility, some models offer additional proprietary transmission modes that permit either higher resolution or faster transmission speed. When operating in these modes, compatibility with the equipment of other manufacturers is not assured.

Standards for CCITT Group IV machines are currently being developed. Group IV will consist of high-speed, high-quality digital devices designed to operate over leased lines, terrestrial microwave facilities, satellite links, or other wideband transmission facilities at horizontal and vertical resolutions of 300 to 400 lines per inch. They will offer the copier-like quality presumably required for the widespread acceptance of facsimile in electronic mail and message systems. In addition, they will be able to function as printers for character-coded data transmitted by computers and word processing systems. Several Group III machines presently offer such capabilities.

Microfacsimile

Basic Concepts

Over the past several decades, a number of businesses have converted large portions of their active and inactive operating records to microfilm, microfiche, or other microforms. Many libraries have likewise microfilmed portions of their collections or purchased micropublications as alternatives to full-size books, journals, and similar materials. As with paper documents, microfilmed business records and library materials stored in centralized repositories may be urgently needed at remote locations, but conventional facsimile systems cannot accommodate such materials directly. Instead, enlarged paper copies of relevant microimages must first be produced on a reader/printer. These paper enlargements can then serve as subject copies for facsimile scanning, but the time-consuming and labor-intensive nature of this indirect approach makes it unsuitable for high volume applications. In addition, reader/printer enlargements may lack sufficient sharpness and contrast for high quality facsimile transmission.

Microfacsimile systems—sometimes called "video-based micrographic systems" or, simply, "videomicrographic systems"—address these limitations by directly scanning the microform images themselves. Such systems were first developed in the 1950s, but attracted little user attention for two decades. Much of this apparent disinterest was attributable to the generally unsatisfactory state of facsimile technology in the 1960s and early 1970s. The earliest microfacsimile systems were custom-developed at relatively high cost for specific applications and offered only marginal performance. Most of them were only operational on an experimental basis designed to demonstrate technical feasibility. Few off-the-shelf products were available, and none of the major micrographics equipment vendors offered such systems. Knowledgeable micrographics systems analysts further questioned the need for such a complicated technology. The most commonly cited business applications involved the transmission of microimages on demand from central files to remote work areas. In a simpler approach to such applications, microform collections can be easily and economically duplicated for distribution to remote sites in anticipation of later reference, thereby minimizing or eliminating the need for on-demand access.

Given this simple and cost effective alternative, microfacsimile concepts gained few adherents until the late 1970s when information systems analysts, concerned about time wasted in document retrieval, became interested in the electronic delivery of documents to managerial and professional workstations. Through the mid 1970s, information processing professionals devoted considerable attention to the development of sophisticated systems for the retrieval of computer-stored data, virtually ignoring paper documents and microfilmed document images as "transitional" information carriers that would eventually be replaced by computer-based information systems. By the late 1970s, however, it had become obvious that documents would retain their importance for many years and that automated document storage and retrieval systems could make a significant contribution to work effectiveness in many applications.

To meet the growing demands of users for convenient and rapid access to document files, a number of micrographics equipment manufacturers have introduced computer-assisted retrieval (CAR) systems that use computers to maintain online indexes to document images stored on microfilm or microfiche. Such systems were originally developed in the late 1960s for library applications, the most famous being Project Intrex that was designed to provide scientists at the Massachusetts Institute of Technology with rapid, automated retrieval of technical publications stored on microfiche. After a decade of relatively slow growth, computer-assisted microfilm retrieval has become commonplace in business applications. Today, the typical business CAR system consists of a minicomputer, one or more display terminals and printers, disk storage for index information, one or more microfilm reader/printers, and specially developed information retrieval software. In the typical retrieval operation, a display terminal is used to search a computer-maintained index for the microform addresses of document images meeting stated parameters. The system responds with the roll or fiche numbers and frame locations of relevant images. The operator then selects the indicated roll or fiche from a nearby storage cabinet or other file and inserts it into a reader/printer for viewing and/or printing.

Most microfacsimile systems include a CAR subsystem that identifies relevant microform images. But rather than being stored in local work files from which they must be manually selected, microfilm rolls, microfiche, or aperture cards are maintained in a specially designed, centralized retrieval unit for automatic selection in response to specific search operations. The selected microforms are directed to a specially designed video scanner that transmits specified images to remote locations. Microfacsimile thus provides fully automated, video-based document delivery. As a significant constraint, microfacsimile costs are high, with typical installation prices ranging from several hundred thousand to over one million dollars.

System Components

Microfacsimile systems are currently being marketed by two broad groups of companies:

1. Manufacturers of automated microform storage and retrieval equipment who offer microfacsimile capabilities as an optional component in a computer-assisted retrieval system. Examples of such companies include Access Corporation, which manufactures automated retrieval systems for microfiche and aperture cards; Infodetics, which manufactures large-scale aperture card retrieval systems for engineering applications; and Ragen Information Systems, which manufactures a unique system for the automatic retrieval of 16mm roll microfilm.

2. System contractors who implement customized microfacsimile systems designed for specific applications. While these system contractors may design special video scanners, retrieval units, or other components for use in microfacsimile applications, they typically specialize in the development of hardware and software interfaces designed to integrate equipment manufactured by other companies. System contractors generally implement microfacsimile as a component in a large-scale document storage and retrieval system that combines computer, micrographics, and telecommunications technologies. As a group, they have been responsible for a number of complex and widely publicized microfacsimile implementations in both government agencies and the private sector. Examples of system contractors include Antone Systems, Integrated Automation, Omex Corporation, Planning Research Corporation, and TERA Corporation.

Regardless of vendor, microfacsimile systems include the same broad groups of components associated with conventional facsimile. The microfacsimile transmitter consists of a video scanner that converts the light intensity variations of successively encountered picture elements in a subject microimage to an electrical signal suitable for transmission to an intended receiver. Available scanners are built to accept one type of microform only, the choices being 16mm roll microfilm, microfiche, or aperture cards. In the typical application, the microfacsimile system receives a request to transmit one or more document images identified by remote users working through a computer-assisted retrieval subsystem. The microfacsimile system selects the appropriate microforms from an automatic retrieval device and mounts it in the transmitter for scanning. Because automatic frame selection and image positioning are utilized, the microforms must usually be produced to rather rigid specifications. No vendors now offer microfacsimile systems configured for manual microform input and image positioning.

Older microfacsimile scanners, some of which remain in use, employed conventional television cameras equipped with relatively expensive image orthicon or less expensive vidicon tubes. These cameras permit rapid image scanning as well as zoom capabilities that can prove useful in engineering and related applications involving graphic documents. Significant disadvantages, however, include their use of analog pixel encoding and their operation at relatively low resolutions. In addition, scanners based on television cameras are vulnerable to a variety of image distortions and can require high voltage power supplies.

To overcome these limitations, state-of-the-art microfacsimile scanners feature solid-state image digitizers composed of CCD or photodiode arrays. The use of digital pixel encoding permits both data compression and video enhancement, the latter technique being used to improve the quality of marginal microimages. Most available microfacsimile scanners operate at a horizontal and vertical resolution of 200 lines per inch, although some vendors now offer scanners that operate at 300 lines per inch for higher image quality. In most cases, digitized images are transferred to a magnetic disk that serves as a temporary buffer pending transmission to remote workstations. The buffer is especially useful for retrieval requests involving multiple document images. In such situations, users working at remote video displays may be able to browse through the disk storage area, examining documents at length or selecting images for printing.

As a component in an automated document storage and retrieval application, the typical microfacsimile system is designed to transmit microimages to remote workstations in five seconds or less. Such rapid transmission requires high-speed communication facilities, and most microfacsimile installations employ coaxial cable to connect central document storage areas to workstations located in the same building or office complex. An increasing number of organizations are equipped with local area communication networks suitable for this purpose, and such communication facilities will likely prove commonplace in the future. Where long distance communication is required, special telephone lines, terrestrial microwave, satellite microwave, or comparable facilities must be used. As with conventional facsimile systems, voice-grade telephone lines can also be used, but required document transmission times will be significantly increased. In such situations, proprietary transmission protocols are employed. At present, microfacsimile systems are designed for operation within a single corporation or institution. There has been some discussion of microfacsimile transmission using CCITT Group III standard facsimile protocols to facilitate interorganizational communication, but such capabilities are not now commercially available.

At the receiving end, transmitted microimages can be displayed on a video screen, printed on paper, or recorded in microform. Unlike conventional facsimile, which takes its name from the paper copies that are its most common form of output, most microfacsimile installations rely on video displays as the primary output device. These video displays, which are also employed in the document-oriented optical video disk systems described in the next section, are high resolution graphics CRT devices. Their characteristics will be discussed in chapter 8. Much of the current popularity of video display output in microfacsimile applications is attributable to the widespread acceptance of so-called paperless information systems. Video displays produce no paper to glut files or cause other records management problems. In many business applications, simple information requests can often be satisfied by consulting displayed document images. As previously noted, video displays can be used to browse through multi-page documents prior to printing, thereby eliminating unnecessary paper consumption. Where microfacsimile is a component in a computer-assisted retrieval system, some vendors offer multi-mode video terminals that can be used for both index searching and document display.

As a potentially significant disadvantage, however, video displays are poorly suited to business or research applications requiring prolonged examination of multipage documents. Such applications are better served by paper copies, and most microfacsimile systems will support a variety of high- and low-speed facsimile printers. In many cases, the end user prefers paper copies for familiarity, portability, and easy reference without special display equipment. As noted above, however, paper copies can pose significant records management problems. One microfacsimile equipment vendor, Ragen Information Systems, offers a unique workstation that addresses this disadvantage. The Ragen 1010, a sophisticated automated document storage and retrieval system, features a proprietary "hard/softcopy" terminal that records incoming documents on an electrostatic print paper using a powdered toner. Individual documents appear under a transparent cover for examination by the requestor. If the document meets the retrieval requirement, the operator enters a command and the toner is fused to the paper, producing a permanent copy. If the document is not relevant, another command is entered and the toner is erased, allowing the print paper to be reused for the next document image.

The technical feasibility of microform output, in which received document images are recorded on microfilm or microfiche, has been demonstrated in several microfacsimile installations. A computer-output microfilm (COM) recorder equipped with raster graphics capability serves as the output device in such applications. Compared to conventional paper copies, microform output offers the traditional records management advantage of conserving space. Document handling may also be simplified at the reception point. One significant disadvantage, however, is that graphics COM recorders are available from a limited number of manufacturers, are much more expensive than most paper printers or video displays, and can require complex site preparation, operator training, and maintenance routines. In addition, they produce conventional silver gelatin microforms that require external development, thus adding worksteps and delays not present with other output options. Once developed, microform copies must be viewed in a reader. In many cases, the end user will eventually make paper copies on a reader/printer, thus defeating the purpose of providing microform output.

Video Disks and Document Storage

Pictorial Documents

The Sears catalog experiment discussed in chapter 3 suggests the potential of video disks—with their high capacity and ability to combine still frames, moving images, color, and sound—as an alternative to books for the publication of pictorial information. The two MCA art programs described in that same chapter are, in effect, the video counterpart of art books. Similarly, Arete Publications has produced a video disk version of its *Academic American Encyclopedia*. Rather than being a simple video recording of the original publication, it combines visual information with music, sound effects, and spoken words in a way that is not possible in a conventional printed reference book.

Many libraries, archives, and other research repositories face the problem of finding a compact, secure, stable, and economical storage medium for collections of photographs and other visual materials. In such applications, video disk systems offer a potentially more versatile alternative to conventional film negatives, paper prints, and slides where rapid retrieval, convenient browsability, and simplified distribution to other institutions are desired. At the Jet Propulsion Laboratory at California Institute of Technology, for example, optical video disks are used in conjunction with a computer-based retrieval system to store planetary photographs produced from spacecraft imaging data. Each disk can store up to 108,000 photographs. In an interesting experiment at the University of Iowa School of Art and Art History, 1,000 black-and-white photographs of woodcuts and engravings were recorded on transmissive optical video disks for use in conjunction with a computer-based retrieval system. A computer program locates video disk images pertinent to user-specified retrieval parameters, activates a disk player to display them on a video monitor, and provides accompanying descriptive information on an adjacent video display terminal. While users found the resolution of displayed video images inferior to that of conventional photographic prints and slides, they considered the video disk system convenient and valuable for research purposes. Similarly, several magazine publishers and other organizations that maintain large picture libraries are planning to implement optical video disk systems for the convenient storage and retrieval of copies of photographs and other illustrative materials. In such applications, the video disk system is designed to facilitate the identification and selection of appropriate photographs by researchers, writers, and others. Conventional photographic negatives, maintained in a separate file, are used for the production of high quality prints. The National Air and Space Museum is currently in the process of converting its photograph collections to a set of video disks for sale to libraries, schools, or individual researchers.

In a commercial application designed specifically for technical and research libraries, the VIDEO PATSEARCH system, developed by Pergamon Press, combines the video disk storage of drawings and other graphic materials from printed U.S. patents with a computer-based system for the storage and retrieval of related textual information. Patent illustrations are recorded on regularly updated collections of optical video disks that are maintained at the user's site. The system's hardware components include a specially designed, microcomputer-based workstation/terminal with two video monitors, a printer, a keyboard, an industrial video disk player, and a telecommunications interface. The terminal is used in a timesharing mode to search the PATSEARCH data base offered through Pergamon's Info-Line Search System or Bibliographic Retrieval Services (BRS). Retrieved textual information pertinent to a given patent is displayed on one of the video monitors. To view accompanying pictorial material not included in the computer-maintained data base, the user is instructed to insert a specified video disk into the player. The technique is similar to the computer-assisted retrieval (CAR) systems developed for use with microfilm or microfiche, but video disks were selected over micrographic storage on the basis of compatibility of components and high-speed frame access.

In a similar application, Mnemos Incorporated uses a proprietary variant of micrographics technology to store up to 6,800 document images on a flexible optical video disk. The source document reduction ratio is 88:1. The disk can also contain up to 4 million characters of machine-readable, computer-processible programs and index data. A special retrieval station—the Mnemos System 6000—combines a microcomputer with a specially designed microform display device. Like conventional optical video disks, the MnemoDisc is produced by stamping copies from a specially prepared master. It is designed as an alternative to conventional micropublishing in applications involving 1,000 or more copies of 1,000 or more pages.

The Problem of Text Storage

The foregoing discussion pertains to the recording and display of graphic images, perhaps with occasional still frames containing titling, a menu of alternatives, instructions, or questions for user interaction. A number of business information specialists and librarians have suggested the more extensive use of video disks for the storage of textual documents. Used in this context, the term "text" denotes the alphabetic characters, numeric digits, punctuation marks, and other symbols commonly encountered in books, journal articles, technical reports, and office documents.

The idea of using video media for document storage is hardly new. Several videotape document storage and retrieval systems were marketed from the mid-1960s through the early 1970s. The most famous of them, the Ampex Videofile, utilized a copier-like input station to record up to 160,000 letter-size pages on a 4,800-foot reel of 2-inch videotape. Retrieval was controlled by a computer, with the resulting document images displayed on a high-resolution video monitor. An electrostatic printer was also offered, as were a variety of other interesting accessories, including a dual-purpose document/data display terminal, a computer-output-to-videotape unit, and a videotape to microfiche printer for archival storage. Similarly, the Infodetics System 2000, a system designed for lower volume applications, could record up to 7,000 pages on a videocassette for later retrieval, display, and/or printing.

Designed to compete with paper files and microforms, these videotape systems offered the theoretical advantages of a compact, high capacity storage medium; the ability to erase, move, or otherwise manipulate specified recorded images; the possibility of transmitting document images to remote locations; and attractive retrieval and display components. In actual practice, however, they proved more complex and expensive than other document storage methods, and their market acceptance was correspondingly limited. Some information specialists contend, however, that many of the limitations of these tape-oriented systems are successfully addressed by video disks. They point to the significant information processing advantages previously discussed in chapter 3: the reasonable cost of video disk players, their ability to operate under computer control and to randomly access specific frames and chapter segments, the wide range of possible display capabilities and visual effects, and the high capacity and durability of the disks themselves. As a dramatic indication of the information storage and retrieval potential of video disk technology, several observers have noted that the entire *Encyclopaedia Britannica* might be contained on a single optical video disk with the individual pages being more quickly and conveniently accessible than in the multivolume printed version.

Drama aside, however, there are several significant impediments to the use of consumer and industrial video disk systems for the storage of textual documents, the foremost being image quality. In the United States, existing consumer and industrial video disk systems record information as a series of television frames that conform to the NTSC resolution standards discussed in chapter 1. Those standards specify a video signal in which each frame consists of 525 horizontal scan lines. As previously noted, the highest quality video components will actually display only about 350 of those scan lines. The resulting images are acceptable for much graphic information where the loss of some detail does not adversely affect overall comprehensibility, but NTSC resolution standards cannot generally accommodate the relatively small characters found in typewritten or typeset text. While characters generated in pica (the approximate equivalent of 12-point) type may be marginally recognizable, the typeset text and footnotes encountered in books, journals, and other library materials cannot be legibly displayed.

Many existing video disks include still frames that contain charts, written instructions, questions, or other text segments. As noted earlier in this chapter, such still frames are composed of large characters especially designed for legible display within prevailing NTSC resolution constraints. Similar special typography is required for the storage of book pages, office records, or other documents. Few difficulties are posed if the documents are being created expressly for video disk applications, but existing documents must be reformatted. This is generally accomplished by recreating the documents, using large characters and more open spacing.

But, unless the text is available in machine-readable form generated by computers or word processors, such reformatting will typically necessitate a prohibitively expensive amount of retyping and/or cutting and pasting. As a potentially more effective alternative, the ITT Research Institute has developed a prototype system in which documents are scanned and the resulting images automatically reformatted by a computer for recording on conventional video disks. The developers claim that the typical book or journal page is reformatted as five or six video disk frames, permitting the recording of about 20,000 pages per conventional two-sided optical video disk.

But even if the problem of image quality could be satisfactorily resolved, other impediments to the widespread use of existing video disk systems for text storage would remain. As noted earlier in this chapter, the video disk mastering process is analogous to the printing of an edition of a book. Using conventional production methods, a single or a few copies of a video disk cannot be economically produced. As a further complication, the production process is time-consuming. This poses few problems for the conversion of books, journals, or other publications where several hundred to several thousand copies are required and production delays can be tolerated. It does, however, prevent the use of video disks for the storage of office documents, archives, manuscripts, and technical reports where, at most, a few disk copies are needed and the desired turnaround time is short.

Document Storage Systems

Recognizing the potential of video disks, several companies are attempting to resolve these problems by developing systems expressly designed for the storage of textual documents rather than being adaptations of products developed for the recording of graphic images in a broad spectrum of consumer and industrial applications. In the early 1980s, IBM, Wang Laboratories, and other computer equipment vendors introduced specially designed video scanners as adjuncts to their office automation product lines. Some of these devices, like the IBM Scanmaster, are styled like the flat-bed facsimile transmitters described in a preceding section (figure 34). Others, like the Wang Professional Image Computer, resemble planetary-type microfilm cameras in providing a flat surface on which documents can be scanned by an overhead image digitizer. Regardless of appearance, these devices scan office documents for storage as digitized video images on magnetic disks, from which they can later be transmitted to facsimile receivers, printers, or high resolution video display terminals.

Implemented as a component in an automated office system, these magnetic video disk systems are designed to integrate the document processing, data processing, and word processing operations of a given office—allowing all three activities to be performed by one system. Thus, a digitized document image might be transmitted to an executive workstation or incorporated into a report generated by a word processing program—an approach that is potentially useful for the manipulation of graphic images or foreign language materials that cannot be conveniently represented in character-coded form. It is important, in this context, to distinguish these image digitizers from optical character recognition (OCR) machines that also scan documents and are widely encountered in word and data processing installations. Unlike OCR scanners, which attempt to identify individual characters for

FIGURE 34

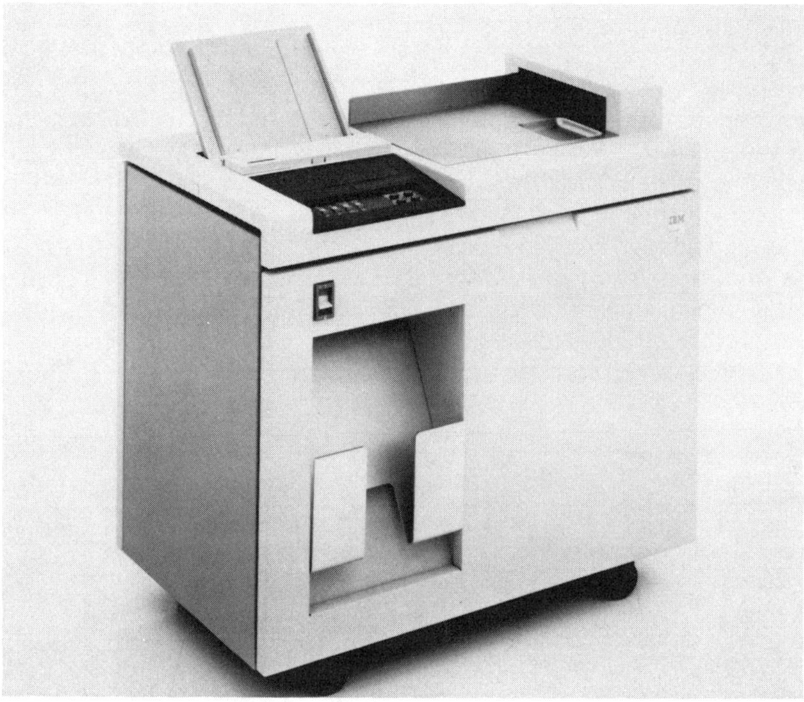

The IBM Scanmaster is an image digitizer which converts documents to a raster format for online storage on magnetic disks. (Courtesy: IBM Corporation)

representation as a 7- or 8-bit code, image digitizers are straightforward facsimile devices that merely encode a document's tonal values without regard to character content.

In addition to their use in document production and dissemination systems, such digitized images might also form the basis for an electronic filing system that permits online document retrieval. At the time this chapter was written, the widespread use of magnetic disks for this purpose was impeded by the large number of bits needed to represent document images in digital form. At a horizontal and vertical resolution of 200 lines per inch—the current industry standard for legibility—a single letter-size page will be divided into approximately 3.8 million picture elements, each encoded as a single bit. Even when data compression techniques are used, the total storage requirement can approach half a million bits per document. To put this total in perspective, the hard disk subsystems available with many microcomputers commonly offer 80 million bits (10 million bytes) of online storage capacity—enough for only about 160 digitized document images. While minicomputers and large-scale computers can support higher density disk drives, most existing computer installations do not provide sufficient magnetic disk capacity for the economical, long-term storage of large quantities of digitized information. A relatively expensive 100 megabyte disk, for example, offers 800 million bits of storage capacity—enough to store the digitized equivalents of half a file drawer of paper documents.

While the storage capacity of magnetic recording materials is constantly improving, many industry observers believe that optical disk technology holds greater promise for the practical implementation of large-scale electronic filing systems based on digitized document images. Compared to magnetic disks, they offer much higher storage capacities at potentially lower costs. Document-oriented optical video disks use the reflective and transmissive information recording methods described in chapter 3, but they differ from conventional consumer and industrial video disks in their use of direct document recording, digital image encoding techniques, and high resolution scanning.

As discussed in chapter 3, optical video disks designed for consumer and industrial applications are stamped from specially prepared masters in a factory. Conversely, optical video disks intended for document storage are designed for direct, in-office recording using special video scanners (figure 35). The acronym

FIGURE 35

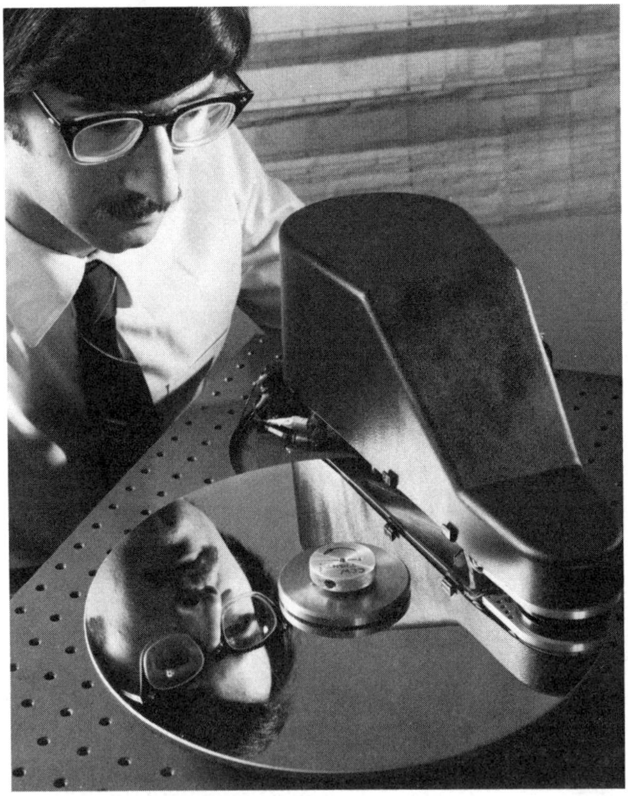

Optical disks like this prototype model, utilize lasers to record and retrieve the digitized equivalents of hundreds of thousands of document images. (Courtesy: Eastman Kodak)

DRAW (direct read after write) is sometimes used to describe this direct recording capability although it more accurately denotes an error-checking methodology that allows the system to verify information immediately after it is recorded on an optical disk. As with the magnetic disk systems discussed above, the document scanner may resemble a facsimile transmitter or a planetary-type microfilm camera. Alternatively, it may be built into a copier-like input station with a glass platen on which documents to be recorded are positioned face down. The scanning mechanism itself may be based on conventional video camera technology or, more commonly, on solid-state CCD arrays or lasers. Regardless of specific technology, the scanner divides a document into the grid-like raster of picture elements characteristic of video-based information systems. Individual picture elements are successively analyzed for their light reflectance properties, which are converted to an electrical signal for transmission to a recording unit (figure 36). The recording unit features a laser that encodes the pixels as microscopic pits in the optical disk's surface. The disks themselves are generally composed of a tellurium alloy, although other recording materials are reportedly being explored by such manufacturers as Eastman Kodak, Drexler Technology, 3M Company, Sony, Matsushita, and Thomson-CSF.

The consumer and industrial optical video disks described in chapter 3 use analog coding techniques to represent individual pixels by variations in the size and spacing of recorded pits. Document-oriented optical video disks, by way of contrast,

FIGURE 36

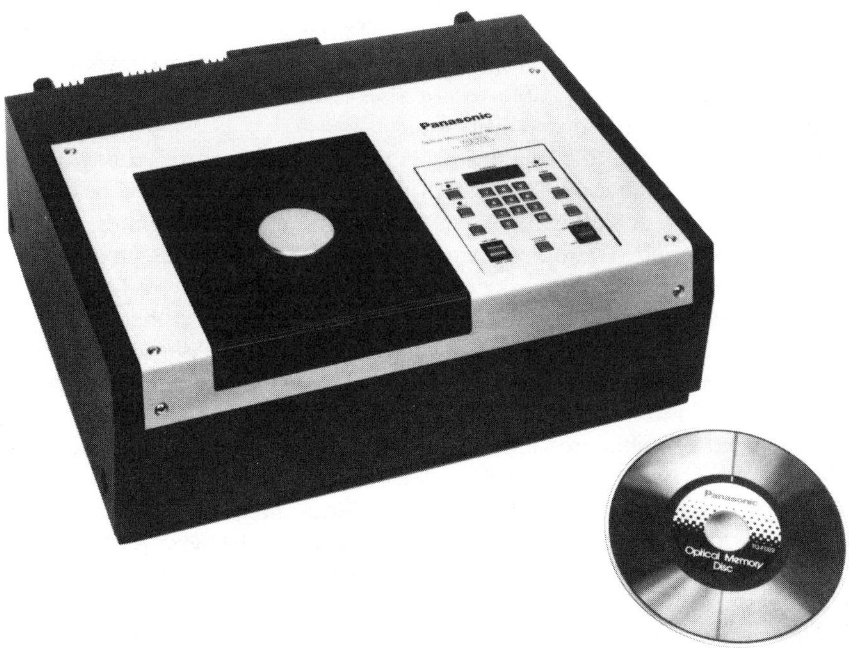

Desktop optical disk systems can store approximately 10,000 letter-size documents. (Courtesy: Matsushita)

employ digital encoding techniques that represent the tonal values of individual pixels as the presence or absence of uniformly sized pits. Such digital coding permits the use of data compression techniques to reduce the amount of disk space required for the storage of individual documents. To provide sufficient image quality, document-oriented optical video disks depart from the NTSC television standard with its inherent resolution constraints. Like digital facsimile devices, most systems offer resolution of 200 horizontal and vertical lines per inch, although some systems operate at 300 horizontal and vertical lines per inch for very high image quality. As with the microfacsimile systems described in a preceding section, specially designed and relatively expensive video monitors can be used to display recorded images. The characteristics of these display devices will be described in chapter 8.

While document-oriented optical video disk systems have received much attention at professional conferences and in the literature of information management, operational systems are just now being introduced. In the first American installation, Xerox Corporation implemented an optical video disk system for the storage of catalog card images at the Cataloging Distribution Service of the Library of Congress. Each optical video disk can store up to 200,000 card images, many of which contain non-Roman characters that cannot be conveniently represented in machine-readable, character-coded form for conventional computer storage. Card image retrieval is computer-controlled, and electrostatic printers permit high quality reproduction on card stock. The Library of Congress has also undertaken a demonstration project in which an optical video disk system developed by Integrated Automation will be used to store journal articles for video display and/or printing. Many journal articles contain photographs or other illustrations that cannot be readily represented in conventional computer-processible form. Even if such representation were possible, conversion of the text of a large journal backfile to machine-readable form on a character-by-character basis would prove prohibitively expensive. Such conversion problems are also characteristic of the large document backfiles maintained by many businesses.

Called Image Link, the system implemented by Integrated Automation uses a solid-state video scanner that operates at resolutions up to 300 horizontal and vertical lines per inch. Following video enhancement and data compression, a laser records the digitized document images on an optical video disk manufactured in France by Thomson-CSF. The disk's storage capacity is 1 billion bytes (8 billion bits). Up to 100 disks can be stored in an automated retrieval unit that operates under computer control to select and display specific images. Depending on resolution and the amount of data compression achieved, the retrieval unit's storage capacity ranges from 1.5 million to 2.5 million letter-size pages. Retrieved document images can be transmitted to high resolution video display terminals, laser printers, graphics COM recorders, or facsimile devices. Various combinations of local and remote workstations can be incorporated in a single equipment configuration.

Several document-oriented optical video disk systems have been demonstrated in prototype at various professional meetings and are described in professional and trade literature. Among the most widely publicized is DOR-MEGADOC, a high capacity system developed in the late 1970s by Philips for use in one of its Dutch research installations. It reportedly uses laser technology to record digitized images of up to 500,000 letter-size pages per optical video disk. Up to 64 disks can be loaded into a "jukebox" type selector mechanism, for a total system capacity of up to 32 million letter-size pages. It is designed as a centralized filing device for office installations, and a single system can support multiple workstations with high resolution video monitors and printers. Recording and access times are said to average two seconds per page. A jukebox-type optical video disk system has also been implemented by RCA under contract to the Department of Defense. At the time this chapter was written, Sony, Matsushita, Hitachi, Fujitsu, and various other companies were reportedly developing similar, high capacity, multi-disk document recording systems.

In a variant approach to high capacity document storage, Omex Corporation has developed an optical storage system that utilizes glass slides rather than disks. Each slide measures 5 by 5 inches and can contain up to 400 million bytes (3.2 billion bits) of data. A laser is used to record information by burning microscopic pits in the slides' tellurium alloy coating. An automated retrieval unit can store up to 2,048 slides for a total online storage capacity of 814 billion bytes (over 16 billion bits)—the equivalent of more than 2,500 conventional disk drives.

With their extraordinary storage capacity, the optical recording media described to this point are primarily designed as replacements for magnetic disks in very high volume electronic filing applications. They will typically serve multiple remote workstations from a centralized installation in a computer room or comparable facility. For the office automation market, several companies have developed self-contained optical video disk systems designed for smaller document collections. As an example, the Toshiba DF-2100 Document Filing System, originally developed by SRI International, is reportedly in use in Japan and has been demonstrated in the United States by the 3M Company at several industry expositions. It uses a laser scanner to record up to 10,000 letter-size office documents on a 12-inch optical video disk. Document recording time is approximately 8 seconds per page, and access times average 10 seconds. Documents are displayed on a high resolution video monitor, and a laser printer is provided for copier-like paper output. The system includes a minicomputer that controls document indexing and image retrieval.

In late 1983, the Panasonic Industrial Company—a Matsushita subsidiary—became the first vendor to market a preconfigured optical video disk recorder in the United States. The Matsushita Optical Document File System stores up to 10,000 letter-size pages on an 8-inch disk. This compact disk can be easily stored in filing cabinets or transported in a briefcase. Designed for office installation, the system features a video scanner that operates at 200 horizontal and vertical lines per inch and can scan a document in about 2 seconds. A laser is used for both recording and retrieval. Individual picture elements are recorded and read as a shading pattern. Retrieved document images can be displayed on a high resolution video monitor, recorded on paper by an electrostatic printer, or transmitted to a remote facsimile receiver using the CCITT Group III standard protocol.

As described in the foregoing paragraphs, document-oriented optical video disk systems are a variant form of micrographics system designed for miniaturized document recording. As such, they are designed to compete with microfilm, microfiche, and other conventional microforms in applications where compact document storage and rapid, automated retrieval are desired. But before such systems can be considered a viable alternative to such well-established information carriers in a broad spectrum of applications, concerns about the stability of optical recording media must be satisfactorily resolved. National standards have been developed that prescribe the manner in which conventional silver gelatin microfilms are to be manufactured, processed, and stored for archival stability. No such standards exist for the media used in optical video disk systems. The recording media currently used in existing document-oriented optical video disk systems consists of tellurium alloys with a projected useful life of about ten years. A number of companies are reportedly working on alternative optical recording media that will offer improved stability, but such materials may not become commercially available before the late 1980s.

Optical Disks for Computer Data

In addition to systems intended for the storage and retrieval of documents images, IBM, Burroughs Corporation, Digital Equipment, and other manufacturers of conventional magnetic disks are reportedly developing optical disks for the storage of the machine-readable, character-coded data generated by computers and word processors. While the high capacity, anticipated low cost, and other advantages of optical data storage has been discussed for a number of years, complex technical problems associated with the production of optical recording materials have delayed the emergence of this product group. In addition to the previously discussed problem of stability, the error rates experienced during optical data recording are a special concern. Compared to document-oriented storage systems where errors typically manifest themselves as relatively innocuous distortions in small portions of a document image, errors in the recording of character-coded letters, numeric digits, punctuation symbols, and other data will result in altered bit patterns that cause entire characters to be represented incorrectly. Acceptable solutions to these problems have been slow to develop, but, in late 1983, Storage Technology Corporation (STC) became the first company to announce an optical disk suitable for data recording.

Like document-oriented systems, these optical data disks use digital encoding and direct recording techniques, but they do not employ the raster format of picture elements characteristic of video recording. Instead, they use lasers to encode individual characters as a pattern of microscopic pits representing predetermined bit sequences. They cannot properly be considered "video" disks, since they do not contain video images, although their information content may ultimately be displayed on the alphanumeric video terminals described in chapter 8.

The currently intense research interest in optical data storage technology is best understood in relationship to available data storage systems. Computer hardware specialists typically recognize a hierarchy of memory types. Primary memory, consisting mainly of semiconductor materials located within the computer itself, is reserved for the storage of data and programs that are under immediate execution by the central processing unit. Primary memory offers very rapid access times, but it is expensive. Secondary memory, consisting of magnetic disks and drums, is used for data and programs that need to be maintained online for immediate access. When needed, such data and programs can be rapidly transferred to primary memory. Tertiary memory is used for data and programs for which the expense of magnetic disk storage cannot be justified. While some mass storage systems use magnetic data cells to maintain large amounts of information online, the most common form of tertiary storage is magnetic tape, a low cost medium that maintains information offline. It is expected that optical data disks will permit large amounts of computer-generated data to remain online for longer periods of time at fairly low cost, thereby replacing magnetic tape in a substantial number of data processing applications. As such, they are of considerable potential interest in businesses, government agencies, and libraries that must maintain very large machine-readable data bases.

Commercially available optical recording materials do not currently offer the erasability and resulting reusability that is characteristic of magnetic recording media. In document storage applications, this limitation presents few significant impediments to user acceptance because the conventional micrographics systems with which optical video disks will compete do not typically offer erasability. The data processing community, however, is accustomed to erasable recording media. In late 1983, Matsushita announced its Erasable Optical Disc Memory System, the first optical disk system capable of deleting previously recorded information. Demonstrated in prototype only, the Matsushita erasable disk features a tellurium alloy with additional submetals that allow the structure of the recording materials to alternate between phases of high and low reflectivity, thereby removing unwanted material. Other vendors are reportedly working on the development of erasable optical recording media for both data and document recording. Pending the availability of such products, optical disks for data storage applications will probably reserve some space for the recording of updates, replacements, or other modifications to previously recorded data. While the old data will not be eradicated, it will be marked in such a way that it can no longer be retrieved. Although this will waste storage space, proponents of optical disk recording argue that space will be sufficiently plentiful and media costs low enough to justify some waste.

Additional Readings

DOCUMENT DISPLAY

Muter, P., et al. Extended reading of continuous text on television screens. *Human Factors* 24: 501–8 (1982).

FACSIMILE

Costigan, D. M. *Fax: Principles and Practice of Facsimile Communication*. Philadelphia: Chilton, 1971.

———. *Electronic Delivery of Documents and Graphics*. New York: Van Nostrand, 1978.

Hunter, R., and Robinson, A. H. International digital facsimile coding standards. *Proceedings of the IEEE* 68: 854–67 (1980).

Musmann, H. G. Comparison of redundancy reduction codes. *IEEE Transactions on Communications* 25: 1425–33 (1977).

Netravali, A. N., and Mounts, F. W. Ordering techniques for facsimile coding: A review. *Proceedings of the IEEE* 68: 796–807 (1980).

Posa, J. G. A fax in every office? *High Technology* 3: 24, 28–29 (August 1983).

Walter, G. O. Technology overview: Raster image telecommunications. *Journal of Micrographics* 15: 30–37 (May 1982).

LIBRARY APPLICATIONS

Algermissen, V., et al. Subminute telefacsimile for ILL document delivery. *Information Technology and Libraries* 1: 274–75 (1982).

McQueen, J., and Boss, R. W. High speed telefacsimile in libraries. *Library Technology Reports* 19: 7–111 (1983).

Saffady, W. Facsimile transmission for libraries: Technology and applications. *Library Technology Reports* 14: 445–532 (1978).

Toney, S. R. Telefacsimile experiment at the Smithsonian Institution. *Serials Librarian* 7: 17–26 (Winter 1982).

MICROFACSIMILE

Barrett, R. Microfilm retrieval and facsimile activities in Japan. *Reprographics Quarterly* 7: 128–32 (1974).

Cohen, H. TV microform/microfiche systems. *ASLIB Proceedings* 35: 19–23 (1983).

Costigan, D. M., and Burger, R. J. Videomicrographics: A positive new trend in online information retrieval. *Journal of Micrographics* 15: 16–24 (1982).

Felton, R. W. Implementing records management systems in large, multiple user environments. *Journal of Micrographics* 12: 331–35 (1979).

French, M. Future applications of the Navy's microfiche image transmission system (MITS). *Journal of Micrographics* 14: 25–31 (1981).

Horder, A. Developments in systems providing remote access to graphic information stores. *Reprographics Quarterly* 13: 51–54 (1980).

Inose, H., Saito, T., and Nakagawa, H. Remote access and retrieval system for visual pattern information featuring microfiche storage and facsimile recording. *Journal of Information Processing* 3: 31–37 (1980).

Sheposh, J. P., and Hulton, V. N. *Implementation of Microfiche Image Transmission System (MITS): A Multifaceted Assessment of Demonstration Installation.* San Diego: Navy Personnel Research and Development Center, 1983. (Available through NTIS).

Walter, G. O. Redundancy reduction and data compaction technology in microform image transmission systems. *Journal of Micrographics* 15: 25–35 (December 1982).

OPTICAL DISKS FOR DOCUMENT RECORDING

Amon, G. J. Archival optical disc data storage. *Optical Engineering* 20: 394–98 (1981).

Barrett, R. Developments in optical disk technology and the implications for information storage and retrieval. *Journal of Micrographics* 15: 22–26 (January 1982).

———. Electronic document handling. *Electronics and Power* 29: 481–84 (1983).

Blom, G. M. Optical disk data storage. *Proceedings of the Society of Photo-Optical Instrumentation Engineers* 318: 43–46 (1982).

Boss, R. W. Optical digital disks as mass storage media. *Videodisc/Videotex* 3: 127–32 (Spring 1983).

Braat, J. Optically read disks with increased information density. *Applied Optics* 22: 2196–201 (1983).

Dinklo, J. A. Digital optical disk systems. In O. Rienhoff and M. E. Abrams, eds., *Computers in the Doctor's Office*, pp. 265–70. Amsterdam: North-Holland Publishing, 1980.

Freedman, D. Optical disks: Promises and problems. *Mini-Micro Systems* 15: 225–28 (October 1982).

Goldstein, C. M. Optical disk technology and information. *Science* 215: 862–68 (1982).

Goldstein, C. M., and Russell, W. D. *The NLM/LHNBC Videodisc Digital Storage Program Status Report*. Bethesda, Maryland: Lister Hill National Center for Biomedical Communications, 1981.

Herzog, D. G. Optical disc utilized as a data storage system for reconnaissance application. *Proceedings of the IEEE 1983 National Aerospace and Electronics Conference*, vol. 2, pp. 1449–59. New York: IEEE, 1983.

Horder, A. *Video Discs: Their Application to Information Storage and Retrieval*. Hatfield, England: National Reprographic Centre for Documentation, 1981.

Kees, B., et al. Ten billion bits on disk. *IEEE Spectrum* 16: 26–33 (August 1979).

Kenney, G. C., et al. An optical disk replaces twenty-five magnetic tapes. *IEEE Spectrum* 16: 33–38 (February 1979).

Lou, D. Y. Characterization of optical disks. *Applied Optics* 21: 1602–9 (May 1982).

Mcleod, J. Optical disk storage technology. *Optical Spectra* 15: 52–54 (November 1981).

———. Optical disks loom as replacement for tape. *Electronic Design* 29: 97–103 (September 30, 1981).

Schipma, P. Videodisc for storage of text. *Videodisc/Videotex* 1: 68–72 (Summer 1981).

Schulman, J. L. Video PATSEARCH. *Information Technology and Libraries* 1: 150–56 (1982).

Suthasinekul, S. Microfilm vs. optical disc as storage medium for document retrieval and dissemination. In A. R. Benenfeld and E. J. Kazlauskas, eds., *Communicating Information: Proceedings of the 43rd ASIS Annual Meeting*, pp. 100–2. White Plains, New York: Knowledge Industries Publications, 1981.

Urbach, P. The Video PATSEARCH system. *Videodisc/Videotex* 2: 30–37 (Winter 1982).

Walter, G. O. Optical digital storage of office and engineering documents. *Journal of Information and Image Management* 17: 27–35 (April 1984).

———. *Video Disks in the Automated Office?* Silver Spring, Maryland: National Micrographics Association, 1982.

———. Videodisc for the storage of office documents and engineering graphics. *Journal of Micrographics* 15: 12–20 (January 1982).

———. Will optical disk memory supplant microfilm? *Journal of Micrographics* 13: 29–34 (July 1980).

OPTICAL RECORDING TECHNOLOGY

Allen, T. H., and Ash, G. S. Optical properties of tellurium films used for data recording. *Optical Engineering* 20: 373–76 (1981).

Bartolini, R. A. Media for high density optical recording. *Journal of Vacuum Science and Technology* 18: 70–74 (1981); reprinted in *Optical Engineering* 20: 382–86 (1981).

———. Optical recording: High density information storage and retrieval. *Proceedings of the IEEE* 70: 589–97 (1982).

———. High density optical recording using laser diodes. *RCA Engineer* 27: 20–27 (May-June 1982).

Bell, A. E. Critical issues in high-density magnetic and optical data storage. *Laser Focus* 19: 61–66 (August 1983).

Brody, H. Materials for optical storage: A state of the art survey. *Laser Focus* 17: 47–52 (August 1981).

Burns, L. L. Slidestore—A laser mass memory for image storage. *Proceedings of the Society of Photo-Optical Instrumentation Engineers*, 1979, pp. 79–83. Bellingham, Washington: Society of Photo-Optical Instrumentation Engineers, 1980.

DiStefano, T. H., ed. *Proceedings of the Symposium on Optical Storage Materials*, 1980. New York: American Institute of Physics, 1981.

Donelson, W. C. Spatial management of information. *Computer Graphics* 12: 203–9 (1978).

Hecht, J. Lasers store a wealth of data. *High Technology* 2: 60–67 (May-June 1982).

Redderson, B. R., and Ralston, L. M. Digital optical data storage and retrieval. *Optical Engineering* 19: 1999–2004 (1980).

Vincent, D., and Lit, J. W. Y. Optical disk in thin films. *Canadian Journal of Physics* 57: 1309–18 (1979).

Watanabe, K., Sato, N., and Miyaoka, S. New optical recording material for video disc system. *Journal of Applied Physics* 54: 1256–60 (1983).

Watkins, J. W., Boudreaux, N. A., and Otten, T. H. Large archival mass memory using optical diskettes. *Optical Engineering* 20: 399–403 (1981).

CHAPTER 7

VIDEOCONFERENCING

As their name suggests, videoconferencing systems utilize video and audio technology to conduct interactive meetings between geographically separate groups of people. As used in this context, the term "meetings" encompasses a broad spectrum of group activities ranging from small group sessions for planning or other business purposes to product introductions, press conferences, stockholders meetings, professional conferences, and educational presentations involving hundreds of participants. Regardless of meeting size, the emphasis on interactivity distinguishes videoconferencing from the mere televising or video recording of such presentations, but videoconferencing should not be confused with those interactive videotext and cable systems that utilize special keypad controllers to select program material or to register opinions. As applied to videoconferencing, interaction involves the verbal exchange of opinions and ideas.

In the simplest form of interaction—widely encountered in large group videoconferences—an audience asks questions or otherwise responds to the remarks of one or more televised speakers. As will be discussed below, the audience itself is rarely televised. Operating in a less restricted mode, small group videoconferences, such as business strategy or project review sessions, attempt to emulate in-person meetings with considerable interchange of ideas among several participants. The televising of all participants provides visual as well as audio cues to support such interaction.

Videoconferencing is a form of teleconferencing, a generic term that denotes the combined use of telecommunications and electronic technologies as an alternative to in-person meetings. Other forms of teleconferencing include audioconferencing—using the familiar conference telephone call to establish a voice link between three or more persons—and computer teleconferencing, a form of computer-based message system in which three or more persons communicate with one another via terminals. In the simplest form of computer teleconferencing, a group leader sends a message to multiple recipients for comment. The messages and individual responses are stored by a computer for online review by the other participants. This, in turn, may provoke responses that are themselves recorded as part of an ongoing dialogue.

Rather than competing with one another, the various forms of teleconferencing should be viewed as complementary business tools that can be used in combination to facilitate communication and interaction among geographically dispersed groups. Computer teleconferencing can often serve as a useful supplement to videoconferencing. As will be discussed in a later section, the effectiveness of simple audioconferencing can often be enhanced by the video transmission of graphic materials. Videoconferencing itself can take any of several different forms, and this chapter begins with a discussion of prevalent approaches and their applications. Later sections will consider the business implications of videoconferencing, reviewing its potential advantages as well as some possible impediments to its acceptance.

Technology Overview

Two-Way Videoconferencing

Much videoconferencing technology is an outgrowth of a series of interesting but unsuccessful experiments with video telephone systems conducted during the 1960s and 1970s. As the name indicates, video telephones transmit the image, as well as the voice, of the user. The most widely publicized of these devices, the AT&T Picturephone, was first publicly demonstrated in 1964 and was commercially available, on a limited basis, in selected U.S. cities through the mid-1970s. Similar devices, most of which failed to develop beyond demonstration models, included Stromberg Carlson's Vistaphone, General Telephone's Pictel, RCA's Videovoice, the British Post Office's Viewphone, and the French Visiophone developed by CIT-Alcatel.

While videoconferencing is a group activity, video telephones were invariably desktop units designed for individual workstations. Picturephone itself featured a 5-by-5.5–inch, black-and-white television screen mounted on a swivelling pedestal. An integral camera provided a head and shoulders view of the user, and the camera could be directed to the desk surface for the transmission of segments of documents or other visual materials—subject, of course, to the resolution constraints discussed in previous chapters. For natural, "hands free" operation, Picturephone offered an integral speaker and microphone, but an adjacent telephone could be used when audio privacy was desired. Plans for more elaborate units called for combinations of conventional and high resolution displays plus integral facsimile transceivers, videocassette recorders, and alphanumeric keyboards for data transmission. Picturephone has been the subject of much technical and sociological discussion, but, despite its considerable potential and seemingly obvious appeal, it proved a commercial failure and is no longer available. Today, several companies market desktop executive workstations that combine a telephone for voice communications with a CRT screen for data communications. While they resemble video telephones in appearance, such devices are designed for computer-generated alphanumeric data, and they cannot display still or moving video images. Their characteristics as computer terminals will be discussed in chapter 8.

Picturephone's trade name and influence survive in the Picturephone Meeting Service (PMS), a full motion, two-way videoconferencing service offered by AT&T. The full motion, two-way variant is the most interesting, complex, and expensive form of videoconferencing. It provides both video and audio coverage of all participants, and offers the most realistic approximation of in-person meetings. It is best suited to planning sessions, project review meetings, or similar small conferences involving two geographically distant groups, each consisting of 5 to 10 persons. Full motion, two-way videoconferencing requires specially designed studio facilities at both meeting sites. The Picturephone Meeting Service offers such facilities on a timesharing basis. Charges vary with distance, but can exceed $2,000 per hour for a coast-to-coast videoconference. Making a substantial long-term commitment to videoconferencing, several large companies and government agencies have designed and constructed their own videoconferencing studios. Examples include Aetna Life and Casualty, Allstate, Atlantic Richfield, Citibank, Exxon, General Telephone, IBM, and M/A-Com. A considerable planning effort is required, and implementation costs can exceed $1 million. Where the volume of videoconferencing activity is high, such an investment may be justified, but for occasional users, timeshared facilities are the preferred alternative.

Whether videoconferencing facilities are custom-developed or rented, certain features are customarily provided:

1. A specially designed conference table provides seating for 6 to 8 participants. Typically, all participants sit on one side of the table, facing a group of video monitors that display participants at the distant site. Off-camera seating may be provided for additional persons along the perimeters of the room.

2. Up to 6 wall- or ceiling-mounted video cameras transmit closeup and overview images of conference participants (figure 37). When none of the participants at a given site is speaking, an overview of the entire group is transmitted. For closeup views, one camera is assigned to each two participants. These cameras are voice-activated and will automatically transmit an image of the speaker and one adjacent person. Remedying a problem encountered in early videoconferencing facilities, special filters are now used to mask extraneous noises that might inadvertently activate a camera. Additional, manually operated cameras may be provided for persons seated away from the conference table.

3. One or more additional cameras are dedicated to the display of blackboards, flip charts, projected visuals, and similar graphic materials. One camera may be directed to a desktop for the transmission of images of three-dimensional objects. The same camera can be used for documents, but, as discussed elsewhere in this book, standard video resolution is typically inadequate for the legible transmission of typewritten or printed text. The facilities' technological components are usually kept as unobtrusive as possible, allowing the participants to focus their attention on the business purpose of the conference.

4. Microphones are strategically positioned on table tops or in other locations. As with cameras, unobtrusive placement is emphasized. Speakers are typically mounted on walls or in ceilings.

5. A bank of video monitors is positioned for comfortable viewing by all participants. One or more of these monitors display images transmitted from the distant conference site. One monitor displays the images being transmitted to the distant site. One or more additional monitors display graphics or other

FIGURE 37

Two-way videoconferencing requires specially designed studio facilities with wall-mounted cameras, concealed microphones, video monitors, and other equipment. (Courtesy: Western Union)

objects that support the speaker's presentation. In an effort to improve the naturalness of videoconferencing, so-called continuous presence systems provide sufficient monitors for the closeup display of all participants at both sites. Because of the expense necessitated by additional equipment and communication facilities, such systems are rarely encountered.

6. Support facilities include a telephone for private voice communication between sites and to coordinate the transmission of visual materials, a computer terminal for electronic message transmission or information retrieval operations, a videocassette recorder, a facsimile transceiver for high resolution document transmission and reception, and such special equipment as electronic blackboards, electronic slide projectors, and video annotators. These devices will be described in a later section.

As with the broadcast video systems discussed in preceding chapters, full motion, two-way videoconferencing requires the transmission of a very large quantity of information at very high speed. Wideband telecommunication facilities are therefore required. As noted in the preceding chapter, a growing number of office automation systems utilize broadband local area networks—communication facilities that use coaxial cable to connect information processing systems within a single building complex or other limited geographic area—which can transmit video signals as well as data and voice, but distance restrictions limit their utility in videoconferencing applications. For the long distance communications characteristic of most videoconferencing, satellite links are most commonly used. Companies such as Satellite Business Systems and American Satellite lease satellite circuits suitable for use by organizations constructing their own videoconferencing facilities. Such facilities must include earth stations for transmission and reception. Timeshared videoconferencing facilities, such as Picturephone Meeting Service, typically include appropriate satellite links and related equipment in their usage charges.

Although satellite transmission costs have fallen steadily over the past decade, they remain surprisingly high. As with digital facsimile systems, data compression techniques are increasingly used to reduce the amount of information to be transmitted in successive video images, with a corresponding reduction in costs. This data compression is performed by a device called a "codec" (coder/decoder). In one of the prevailing approaches to data compression, the codec compares successive frames and transmits only the changes encountered in them. Since videoconferences—like most business meetings—are rarely characterized by frantic action, this method typically yields a significant signal reduction without much loss of image quality. Alternatively, the codec may encode high detail areas of each video image, ignoring the background areas. The continuing development of both techniques has reduced transmission bandwidth requirements from the 90 million bits per second required for uncompressed video images to less than 1 million bits per second. Continuing progress is expected.

One-Way Videoconferencing

Full motion, one-way videoconferencing with two-way audio capabilities offers a less expensive alternative to the two-way systems discussed above. But while two-way systems are designed to facilitate problem solving or the exchange of information between two relatively small groups, one-way videoconferencing is best suited to formal televised presentations by a single speaker or a panel of participants followed by questions from an audience located in one or more geographically distant viewing rooms. It is particularly useful for product introductions, stockholder meetings, educational sessions, professional conferences, and similar special events.

Facilities likewise differ from those employed in two-way videoconferencing. As a special event, the one-way videoconference is formally produced rather than spontaneous. Elaborate and careful planning is required, and, where in-house expertise is lacking, companies such as Robert Wold, Videonet, Video Star, Pyramid Video, and Bonneville International offer consulting services ranging from the provision of conferencing and telecommunication facilities to full production responsibility. In addition, several public television stations have recently established videoconferencing production subsidiaries.

Regardless of the particular delivery methods used, the specially equipped videoconferencing rooms described in the preceding section are typically replaced by a television studio or comparable conventional production facilities. The audience may be seated in small viewing rooms or large auditoriums in one or more locations. In 1983, for example, the American Library Association used the services of the Public Services Satellite Consortium (PSSC) to broadcast a one-way, 5-hour videoconference to audiences in 117 libraries in 43 states. In 1982, a shorter videoconference reached 62 sites in 30 states. Similar meetings have been sponsored by other professional associations and educational organizations. Regardless of audience size and location, appropriate video monitors and sound systems are provided at each viewing site. Projection television systems may be used for large-screen display. Floor microphones are provided for audience questions which are transmitted to the main site via telephone lines. The audience itself is not televised.

Recognizing the economic potential of one-way videoconferencing—as well as its potentially adverse impact on conventional meetings—several major hotel chains have established videoconferencing facilities with production studios, satellite transmission and reception equipment, and appropriately equipped viewing rooms. The oldest and largest of these services, the HI-NET network operated by Holiday Inns, has more than 300 locations in over 40 states. Similar services have been introduced by the Hilton, Marriott, Hyatt, and Westin hotels. Using international telecommunication facilities provided by Satellite Business Systems, Intercontinental Hotels provides videoconferencing services between New York and London. Given the growing number of companies with overseas business connections, interest in international videoconferencing is likely to increase. As with other aspects of information processing, however, some European and Latin American countries, concerned about the national security and other implications of transborder data flow, have discouraged such developments.

Within the continental United States, hotel-based videoconferencing costs vary with the services and support utilized, but can be as low as $10 to $30 per participant, depending on the number of sites and participants involved. With one-way videoconferencing, unit costs vary inversely with the number of participants.

Nonmotion Systems

As discussed in the preceding sections, codecs can effectively compress video signals to reduce transmission requirements in two-way, full motion videoconferencing. One-way videoconferencing permits further savings by eliminating a major portion of the video component and spreading costs over a relatively large audience. But, given its expense, full motion, two-way videoconferencing—the most versatile variant—is likely to be restricted to a small number of very large corporations. One-way, full motion videoconferencing, while less expensive, is not suited to the small group meetings that constitute most organizations' conferencing requirements. In a drastic simplification of videoconferencing concepts that can significantly broaden the potential range of users, slow-scan (freeze-frame) and audiographic systems permit significant cost reductions by transmitting still frames rather than moving image. Such nonmotion videoconferencing systems rely heavily on two-way audio communications for interactivity. Because ordinary telephone lines are used, costs are much lower than for systems using full motion video.

Conforming to the broadcast television standards, full motion, one- and two-way videoconferencing transmits continually changing images at a rate of 30 frames per second. Slow-scan television systems, by way of contrast, transmit images at a slower rate, thus requiring less bandwidth and permitting the use of telephone lines rather than satellite or other high-speed communication facilities. In the simplest equipment configuration, a slow scan television system consists of a transmitter that accepts input from an attached video camera. In a typical application, a camera mounted on a vertical column photographs prepared visuals, graphics, or similar objects positioned on a copyboard or other flat surface. The resulting video images are displayed on an attached monitor for previewing by an operator who pushes a button to freeze a given frame for transmission over telephone lines to a remote site. Available systems may use either analog or digital pixel encoding. Transmission time varies with resolution. Simple analog systems can transmit a frame in as little as 36 seconds with a resolution of 256 horizontal scan lines, each consisting of 240 picture elements. When resolution is increased to 256 horizontal scan lines of 480 picture elements each, transmission time is correspondingly increased to 78 seconds per frame. When operating at 512 horizontal scan lines of 480 picture elements each, the required transmission time is 156 seconds per frame. As discussed in chapter 6, such resolutions are too low for the legible transmission of typewritten or printed documents. Facsimile continues to be the technology of choice for such applications.

At the receiving site, video images are displayed on a monitor. With the most primitive equipment configurations, scan lines are displayed as they are received—the video image being built up over a period of 35 seconds or longer as discussed above. More sophisticated monitors are equipped with multiframe memories which can store several images for display as completed frames. Multiframe memories also allow the user to return to a previously displayed frame without time-consuming retransmission. Several companies manufacture printers that can make paper copies of displayed images. Received images can also be recorded on videotape. The most sophisticated slow scan television systems incorporate microcomputers that permit the preparation and storage of visuals prior to transmission.

Slow scan television systems can transmit images of videoconference participants as well as visuals and other objects (figure 38). As discussed above, such images may be manually selected after previewing on a local video monitor. Alternatively, a video camera may automatically transmit images at specified intervals. In either case, the images are received at the viewing site as a series of still pictures. In a highly simplified version of freeze-frame videoconferencing, a system developed for the U.S. Army's Defense Advanced Research Projects Agency transmits highly stylized images of conference participants. Making very extensive use of data compression techniques, this approach permits transmission over ordinary telecommunication facilities. It is specifically designed for defense emergencies when satellite links or other high bandwidth telecommunication facilities may not be available.

Audiographic conferencing, a new and much publicized variant of nonmotion videoconferencing, combines two-way audio with devices for the transmission of graphic images. Intended primarily for business strategy meetings, project review sessions, or other small group interaction, audiographic conferencing relies heavily on prepared visuals and documents. No attempt is made to transmit images of moving subjects. Audiographic conferencing can consequently be viewed as either a simplified type of videoconferencing or an enhanced form of audioconferencing.

Some of the devices used in audiographic conferencing are encountered in conventional videoconferencing as well. Slow scan television equipment, for exam-

FIGURE 38

As an economical alternative to full motion systems, slow scan television technology can be used to transmit a succession of still-frame images of videoconferencing participants or objects. (Courtesy: Colorado Video)

ple, can be used for the transmission of charts, diagrams, or other graphic materials to remote color television monitors. Facsimile transceivers are used for the high resolution transmission of paper documents. In some specially designed facilities, the facsimile transceiver is inset in the conference table for more convenient access by participants. As discussed in the preceding chapter, facsimile output can be displayed on high resolution video monitors as an alternative to being printed on paper.

Electronic stylus systems, a variant form of facsimile, permits the transmission of sketches or handwritten messages. A message, written on a sensitized surface at one location, is transmitted to a remote device that records it on paper. Such systems, which are manufactured by such companies as Telautograph Systems and Infolink, have been successfully used in a variety of business applications for several decades. Their use in audiographic conferencing provides communication capabilities that can effectively augment prepared visuals and documents. Similar in concept, the electronic blackboard—of which the Gemini model offered by AT&T Information Systems is the best known example—was developed specifically for videoconferencing. Resembling a conventional chalkboard, it features a touch sensitive surface which transmits drawings or handwriting, as it is created, to a remote video monitor. More advanced electronic writing devices, like the Telewriter II developed by Optel Communications, permit much greater control over the display of written information at the remote site (figure 39). The user can select the display color,

FIGURE 39

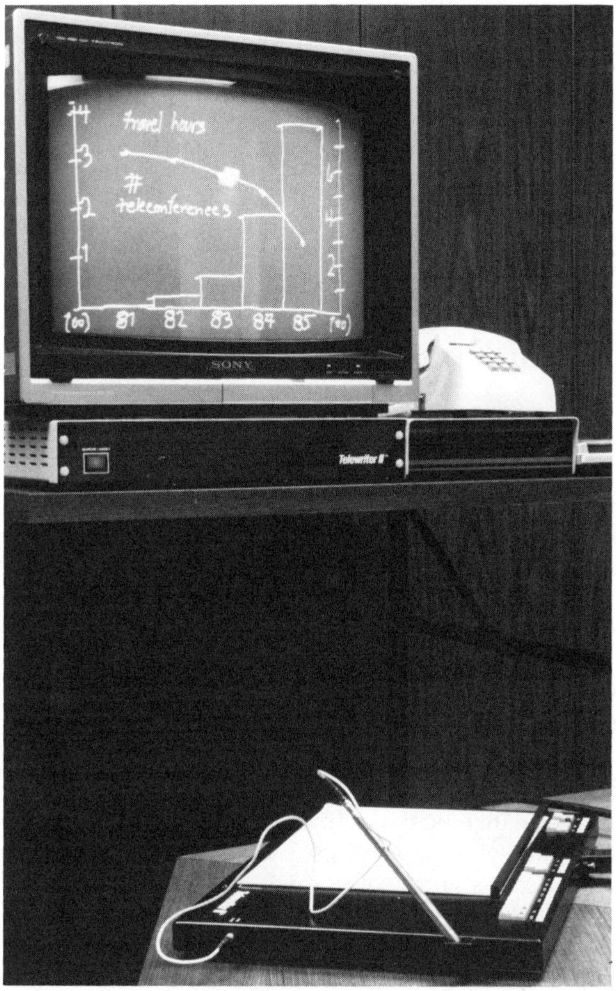

Used in audiographic conferencing, the Telewriter II is an "electronic blackboard" system which transmits handwritten information from one site to another. (Courtesy: Optel Communications)

address specific points on the remote monitor, or erase all or part of the displayed information. At the receiving site, information can be added to the transmitted material and a corrected version returned electronically to the creator. An internal memory can store up to 15 pages, permitting the advance preparation of visual materials. Auxiliary printers and storage devices are optionally available. A portable model can be conveniently passed among the participants at a given site.

A special class of electronic blackboards, called "video annotators," permit the superimposition of hand drawings on video images. In audiographic conferencing, prepared visuals can be transmitted via slow-scan or freeze-frame methods while handwritten markings are added interactively in real time. These devices can enhance the naturalness and, consequently, the effectiveness of audiographic conferencing by allowing participants to emphasize or modify portions of displayed information, just as they might at a conventional in-person meeting. With some systems, the annotations can appear in several different colors.

Like conventional meetings, videoconferencing—in either its full motion or audiographic variants—may utilize slides or other prepared visual materials distributed to the conference sites in advance of the event itself. For videoconferencing applications, several companies market voice-activated slide projectors that can be controlled by a speaker at a remote site. When operating under computer control, videocassette recorders, video disk players, and microfiche retrieval equipment can likewise be controlled remotely.

Business Significance

Rationale

Business interest in teleconferencing in general, and videoconferencing in particular, is one facet of the emphasis on white collar productivity improvement that has characterized office automation programs since the late 1970s. Departing from traditional office automation efforts, which were primarily designed to increase clerical work output, information systems analysts and productivity improvement specialists are giving increased attention to productivity improvement among managerial and professional personnel. While clerical employees are more numerous, managerial and professional salaries constitute the bulk of many organizations' payrolls, and they are responsible for decision making that directly affects the mission and profits of a business or other organization.

Contrary to the textbook view of managers as highly efficient, scientific planners, several studies indicate that the typical manager's workday consist of a surprisingly large percentage of time-wasting activities. Travel is among the most frequently cited examples. Many managers and professional employees spend a very substantial percentage of their time travelling to meetings in field offices, branch locations, manufacturing installations, or other facilities within their organizations. The direct cost of this travel—including air fare or other transportation, lodging, meals, and related expenses—is both considerable and increasing. Indirect costs, consisting largely of the loss of productive work time in transit, can prove equally or more significant. Such lost work time is commonly aggravated by difficulties in making connections for travel outside of major cities, increasingly common flight delays or cancellations, which can disrupt meeting schedules, and the unavailability of all required work materials on arrival at the meeting site. As a further complication, the travelling employee's return to the office is often greeted by the need to deal with urgent matters that arose during his or her absence. Furthermore, extensive travel may not prove desirable or even possible for certain managerial employees, such as those with young families or health problems.

Videoconferencing is designed to address these problems by minimizing or eliminating travel for meetings that do not require in-person interaction. Frequently cited examples include training sessions and product introductions, which are well suited to one-way, full motion videoconferencing, and planning sessions, project reviews, or similar small-group meetings for which two-way, full motion videoconferencing or one of the nonmotion alternatives can often be successfully used. Unlike travel that necessitates an interruption of managerial work schedules for even the shortest meetings, videoconferencing allows normal work activities to be resumed within the same half day.

Organizations that make extensive use of videoconferencing, including those companies and government agencies that have constructed their own videoconferencing facilities, presumably expect cost justification through savings in direct and indirect travel costs. As with all information processing technologies, however, a detailed analysis of an organization's conferencing requirements is required to confirm such justification. In assessing the potential of videoconferencing, such an analysis must consider all teleconferencing options, plus other technological and procedural approaches. Comparing rising travel costs and managerial salaries to the declining costs of the telecommunications and electronics technology on which videoconferencing is based, long-term costs appear especially favorable. While full motion, two-way videoconferencing is likely to remain too expensive for many organizations for some time to come, the audiographic or freeze-frame alternatives can prove surprisingly cost-effective. Several organizations have likewise reported savings by substituting full motion, one-way videoconferencing for conventional sales meetings or other large-group conferences.

Videoconferencing can offer significant advantages when compared to conventional in-person meetings:

1. Because videoconferencing requires careful planning and preparation, it often results in more effective meetings with better formulated agendas. Realizing the expense associated with the construction or rental of videoconferencing facilities, participants are likely to be on time and to concentrate on the specific purpose of the meeting, without the irrevelent digressions and tangential discussions that can impede effective group interaction. A potentially significant reduction in costs can result because videoconferences, which are often shorter than their in-person counterparts, allow participants to resume their normal work activities sooner.

2. The time and expense associated with travel necessarily limits the number of employees who can participate in conventional meetings, while physical constraints limit the amount of documents and data that managers can carry to meetings at remote locations. No matter how careful their preparation, travelling managers often find that a given meeting could benefit substantially from the specialized knowledge of a given employee or from information left back at the home office. Videoconferencing can permit broader participation in meetings, and it allows additional personnel or information to be brought into a meeting as required.

3. With the exception of full motion, one-way videoconferencing for large audiences where considerable advance preparation is required, videoconferences can often be arranged on shorter notice than can be accommodated when travel is involved. This is especially the case with audiographic conferences,

where the least specialized facilities are required. Follow-up meetings can likewise be scheduled more readily.

4. Taking a broader perspective, videoconferencing can increase the frequency of communications between an organization's headquarters and geographically dispersed facilities, thereby reinforcing centralization and organizational unity.

Limitations

Some of the earliest and strongest supporters of videoconferencing systems were surprised to find that their organization's videoconferencing activity fell well below anticipated levels. Their initial expectations were unrealistic. While videoconferencing offers potentially significant advantages, it is not suitable for all applications. It is primarily useful for problem solving, information exchange, or—in the case of the full-motion, one-way approach—formal presentations followed by questions from an audience. Sales contacts, delicate negotiations, and similar interactions continue to require personal presence for greatest effectiveness. Likewise, videoconferencing is primarily designed for intra-organizational communications. Prevalent incompatibilities among existing facilities and equipment, combined with logistic constraints, generally prohibit inter-organizational meetings.

As with all information processing technology, the effective utilization of videoconferencing can be constrained by behavioral considerations. Teleconferencing technologies can have a significant impact on group interaction. Traditional organizational barriers and hierarchical authority relationships can be eroded by greater access to telecommunication facilities. Aggressive personalities, who dominate in-person meetings, may feel uncomfortable with videoconferencing, given the physical distance between participating groups. Just as many Picturephone users took time to improve their appearance and tidy up their desks before answering a call, some videoconferencing participants, accustomed to the unrealistic world of television entertainment, may feel self-consciously embarrassed by their appearance on a video monitor. Resistance to the freeze-frame approach, for example, is sometimes encountered from participants who are concerned about being photographed in potentially unflattering poses. Some of these attitudes and behavioral constraints will be overcome by experience; participant preparation and orientation is essential to the effective use of any technology.

Additional Readings

BUSINESS APPLICATIONS

Ancipink, P. Video teleconferencing: Creating the illusion. *Best's Review* 81: 94+ (October 1983).

———. Teleconferencing—Business or show biz? *Best's Review* 84: 60–62, 64 (May 1983).

Borden, J. Videoconferences: An alternative, yes—A solution, maybe. *Successful Meetings* 31: 33–35 (December 1982).

Cutting, B. Anatomy of a videoconference. *Marketing Communications* 6: 42–43 (October 1981).

Darragh, W. R. Videoconferencing update. *Journal of Information Management* 4: 52–57 (Spring-Summer 1983).

DeBaldo, P. Video teleconferencing: Improved communication and decision making. *Telecommunications* 17: 82–83, 93 (January 1983).

Duncan, G. Videoconferencing takes the meeting to the sales force. *Sales and Marketing Management* 129: 123–32 (November 15, 1982).

Edwards, M. Stay-at-home conference: More than just an energy saver. *Infosystems* 28: 48–54 (August 1981).

File, K. N. Teleconferencing: A case study. *Office* 94: 82–91 (November 1981).

Fischell, D. R., and Stockbridge, C. The QUORUM teleconferencing system: Going the distance for business customers. *Bell Laboratories Record* 60: 278–83 (December 1982).

Gold, E. M. Teleconferencing: Communications bridge between geographically dispersed sites. *Telephony* 20: 30–32 (July 26, 1982).

Hansell, K. J., Green, D., and Ebring, L. Survey examines benefits of videoconferencing. *Telephony* 20: 37–39 (July 26, 1982).

———. Videoconferencing in American business: Perceptions of benefit by users of intra-company systems (a first look at user responses). In *Fifteenth Annual Electronics and Aerospace Systems Conference Record*, pp. 227–34. New York: IEEE, 1982.

Kelly, C. W. Video teleconferencing for crisis applications. *Signal* 36: 27–36 (July 1982).

Kleinberg, E. M. Teleconference: The future sales meeting media. *Industrial Marketing* 66: 61 (November 1981).

Malmen, R. L. Office automation at Allstate. *Best's Review* 83: 64–68 (November 1983).

Miura, A., et al. Video teleconferencing brings new direction to business in the 1980s. *Communication News* 10: 52–54 (February 1982).

Monahan, P. A. Teleconferencing grabs attention as it battles Hollywood image. *Bank Systems and Equipment* 20: 99–110 (October 1983).

Prince, S. Videoconferencing: Corporate satellite communications comes of age. *Marketing Communications* 7: 27–32 (July 1982).

Romei, L. K. Will the concept fly when the boss can't. *Modern Office Procedures* 28: 122–32 (June 1983).

Schiff, F. W. Flexiplace: An idea whose time has come. *IEEE Transactions on Engineering Management* 30: 26–30 (1983).

Seaman, J. Teleconferencing: Shortcut to business communication. *Computer Decisions* 13: 56–66 (November 1981).

ECONOMIC CONSIDERATIONS

Dawson, R. Fifteen hours of meetings per month pay for videoconference gear. *Bank Systems and Equipment* 19: 107, 112 (August 1982).

Hansell, K. J., Green, D., and Ebring, L. Videoconferencing boosts productivity. *Telephony* 20: 38–40, 44, 69 (August 2, 1982).

Keiper, R. What's needed to justify corporate teleconferencing. *Office* 96: 48–50 (November 1982).

Lowndes, J. C. Teleconferencing systems expected to reduce costs. *Aviation Week* 114: 322–33 (June 8, 1981).

EDUCATIONAL AND POLICY CONSIDERATIONS

Call, I. S. Videoconferencing: A new medium for communication. *Audiovisual Instruction* 23: 20–21 (January 1978).

Carter, L. J. Videoconferences via satellite: Opening Congress to the people? *Science* 197: 31–33 (July 1977).

Dutton, W. H., Fulk, J., and Steinfield, C. Utilization of video conferencing. *Telecommunications Policy* 6: 164–78 (September 1982).

Johansen, R., et al. *Electronic Education: Using Teleconferencing in Postsecondary Organizations.* Menlo Park, California: Institute for the Future, 1978.

Reilly, T. M. The extended classroom. *Datamation* 29: 199–200 (April 1983).

Salo, A. C. Special report—ALA-TV. *Information Technology and Libraries* 2: 302–5 (1983).

HUMAN FACTORS

Brown, E. F., et al. Some objective and subjective differences between communication over video-conferencing systems. *IEEE Transactions on Communications* 28: 759–64 (1980).

Carey, J. Interaction patterns in audio teleconferencing. *Telecommunications Policy* 5: 304–11 (1981).

Dickson, E. M., and Bowers, R. Human response to video telephones. In L. Kirchmayer, H. Linstone, and W. Morsch, eds., *A Technology Assessment Primer*, pp. 148–60. New York: Van Nostrand, 1975.

Duncanso, J. P., and Williams, A. D. Videoconferencing—Reactions of users. *Human Factors* 15: 471–85 (1975).

Thompson, G. B. Shared space—A vital concept in successful teleconferencing. *Telephony* 203: 24 (July 26, 1982).

Turoff, M., and Hiltz, R. S. *The Network Nation: Human Communication Via Computer*. Reading, Massachusetts: Addison-Wesley, 1978.

INTERNATIONAL APPLICATIONS

Broderick, J. The problems of corporate conferencing in Latin America. *Satellite Communications* 6: 72–77 (August 1982).

Helfer, E. Intercontinental communication. *Public Relations Journal* 39: 24–26 (February 1983).

Mayo, C. Overseas videoconferencing: New markets for digital satellite service. *Telecommunications* 17: 102–4, 111 (June 1983).

Mokhoff, N. They said it couldn't be done: The global video conference. *IEEE Spectrum* 17: 44 (1980).

PICTUREPHONE

Dickson, E. M., and Bosers, R. *The Video Telephone: Impact of a New Era in Telecommunications: A Preliminary Technology Assessment*. New York: Praeger, 1974.

Noll, A. M., and Woods, J. P. Use of Picturephone in a hospital. *Telecommunications Policy* 3: 29–36 (1979).

SLOW SCAN TELEVISION

Flynn, R. SSTV today. *QST* 67: 11–14 (June 1983).

Swift, D. Slow scan brings students and faculty together in University of Hawaii experiment. *Communications News* 20: 32–33 (August 1983).

VIDEOCONFERENCING TECHNOLOGY

Anastasiou, D., et al. Series/1-based videoconferencing system. *IBM System Journal* 22: 96–110 (1983).

Brody, H. Reach out and see someone. *High Technology* 3: 53–59 (August 1983).

Jones, G. E. Graphics teleconferencing. *Computer Graphics World* 6: 66–70 (August 1983).

Kikuchi, M., and Yoshikawa, M. New videoconference system. *Japan Telecommunications Review* 22: 112–19 (1980).

Livingstone, D. Teleconferencing. *Computerworld* 16: 65–67 (December 1, 1982).

McCartney, L. Teleconferencing comes down to earth. *Datamation* 29: 76–78 (January 1983).

Miller, J. Videoconferencing comes of age. *Communicator's Journal* 1: 16–19 (July-August 1983).

Munsey, W. Wide-band versus narrow-band video-conferencing: The user must decide. *Telecommunications* 15: 47–50 (February 1981).

Speter, K. M. Video—The added dimension in communications. In *Intelcom 80 Conference Proceedings*, pp. 420–22. Dedham, Massachusetts: Horizon House, 1980.

Thackray, J. You can't play if you don't know how. *Datamation* 28: 90–96 (October 1982).

Ungaro, C. Teleconferencing focuses on a new era. *Data Communication* 12: 85–97 (September 1982).

Watanabe, T. Teleconferencing in Japan—Use of audio conference systems and evolution towards video. *Telecommunications Policy* 3: 290–96 (1979).

Wilk, E. S. Video-conferencing: When does it help? *Computerworld* 16: 39–46 (September 29, 1982).

Wright, B. A. The design of Picturephone Meeting Service (PMS) conference centers for video teleconferencing. *IEEE Communications Magazine* 21: 30–36 (March 1983).

CHAPTER 8

VIDEO DISPLAY TERMINALS

Chapter 1 surveyed recent developments in television set technology, emphasizing color displays suitable for use as broadcast or cable receivers as well as for operation with the videocassette recorders, video disk players, and other video peripheral devices described elsewhere in this book. While such applications account for the majority of installed display devices, video displays for computer-generated data are an increasingly important and commonplace product group. Since the late 1960s, interactive computer systems have made extensive use of video displays as an alternative to paper output devices. Compared to most printing terminals, video displays offer the advantages of quieter operation, higher output speeds, and lower purchase and operating costs. Where selective paper output capability is required, most video displays can be equipped with an auxiliary printer.

As noted in the preceding discussions of cabletext and videotext systems, modified television receivers can function as data displays, and some low cost personal computers manufactured by Apple, Atari, Commodore, Tandy, and other companies are specifically designed for attachment to a color television set. But television receivers are primarily designed to display graphic images, and their ability to legibly display the alphabetic characters, numeric digits, punctuation marks, and other symbols encountered in computer-generated textual data is limited by prevailing broadcast resolution standards and impairments introduced by the receiver's RF modulator. As discussed in preceding chapters, these constraints require using relatively large characters that ultimately restrict the amount of information that can be displayed in a given video image. When connected to a microcomputer, for example, a typical color television receiver will display 16 to 20 lines, each containing 30 to 40 characters (figure 40). The display format in most business computing applications, however, provides 24 lines, each containing 80 characters. When compared to conventional television receivers, the video monitors and component television systems described in chapter 1 can offer significantly improved image quality, but most computer applications are best served by video devices designed specifically for data display.

These devices—which are variously termed "video display terminals" (VDTs), "video display units" (VDUs), or simply "computer displays"—resemble conventional television receivers in appearance but differ in construction, capabilities, and intended applications. Combining video and telecommunications technology, they are exclusively designed for interaction with computers. They are not equipped with a tuner for broadcast video signals, and they will not operate with videocassette recorders, video disk players, or similar devices. Like ordinary television receivers and video monitors, video display terminals may be attached to local microcomputers. Alternatively, they can be used to access remote computers on a timesharing basis. In either case, they are increasingly familiar devices in business, government agencies, schools, libraries, and other organizations where they are widely used for programming, data entry, information retrieval, word processing, electronic mail, and similar computer applications. In homes, video display terminals are commonly connected to microcomputers. They can also be used to access CompuServe, The Source, and other home information services described briefly in chapter 5. Several companies have recently introduced low cost video display terminals designed specifically for such consumer applications, and the home terminal market is expected to expand significantly in the coming years.

This chapter discusses the current state of the art and likely future development of video display terminals, emphasizing features of significance for the selection of equipment for various types of applications. The chapter begins with a description of terminal technology and components. Later sections discuss performance characteristics for textual and graphics applications.

Terminal Technology

Terminal Architecture

As applied to computer systems, the term "architecture" denotes the types and interrelationship of components used in a particular equipment configuration. The typical video display terminal consists of a combination of control and memory, circuitry, a display screen, a keyboard or related input mechanism, a communications interface, and a power supply. The display screen—usually a cathode ray tube (CRT)—will be discussed in a later section, as will the keyboard and communications interface. For North American installations, most video display terminals are equipped with a 120 volt, 60 Hz AC power supply. Most vendors offer a 220/240 VAC, 50 Hz configuration for overseas markets.

With respect to internal electronic circuitry, all newly manufactured video display terminals are controlled by microprocessors and feature computer-like, electronic memories. The microprocessor consists of highly miniaturized computing circuitry that initiates and supervises particular terminal operations. Read-only memory (ROM) circuits provide permanent storage for programs on which the terminal's operating capabilities are based. These programs—which are termed "firmware" to distinguish them from conventional software commonly stored on disks or tape—are placed in ROM by the terminal's manufacturer. Random-access memory (RAM) circuits store the data to be displayed on the terminal's screen at a given moment. The content of random-access memory is determined by specific computer interaction and changes as new data are transmitted or received. The video display terminal must at least be equipped with sufficient random-access

FIGURE 40

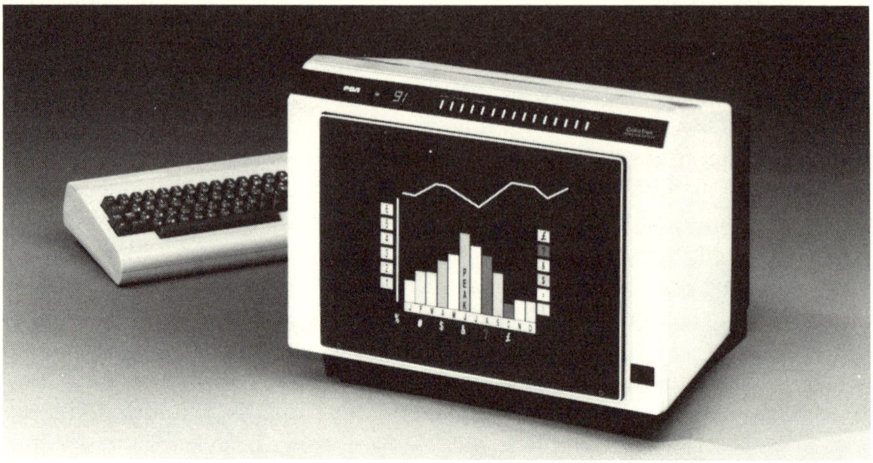

Designed for home applications, several newer television receivers feature input jacks for the simplified connection of microcomputers, although display quality is limited by prevailing television broadcast standards. (Courtesy: RCA Consumer Electronics)

memory for one screenful of data. Some advanced models are equipped with multiscreen memories, allowing them to recall previously displayed data to the screen. With such devices, the video screen serves as a kind of "window" into a portion of memory.

While they share a common purpose, the particular microprocessors and memory circuits used by available terminals differ in complexity. These differences determine a given terminal's innate information processing capabilities, causing it to be categorized as "dumb," "smart," or "intelligent." As its name suggests, a dumb video display terminal is the simplest of interactive data communications devices. It has no innate information processing capabilities and can only function when interacting with an external computer. Although it is controlled by a microprocessor, it is not programmable, and its internal random-access memory is limited to the storage of one screenful of data. When the screen is full, the entry or reception of new data displaces an equivalent quantity of information stored in the terminal's memory and display. The displaced information is "lost" and can only be redisplayed by reexecuting the appropriate computer operations. Displayable information is typically limited to alphanumeric characters. Graphic or color display capabilities are not provided.

Dumb terminals were once the dominant type of video display device for interactive computing applications, and the longevity and popularity of older models indicates their continued importance. While some applications require the more sophisticated devices described below, dumb terminals are well suited to a broad spectrum of home, business, school, and library requirements. They are especially useful in information retrieval, electronic message transmission, and other timesharing applications where straightforward, economical data communication capabilities are desired. Prices have fallen steadily since the late 1970s, and dumb video display terminals can now be purchased for less than $500—placing them within the reach of many home users.

Distinctions between dumb and smart terminals cannot be clearly drawn, and some observers contend that the smart terminal is more a marketing concept than a product group with well-defined attributes. Taking the simplest view, a smart terminal is essentially a dumb terminal with special features. It is typically equipped with a more powerful microprocessor that gives it a broader range of communications and display capabilities. As will be detailed in later sections, a smart terminal can often transmit data in blocks rather than as individual characters; display data in various sizes, intensities, or even colors; display a formatted screen with prelabelled areas; or split the screen area into two or more sections that can be controlled separately. It may also be equipped with a large random-access memory capable of storing two or more screens of data. Such features are especially useful in data entry applications.

But while their special features set them apart from simpler dumb devices, smart terminals are not programmable and are incapable of standalone operation. To perform information processing functions, they must be connected to an external computer. Most smart terminals are currently priced from $100 to $200 higher than dumb models. As with television sets, recent market entries by Asian manufacturers—notably, the Taiwanese and Koreans—have increased competition and lowered prices. Given the steadily falling cost of electronic circuitry, the already modest price differential between dumb and smart models will eventually vanish, causing smart terminals to supplant dumb terminals in straightforward interactive computing applications where programmability for local information processing is not required.

While dumb and smart terminals are exclusively designed for interaction with an external computer, intelligent terminals are fully programmable devices equipped with powerful microprocessors and sizeable internal memories intended for the storage of both data and programs. They are capable of both standalone information processing operations and data communications. The earliest intelligent terminals were relatively expensive, special-purpose devices designed for data entry and similar applications where local programs verified the accuracy of information and performed minor calculations prior to transmission to a remote computer.

While such devices remain in use, applications requiring intelligent terminals are increasingly utilizing microcomputers equipped with additional hardware and software components designed to permit electronic communication with an external computer. A telecommunications software package, purchased on a diskette or a read-only memory circuit board, enables the microcomputer to emulate one of the more commonly encountered dumb or smart terminals. For a given microcomputer, these additional components may be available from the microcomputer manufacturer or from other sources. In a variant approach, several vendors offer upgrade kits to convert dumb or smart terminals to microcomputers.

In most cases, a microcomputer turned intelligent terminal operates as a standalone information processing device, executing prewritten software packages or customized programs. Depending on the equipment configuration selected, the cost of a microcomputer system suitable for home, school, business, or library applications will range from about $1,000 to more than $6,000. The microcomputer itself is often the least expensive component. Total system costs are significantly increased by the addition of required input, output, and storage devices. With most models, intelligent terminal capabilities are an optional feature consisting of a communications interface device and a terminal emulation software package. The relatively low cost of these components—typically, $200 to $600 in addition to the cost of the microcomputer itself—appeals to many home users, allowing them to expand their local information processing capabilities by accessing remote computing services on a timesharing basis. Rather than purchasing two separate pieces of equipment in applications where local information processing and terminal operations are both required, a growing number of businesses, government agencies, schools, and libraries are acquiring microcomputers equipped with data communications capabilities as an alternative to conventional dumb or smart terminals.

In addition to permitting straightforward timesharing operations, such intelligent terminals can be used to obtain or "download" information from larger computers for local manipulation. A growing number of vendors have introduced programs designed to facilitate such downloading, allowing microcomputers to use programs and data files developed for larger systems. As previously discussed in chapter 5, the downloading of telesoftware by intelligent terminals is either currently offered or being planned by a number of videotext systems.

While heavy duty models have been developed for use in factories and similar harsh environments where dust, corrosive liquids, or similar contaminants pose special problems, the typical dumb, smart, or intelligent video display terminal is a desktop device designed for operation in a broad range of office and home environments. Although the exact dimensions of particular models are influenced by such factors as screen measurements and keyboard layout, most conventional video display terminals are about the size of a television set. As long as video display terminals were relegated to data entry departments or centralized office locations, few users were concerned with their installation space requirements. With the increased recent attention given to office automation, however, video display terminals have become an increasingly common fixture on the desks of individual office workers. In some organizations, every managerial and clerical workstation is equipped with a terminal that must compete with telephones, microfiche readers, and office supplies for a limited amount of available desk space. Recognizing this, a growing number of manufacturers have redesigned their product lines, introducing relatively unobtrusive models with reduced base measurements. Several North American and European manufacturers have developed very compact desktop display terminals designed for occasional use in offices or homes. Some of these devices offer videotext compatibility in addition to conventional data communications capabilities. While such terminals often compromise keyboard design and screen measurements, they require little desk space and are sufficiently low priced to encourage purchases.

While portable printing terminals have been available for over a decade, satisfactory portable video displays are a relatively recent development. Since the late 1970s, several vendors have offered portable dumb and smart terminals with small CRT displays. Patterned after the portable electronic test equipment used by computer technicians, these portable devices feature a metal suitcase containing the electronic components, display screen, power supply, and data communications interface. The keyboard is located inside a removable cover. Since the mid-1970s, a number of companies have manufactured hand-held display terminals designed for data entry in inventory, sales, field service, and similar business applications. Styled much like a calculator, these devices utilize the compact liquid crystal display or light-emitting diode display technologies described in a later section. A numeric keypad with special command keys must be used in the shifted position for the entry of alphabetic characters, making these devices inconvenient for nonnumeric applications. In the early 1980s, however, several manufacturers introduced slightly larger models with full alphanumeric keyboards suitable for both data entry and information retrieval operations. Compact enough to fit easily into a briefcase, these terminals feature a liquid crystal display of up to 40 characters in length and an integral communication interface suitable for connection to an ordinary telephone jack. Additional features, such as an electronic calendar or digital alarm clock, may also be included.

Where both local information processing and data communications capabilities are desired, most of the rapidly increasing number of portable microcomputers can be configured as intelligent terminals. Like the CRT-based portable terminals described above, the most popular configuration features a plastic or metal suitcase that houses a microprocessor, electronic memory circuits, a display screen, a communications interface, a power supply, one or more floppy disk drives for auxiliary data storage, and—with one available model—an integral printer. The display screen is typically a 9-inch cathode ray tube, although smaller and larger displays have been used. The keyboard is built into a removable screen cover. The case includes a carrying handle and is compact enough to fit under most airline seats. Prices currently range from $1,500 to over $3,000, depending on the particular equipment configuration selected. With most models, intelligent terminal capabilities are an optional feature that will increase the cost by approximately $200 to $600.

As an alternative configuration, several manufacturers offer microcomputers that are compact enough to fit into an ordinary briefcase. About the size of a portable manual typewriter, they feature a microprocessor, internal memory, a power supply, a communications interface, and a full alphanumeric keyboard. Liquid crystal or other flat panel displays offer a compact alternative to relatively bulky cathode ray tubes, although only a few lines of data may be displayed at a time and the number of characters per line is likewise limited. For auxiliary data storage, a microfloppy disk drive, which uses compact diskettes measuring 3.5 inches in diameter, or a microcassette recorder may be provided. Some manufacturers also offer a compact printer. At the time this chapter was written, prices for such portable microcomputers began at slightly less than $1,000 and ranged upward to $10,000. Designed for managerial and professional applications, the most expensive devices offer more powerful computing capabilities and use more exotic display technologies. Lower priced models are suitable for home or office use. As noted above, intelligent terminal capabilities will increase these prices by an estimated $200 to $600.

Whether it is designed for desktop operation or portability, the typical dumb or smart video display terminal is offered in a keyboard send-receive (KSR) configuration, meaning that it includes a keyboard and can transmit data to, or receive data from, a remote computer. It is the most important video equipment configuration for computer-user interaction. Where interaction is not required, most video terminals are available in a receive-only (RO) configuration that provides display capabilities, but omits the keyboard. Widely encountered in airports, hotels, and other public places, receive-only display terminals resemble the video monitors discussed in chapter 1. They are, in fact, a special class of video monitors designed specifically for the display of computer-generated data. In an increasingly common application, some microcomputers are sold with a microprocessor and memory circuitry built into a keyboard designed for attachment to an external, receive-only video display terminal. Most dumb and smart video display terminals can also be equipped with a floppy disk drive or magnetic tape recorder for the offline preparation of data prior to transmission or for the storage of received data in machine-readable form. But the cost of such automatic send-receive (ASR) configurations can approach that of an intelligent terminal without offering the programmability and standalone information processing capabilities of a microcomputer. With the proliferation of microcomputers, the availability and popularity of ASR terminal configurations have declined noticeably. As noted above, intelligent terminals are commonly equipped with one or more floppy disk drives.

As previously discussed, dumb, smart, and intelligent video display terminals can be configured with an auxiliary printer for the selective hard-copy output of displayed data. A variety of printers are available for this purpose, and most video display terminals are equipped with an industry-standard printer interface. In most cases, a screenful of displayed data can be dispatched to the printer. Alternatively, display and printing can occur simultaneously. With some models, the interface is equipped with a small internal memory that permits data communication and printing at different rates.

In an equipment configuration noted briefly in chapter 7 a growing number of vendors offer a special communications workstation equipped with both a video display terminal and a telephone (figure 41). Voice and data communications capabilities are not integrated, however, and these devices should not be confused with video telephone systems. Instead, they provide a single piece of equipment that can be used for either voice or data communications, enabling the office worker to make telephone calls, access electronic messaging systems, or retrieve information from external data bases. With some models, a smart video terminal is equipped with sufficient random-access memory to store a directory of frequently called telephone numbers for either persons or computer services. On the user's command, the terminal will automatically dial an indicated number. If the dialed number is busy, the terminal will automatically redial it at a later time. Prices for these special workstations vary with the model selected but are about twice those for a video display terminal alone.

Controls and Keyboard

As will be described more fully in a later section, most video display terminals support a variety of communications capabilities and visual attributes from which the user can select those required for a particular application. With the earliest models, the user selected the desired communication speed, line mode, and other operating parameters by setting groups of switches in predetermined positions indicated on diagrams printed in the terminal operator's manual. The switches themselves were often inconveniently located behind the terminal, and the positions appropriate to particular operating configurations had to be memorized or the manual consulted each time a change in operating parameters was required. Most newer dumb

FIGURE 41

A growing number of vendors offer special communication workstations which combine a video display terminal with a telephone, thereby offering a choice of voice or data communications. (Courtesy: Northern Telecom)

terminals—and many smart models—feature dedicated control buttons or keys labelled with the operating parameters that they initiate. Because the keys are clearly marked and located on the front of the terminal, this approach is certainly more convenient in applications requiring communication with multiple computers and the frequent changing of operating parameters. But, given the versatility of many newer terminals, the number of required control buttons can prove excessive. In addition, buttons and keys require space and must be carefully positioned to avoid inadvertent depression during normal keystroking operations.

To overcome this difficulty, many smart and intelligent terminals have replaced conventional control buttons and keys with a "set-up mode" in which operating parameters are selected from one or more menus of alternatives displayed on the video screen. The set-up menus and corresponding control programs are stored in the terminal's read-only memory. With some models, the user selects particular operating attributes by pressing specified combinations of alphanumeric keys. In a more common approach, the terminal is equipped with special function keys, which are assigned meanings in the context of particular set-up operations. These keys—which are simply labelled F1, F2, F3, and so on—may be grouped in a cluster to the right or left of the main keyboard section. As an increasingly popular alternative, function keys may be aligned in one or more rows at the top of the keyboard, permitting the display of corresponding labels in the bottom portion of the video screen. These labels change with each set-up menu. Depending on the control program used, function keys may be used to select operating options or to initiate the display of more detailed menus.

As the focal point for user interaction with external computers, terminal keyboards have received considerable recent attention from equipment designers, ergonomics specialists, occupational health specialists, and others interested in improving the effectiveness with which people use machines to accomplish information processing tasks. Through the late 1970s, most equipment manufacturers integrated the terminal keyboard and video screen in a single chassis that forced the user to prolong rigid postures, straining neck, back, and arm muscles. To minimize the associated operator discomfort and fatigue, most newer terminals are equipped with detached keyboards that are connected to the terminal's video monitor by a coiled cord. By altering the position of the detached keyboard, the operator can assume a variety of postures—an important factor in reducing the potential for fatigue in data entry and other business applications where video display terminals are used during major portions of the workday.

Much recent attention has likewise been given to keyboard height and slope. Following the recommendations of human engineering specialists, a growing number of newer terminals feature modestly sloped keyboards with a very low profile. Such features are essential in display terminals designed for the European market where there is much greater sensitivity to ergonomic considerations and where labor unions and other worker's groups have played a more active role in terminal equipment design than in the United States. The widely publicized guidelines developed by the German Institute for Standardization emphasize very low profile keyboards with the height of the middle row measuring less than 30mm (about 1.2 inches) above the desk surface and the overall slope measuring less than 15 degrees. An increasing number of video display terminals sold in North America are advertised as ergonomically designed devices conforming to these German standards, although such terminals are generally more expensive than less thoughtfully designed models. An increasing number of newer video terminals also feature sculptured keycaps with matte texture for a positive feel and low reflectivity. A relatively recent enhancement is the provision of adequate space for palm rests in the lower front portion of the keyboard. German guidelines require a palm rest to reduce static muscle loading where keyboard height exceeds the recommended 30mm. The recommended palm rest depth is 50mm to 100mm (approximately 2 to 4 inches).

In addition to its physical design, a keyboard's effectiveness depends heavily on the arrangement of the keys themselves. The keyboards of most newer video display terminals consist of three functional segments: a main alphanumeric section, an auxiliary numeric pad, and a control key cluster. The main alphanumeric keyboard consists of sixty or more keys representing alphabetic characters, numeric digits, punctuation marks, the carriage return, and special symbols. The familiar QWERTY arrangement of alphabetic keys, which takes its name from the order of the leftmost characters in the keyboard's second row, is standard with all video display terminals sold in North America, although some vendors offer a Dvorak keyboard as an optional layout. Proponents of the Dvorak keyboard contend that it offers improved keystroking efficiency and speed, but few data entry personnel or typists are trained to use it.

A minority of video display terminals sold in Europe are configured with a slightly different arrangement of alphabetic characters—the French AZERTY and

German QWERTZ keyboards are examples—but foreign keyboards are most notable for the availability and location of keys representing accented characters, diacritical marks, and other special symbols. Most video display terminals sold in the United States can be optionally ordered with foreign keyboards, and such equipment configurations are of special interest to research libraries where computers will be used to maintain bibliographic data from international sources. Where accent marks and related symbols are involved, many terminal equipment vendors employ a layout recommended by the European Computer Manufacturers Association (ECMA).

Country and language aside, the most significant differences in the layout of a keyboard's main alphanumeric section concern the manner in which numeric digits, punctuation marks, and special symbols are paired. Used in this context, pairing denotes the combination of character symbols on keytops so that one or the other will be transmitted, depending on whether the shift key is depressed or released. The pairing pattern is of special importance for efficient touch typing. In 1971, the American National Standards Institute (ANSI) proposed a keyboard layout in which characters and symbols are paired in a manner that roughly corresponds to their adjacency in columns of the symbol chart of the American Standard Code for Information Interchange (ASCII), a communications code used by many terminals. So, for example, the numeral *2* and the double quote symbol are adjacent to one another in the ASCII chart and are paired on a keytop in the first row of the terminal keyboard. The same pairing applies to the numeral *3* and the sharp symbol, the numeral *4* and the dollar sign, and so on. This keyboard layout is variously described as an ANSI keyboard for the organization which developed it, as a bit-paired arrangement because it is derived from the pattern of logical bits in the ASCII code chart, or as a "programmer's" keyboard because of its traditional popularity in equipment used in data processing.

Some typewriters employ a keyboard layout similar to the ANSI layout, but terminal keyboards described as typewriter-paired use the same arrangement as the popular IBM Selectric typewriter. This layout is widely preferred in business, library, school, and home applications, especially where the terminal will be used by touch typists with work experience in an office rather than a data processing environment. A distinctive feature of the typewriter-paired arrangement is the grouping of four frequently used punctuation marks—the colon, semicolon, apostrophe, and double quote—on two keys located at the extreme right of the home row. Recognizing that video display terminals are now widely used for word processing and text-oriented applications, an increasing number of vendors offer the typewriter-paired arrangement as a standard feature.

In addition to these commonly encountered arrangements, some video display terminals can be optionally equipped with single keys or entire keyboards designed for special applications. The most common of these special keyboards supports the unusual character set used in the APL programming language. Some vendors also offer keyboards for Hebrew, Cyrillic, or other non-Romance languages.

When present as a standard or optional feature, a numeric keypad is located to the right of the main alphanumeric section. As its name suggests, it provides a calculator style arrangement of ten numeric keys, possibly supplemented by a minus sign, comma, asterisk, and/or carriage return key. Although it replicates keys provided in the main alphanumeric section, the numeric pad is designed to facilitate the entry of quantitative data. It permits the entry of numeric data even when the main alphanumeric section is locked into the shifted position.

There is little uniformity in the placement of control keys, but newer video display terminals increasingly cluster them at the extreme right or left of the keyboard. This cluster typically includes the Escape (ESC) and Control (CTRL) keys—both of which are used in combination with other keys to initiate specific terminal operations or to transmit special characters—and a cursor control pad used to position the cursor, the small block of light or underscore that marks the screen location where characters will be displayed. Cursor control keys are invariably labelled with directional arrows. A compass arrangement with dedicated keys for each direction is typically preferred, although a surprising number of otherwise thoughtfully designed terminals arrange cursor control keys in a single line at the top or bottom of the keyboard. Still others pair the up/down and left/right controls, necessitating the frequent use of the shift key.

Some video display terminals feature spaces or raised dividers that separate the various keyboard sections. Others use different colors to identify the various key groups.

As an alternative to control key clusters, a relatively small—but widely publicized—group of video display terminals are equipped with special controls that initiate cursor movement and facilitate the selection of options from a displayed menu. As a primitive example, some older terminals were equipped with thumbwheels for vertical and horizontal cursor movement. Joysticks, a generally more acceptable alternative best known for their use in video games, are widely encountered in computer graphics applications. A joystick consists of a vertical shaft that can be tilted in various directions to position the cursor or draw lines and shapes on a video screen. As an alternative to the joystick, a trackball is a moveable sphere mounted on rollers. The operator rotates the sphere to move the cursor to a desired screen location.

A mouse, a hand-held control unit that has attracted much recent attention for its use in microcomputer systems designed for managers and professional persons who are uncomfortable with typing, consists of a small box with wheels or bearings mounted in the bottom. When the mouse is rolled along a desk top or other flat surface, the cursor moves along the video screen in the corresponding direction. Because the cursor moves in the same direction as the operator's hand, a pointing action is simulated. The mouse is typically equipped with one or more buttons programmed to initiate particular operations, thus minimizing the need to resort to the keyboard once the cursor is positioned.

As a more sophisticated and expensive alternative, some video display terminals are equipped with touch-sensitive screens that respond to actual pointing (figure 42). They feature light sensors or similar mechanisms that detect the screen location of a finger or other pointing object and perform an indicated operation, such as cursor movement, at that location. Touch-sensitive screens can also facilitate the selection of options from displayed menus. As an older approach to pointing, a hand-held light pen can be used to position the cursor and select options from a displayed menu. The light pen is equipped with a photocell that detects light emitted by the video screen while electronic circuitry determines the specific screen location. Although they are relatively light and compact, light pens can prove awkward

FIGURE 42

As an alternative to the keyboard in business applications where users' typing skills are limited, some video display terminals feature touch-sensitive screens. (Courtesy: Four-Phase Systems)

and uncomfortable in prolonged use, and, because they detect light, they cannot be used to position the cursor in a blank area of the terminal screen.

Communications Characteristics

When communicating with an external computer, video display terminals transmit and/or receive digital data in the form of electrical signals that consist of a series of on/off pulses. Where textual information is involved, predetermined combinations of these pulses—which, in data processing terminology, are called "bits"—encode individual characters intended for transmission and/or display. In computer code charts, these bits are represented by the symbols "1" and "0," respectively. Two major coding systems define the number and position of the bits which make up individual characters:

1. The majority of video display terminals utilize the American Standard Code for Information Interchange (ASCII), which is defined in American National Standards Institute standard X3.4-1968 and is recognized by both the International Standardization Organization (ISO) and the Comité Consultatif International Téléphonique et Télégraphique (CCITT) as an accepted variant of International Alphabet No. 5. The ASCII code uses 7 bits to represent each character. These 7 bits are typically accompanied by 3 additional bits: a parity bit, which is used for error checking, and 2 "framing" bits that indicate the beginning and end of a character. Transmission systems that employ such framing bits are termed "asynchronous" because the sending and receiving devices need not be synchronized. ASCII asynchronous video display terminals are manufactured by dozens of companies and can be used with many types of computers. The simplest models are sometimes described as "glass teletypes" because they emulate the communication characteristics of the once popular Teletype Model 33 printing terminal. While Teletype compatability is still supported, many newer models offer special visual attributes or other features designed for use with specific computer systems. These capabilities will be described in a later section.

2. A second group of video display terminals utilizes the Extended Binary Coded Decimal Interchange Code (EBCDIC) which uses 8 bits to represent individual characters. Most EBCDIC terminals employ bisynchronous transmission techniques, which do not require framing bits. As a result, they are capable of faster transmission than their asynchronous counterparts, but are more complex and expensive. Most bisynchronous video display terminals are designed for communication with large IBM computers. The IBM 3270 Series display terminals are the most widely encountered examples. A growing number of vendors market terminals designed for compatibility with one or more 3270 Series models.

Because they utilize a different number of bits and different transmission methods, ASCII and EBCDIC terminals are incompatible with one another. Recently, however, several manufacturers have introduced video display terminals capable of either ASCII asynchronous or EBCDIC bisynchronous communications. Some microcomputers can likewise be equipped with software packages designed to support either mode of data communications.

Regardless of the particular coding scheme or transmission methods used, video display terminals operate online to an external computer. Sometimes, the terminal and computer are located within a few hundred feet of one another and are connected by a specially designed cable that transmits successive bits as the presence or absence of electrical pulses. This is typically the case, for example, where video display terminals are attached to microcomputers in home or office installations. In most timesharing applications, however, the video display terminal and computer are separated by a considerable distance, and telephone lines serve as the data communications link. As discussed in chapter 6, telephone lines were originally designed for transmission of the continually varying analog signals characteristic of the human voice. The terminal's digital signals must then be converted to analog form prior to transmission. This conversion is accomplished by a modem that may be an integral part of the video display terminal, but is more often a separate device. Modems establish an electrical connection between a terminal, a telephone line, and a telephone instrument. Using the telephone, the terminal operator dials the number of the desired computer and activates a switch that permits data communications. With some integral modems, phone numbers can be dialed through the terminal keyboard, and a separate telephone instrument is not required.

As an alternative to conventional modems, acoustic couplers consist of a microphone and speaker in rubber cups designed to cradle a telephone handset. The coupler's speaker is aligned with the telephone's microphone, and the coupler's microphone is aligned with the telephone's speaker. The coupler converts the terminal's electrical, digital signal to audible, analog tones for transmission over telephone lines.

As with other types of computer equipment, the communication speeds of video display terminals are typically reported in either of two measures: bits per second or bauds. Terminals transmit information by altering the amplitude, frequency, phase, or other condition of cables, telephone lines, or other telecommunication facilities. As noted above, successive alterations in line conditions represent the digital pulses or bits that encode individual characters. As the phrase indicates, bits per second is a measure of the rate at which successive individual bits are transmitted. The term baud denotes the number of times a given line condition changes in a second. As long as each change reflects one bit, a given terminal's baud and bit rates will be identical. This is the case with the vast majority of available devices, but certain high-speed terminals utilize sophisticated coding schemes that transmit more than one bit per baud. Such devices are rarely encountered in video display applications, however, and, for all practical purposes, the two speed measures can be used interchangeably.

Unlike printing terminals with their mechanical constraints, video terminals are electronic devices, which can display data at very high speeds. Most available models are capable of operating at a variety of speeds ranging from 50 to 19,200 bits per second. The actual speed selected for a given application will depend on the requirements of the host computer system and the nature of the transmission facilities employed. With ordinary telephone lines, for example, transmission speeds are typically limited to 1,200 bits per second or lower. As with the other video transmission systems, coaxial cable or other wideband communication facilities permit faster speeds, although the reception of multiple screens of data at very high rates is of questionable utility in applications where the operator is expected to intellectually assimilate the displayed information.

Regardless of speed, most video display terminals communicate in a conversational mode in which lines of characters are transmitted following each carriage return. Some smart and most intelligent video display terminals are also capable of buffered transmission in which all or parts of a screen are first entered into the terminal's random-access memory for editing prior to transmission in a block. To facilitate error correction and data modification prior to transmission, terminals capable of such block-mode transmission typically feature dedicated function keys that permit the insertion or deletion of lines and/or characters. Block-mode transmission is especially useful in data entry applications where the terminal displays a formatted screen consisting of labelled areas followed by blank spaces for the entry of specific items of data. The operator enters the required information, proofreads it, makes any required changes, then initiates transmission.

Display Capabilities

Alphanumeric CRT Displays

Despite the considerable recent attention being given to alternative display technologies, the cathode ray tube remains the overwhelmingly dominant video display technology. As with the television receivers and video monitors discussed in chapter 1, CRT-based terminals use an electron beam to display information by illuminating the phosphorescent surface of a video screen. In most cases, the displayed image lasts only a fraction of a second, and the screen phosphors must be repeatedly re-illuminated or "refreshed." CRT terminals are commonly categorized as alphanumeric or graphic, depending on the type of information which they can display. Alphanumeric CRT terminals, the focus of this discussion, can display alphabetic characters, numeric digits, punctuation marks, and other symbols commonly found in textual information. Graphic CRT terminals, which have a much broader range of display capabilities, will be discussed in the next section.

As with television receivers, the screens of video display terminals are measured diagonally, the most commonly encountered size for alphanumeric CRT devices being 12 inches. Most vendors offer at least one model with a 14- or 15-inch screen, but larger screens are rarely encountered in alphanumeric applications. For group display, several companies offer video projectors that operate with large, wall-mounted screens. A growing number of compact terminals are equipped with 9-inch CRT screens, and several portable microcomputers feature screens that measure from 5.5 to 7 inches diagonally.

Regardless of size, the CRT screens of video display terminals designed for most data processing applications feature the same 1.33:1 (horizontal to vertical) aspect ratio encountered with conventional television receivers. Video display terminals with a vertical screen orientation are sometimes used in word processing systems. Such screens measure approximately 15 inches diagonally and are designed to display the equivalent of a letter-size page, enabling an operator to visualize a typed document prior to printing. For applications involving a combination of word and data processing, at least one terminal manufacturer offers a tiltable screen, which can be oriented either vertically or horizontally.

While the resolution of conventional television receivers and other video devices is measured in lines or picture elements per given linear dimension, the resolution of alphanumeric video terminals is commonly expressed in terms of the number of lines of data that can be displayed on the screen at one time and the number of characters that can be displayed in each line. Although there are no written standards governing display format, most horizontally oriented alphanumeric CRT terminals will display 24 lines of data, each line containing up to 80 characters. In some cases, one or two additional lines are provided for the display of status or prompting information. As noted in the introduction to this chapter, the ability to display 80-character lines clearly distinguishes video display terminals from conventional television receivers when the latter are utilized as computer display devices. It also gives CRT terminals a clear advantage over the alternative display technologies to be discussed in a later section. A growing number of alphanumeric CRT terminals can display 24 lines of up to 132 characters each, emulating the data format commonly associated with computer printouts. The vertically oriented alphanumeric CRT terminals mentioned above can display 50 or more lines of data, each consisting of up to 80 characters.

Screen format aside, the size of the displayable character set and the method of character generation vary from model to model. When the 7-bit ASCII code is used, the typical alphanumeric video terminal can display 96 to 128 different characters. Terminals using the 8-bit EBCDIC code can typically display up to 256 different characters. In terms of character generation methodology, most alphanumeric CRT terminals are dot matrix display devices that form individual characters by illuminating points on the video screen in a predetermined pattern. These terminals are typically equipped with character generation tables stored in read-only memories. On receipt of an incoming character code, the terminal's microprocessor looks up the appropriate dot matrix pattern for display. Some models are equipped with two or more different character generation tables for greater versatility. The additional tables may contain foreign character sets, scientific character sets, or other special symbols. For an additional charge, many terminal manufacturers will provide special character sets according to customer specifications.

Regardless of a terminal's displayable character repertoire, the legibility of individual characters varies directly with the number of dots in the matrix. At the time this chapter was written, matrix sizes for available video display terminals ranged from 5 (horizontal) by 9 (vertical) dots to 9 (horizontal) by 13 (vertical) dots. While a matrix of 45 dots is generally acceptable for the legible display of uppercase alphabetic characters and numeric digits, larger matrix sizes are preferred for smaller lowercase characters and special symbols. Larger matrix sizes are especially useful for the display of the descenders associated with the lower case *p*, *q*, and *y*. Regardless of matrix size, recommended character width to height ratios range from 1:2 to 7:10.

As an alternative to dot matrix technology, some alphanumeric video display terminals use the stroke method of character generation in which an electron beam draws characters on the phosphorescent surface of the CRT screen. The result is a fully formed, highly legible character, but, because of slowness and high cost, stroke generation displays are commonly reserved for graphic applications. In another approach to high quality video display, DatagraphiX terminals use the proprietary Charactron-shaped beam tube that generates characters by selectively directing an electron beam through a specially designed stencil containing the displayable character set. The resulting characters are fully formed and very sharply defined. As might be expected, video displays utilizing this character generation technique are more expensive than dot matrix devices.

The majority of alphanumeric CRT terminals are monochrome display devices—that is, the phosphorescent screen displays characters in a single color on a dark background. The Electronics Industries Association (EIA) has identified and developed standard alphanumeric designations for several dozen available phosphors. While most of these are designed for use in oscillographs, radiographs, CRT scanners, and similar instruments, three are widely utilized for the display of computer data. Through the late 1970s, many video display terminals featured the bluish-white (EIA designation P4) phosphor. Since the early 1980s, terminal equipment manufacturers and users have generally preferred the higher contrast offered by the bright green (EIA designation P39) phosphor. Although they have proven popular in European applications for several years, video terminals utilizing an amber (EIA designation P41) phosphor have only recently become widely available in North America. Advocates of amber phosphors cite their restful properties, an important consideration in applications involving prolonged use of video displays. Regardless of phosphor, better video terminals—like conventional television receivers—feature contrast and brightness controls that allow the operator to adjust display attributes to suit individual preferences.

As will be discussed later in this chapter, graphics display terminals are often equipped with color cathode ray tubes, and—as discussed in chapter 5—color displays are essential in videotext applications where graphics play an important role in information transfer. In the past several years, however, several manufacturers have introduced reasonably priced color and other advanced display terminals designed for alphanumeric applications (figure 43). Compared to the graphics terminals discussed later in this chapter, their color repertoire and fidelity are limited, but they are suitable for straightforward applications where a multicolor presentation can effectively highlight important information and clarify relationships among displayed data, while enhancing pattern recognition and making the display more appealing. They are primarily intended for business applications involving managerial reports and illustrated arguments.

In the absence of color, an increasing number of monochrome display devices

FIGURE 43

Advanced alphanumeric display terminals can combine split screen features, varied character intensities, simple graphics, and reverse video to present information more effectively. (Courtesy: IBM Corporation)

have special effects to highlight and separate data. The most common of these attributes is the selective display of information in reverse video—that is, as dark characters on a light background. In data and word processing applications, reverse video is widely used for headings, data labels, and instructions requiring special emphasis. Some newer alphanumeric CRT terminals, however, provide reverse video as the normal display mode. Proponents of these devices contend that negative appearing displays cause the pupil of the eye to widen, with a resulting reduction in the operator's depth of field, some blurring of images, and accompanying visual fatigue. With positive appearing displays, they argue, the pupil remains small and a sharp focus and depth of field are maintained. In data entry and word processing applications, positive appearing displays also eliminate the repeated visual accommodations associated with the alternate viewing of positive appearing source documents and a negative appearing video screen. As a further advantage, positive appearing displays are generally less affected by ambient light reflections.

In addition to reverse video, other visual attributes can be used to emphasize headings, highlight specific data segments, and/or improve the appearance of displayed information. Many available video terminals will display specified data in higher or lower intensity, larger or smaller characters, and with or without underlining. Blinking can likewise be used to call attention to particular portions of the screen. Depending on the model, these visual attributes may be applied on a line-by-line, word-by-word, or character-by-character basis. As with all special display capabilities, visual attributes must be activated by programs specifically designed to take advantage of them. To facilitate learning and operation, a growing number of commercially available computer software packages utilize the special display capabilities of particular video terminals.

Graphic CRT Displays

A growing number of essentially alphanumeric video terminals can display special block characters which can be combined to form bar charts, line graphs, histograms, and other straightforward graphic presentations (figure 44). True graphic terminals, however, are specifically and primarily intended for the display of designs or other pictorial images. Most available models are also equipped with character generation circuitry that permits the display of conventional alphanumeric data, but—in the typical application—such alphanumeric data occupies a small portion of the total display area and exists to supplement or complement pictorial information. Few true graphic terminals are being extensively used for data entry, information retrieval, word processing, or other alphanumeric applications, but some observers contend that the declining cost of electronic components, combined with the growing popularity of computer-generated graphics, will eventually render purely alphanumeric video terminals obsolete.

Such predictions aside, graphic display terminals are an unquestionably expanding product group that can support a variety of applications. The earliest graphic displays were designed for scientific and technical applications in such fields as design engineering, aerospace, medical research, and land resources management. Their importance has increased with the growing popularity of computer-aided design and computer-aided manufacturing (CAD/CAM) systems in engineering, architecture, and related fields. In most scientific and technical applications, the

FIGURE 44

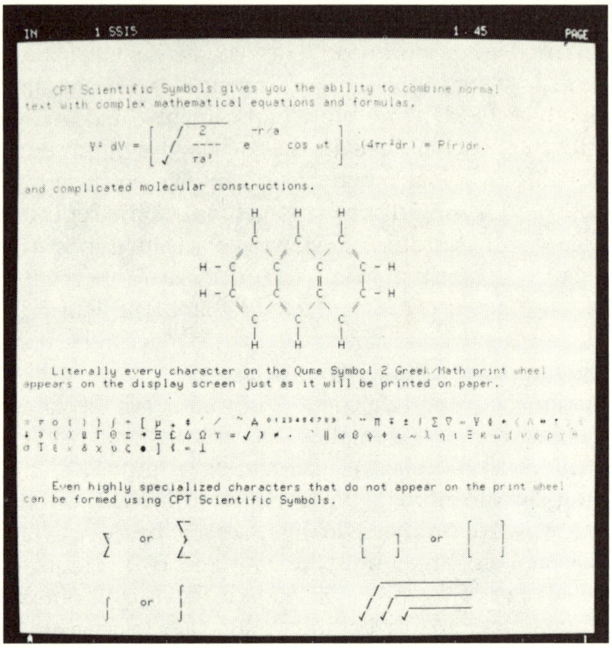

Special designed alphanumeric terminals can display scientific symbols and foreign character sets as well as conventional text. (Courtesy: CPT Corporation)

graphic video display terminal is one component in an elaborate computer hardware and software configuration. As a product group, they are complex and relatively expensive instruments that use a greater variety of display technologies and offer a broader range of capabilities than graphic displays designed for business, educational, or home applications.

In business, graphic video displays are increasingly used for management reporting and data analysis. In too many applications, computers generate far more data than users can readily digest. Compared to conventional tabular displays or printouts, graphic presentations can increase the speed at which information is absorbed by delineating patterns, clarifying trends, and highlighting exceptional conditions (figure 45). In this respect, graphics are particularly useful for statistical or financial analysis. A growing number of graphic software packages are available for computers of all types and sizes, and most computerized decision support systems include a graphics component. Some software packages designed for alphanumeric applications also include a graphics component that is designed to simplify training and use. As an alternative to conventional menus containing words or phrases, these software packages display images called "icons," which represent particular computer operations from which the user can select. In another important business application, graphic video displays can be used in conjunction with computer-stored data and appropriate software to create presentation aids or reproduce images transmitted from paper files, microfilm storage, or optical disk systems for later reproduction on mylar transparencies or photographic media.

In computer-assisted instruction and similar educational applications, graphics are widely used to gain and hold the learner's attention. Graphics are a dominant element in educational software packages designed for young children, and educational programming languages such as LOGO and PILOT include an extensive graphics component. Their extensive use in recreational computing and videotext systems reflects the importance of graphics in home applications.

While many educational and home applications use conventional television receivers, technical and business applications require display devices specifically

FIGURE 45

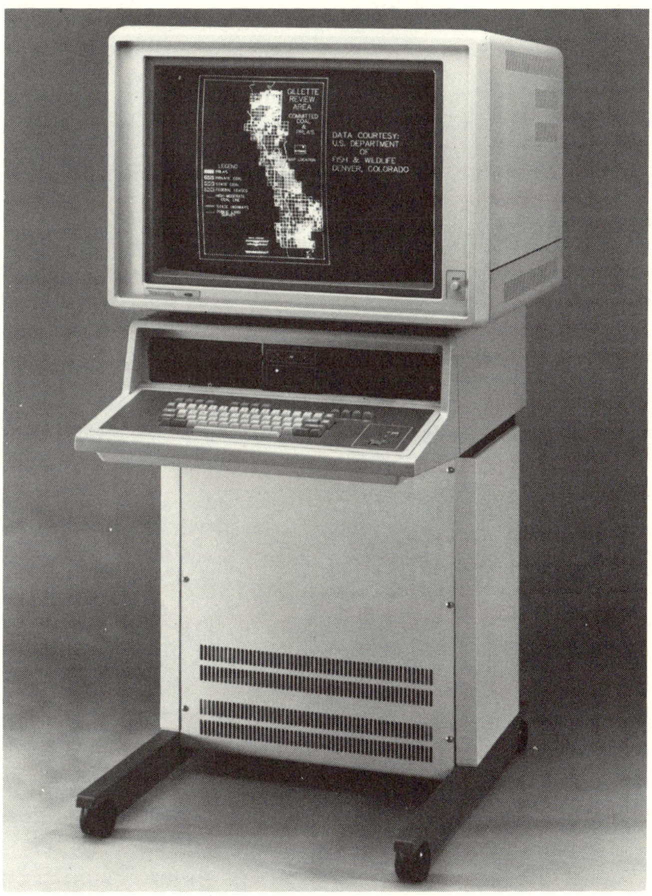

Graphics terminals are designed for the high resolution display of charts, maps, designs, or other complex pictorial images in scientific, technical, and business applications. (Courtesy: Tektronix)

designed for computer-generated images. As with alphanumeric terminals, most available graphic displays use CRT technology. Typical screen sizes, measured diagonally, range from 13 to 25 inches, with most models measuring 19 inches or less. Most models likewise feature a horizontal screen orientation with the 1.33 to 1 aspect ratio associated with conventional television receivers and alphanumeric video displays. While other aspect ratios and vertically oriented screens are available, the horizontal display of graphic images is well suited to the panoramic nature of human vision.

The oldest type of graphic video display device, the direct view storage tube (DVST), uses a combination of electron beams to plot points and draw lines on a CRT screen. The CRT features a high persistence phosphor that maintains the displayed image on the screen without the periodic redrawing or refreshing associated with conventional cathode ray tubes. Because the image is stored on the screen itself, little internal memory is required, and terminal prices are relatively low. Since the displayed image need not be periodically refreshed, flicker is eliminated. In addition, direct view storage tubes offer high resolution potential. Available models can display up to 4,096 lines of up to 4,096 picture elements each for a total of almost 16.8 million plottable points.

As significant disadvantages, however, direct view storage tubes display monochrome graphics that are characteristically low in both contrast and brightness. As a further limitation, they can only display outlines. Solid figures cannot be depicted. In addition, their slow drawing speeds, combined with the inability to selectively erase portions of a displayed image, make them unsuitable for interactive graphic applications or those requiring the display of rotating images. As a final point, storage tube life is typically shorter than that of conventional CRTs, although the service life of recent models has improved considerably.

Direct view storage tubes are widely encountered in scientific and technical applications, but they are a progressively smaller component in a graphics display market that is currently dominated by vector refresh and raster scan technologies. Vector refresh displays—also known as vector writer, stroke refresh, or stroke writer displays—resemble direct view storage tubes in their use of an electron beam to plot points and draw lines at coordinates dictated by graphics software. But unlike high persistence storage tubes, the images generated by vector displays fade quickly and must be refreshed at frequent intervals, typically 30 to 60 times per second. For this purpose, vector refresh terminals are equipped with sufficient internal memory for the storage of plotting information relevant to displayed images. Compared to direct view storage tubes, vector refresh terminals offer the fast drawing speed and selective erasure capability essential to interactive graphics applications. Displayed images are high in both contrast and brightness. High resolution models can display as many as 4,096 horizontal lines with as many as 4,096 picture elements per line. While primarily intended for monochrome display, some models provide two or three colors. Where the color display of computer-generated graphics is required, however, raster scan technology offers superior capabilities.

Raster scan terminals, the current focus of industry and user interest, are increasingly encountered in a wide range of scientific, technical, business, and educational applications. They resemble conventional television receivers in displaying images as a series of horizontal scan lines composed of individual picture elements. Raster scan terminals are equipped with relatively large "bit-mapped" memories that store binary-coded tonal values corresponding to successive picture elements. With monochrome displays, each picture element is represented by a single bit. Grayscale or color displays use multiple bits for each picture element. In either case, an electron beam sweeps across successive horizontal scan lines energizing individual picture elements according to the coded pattern. When the last line is drawn, the beam returns to the top of the screen and the image is refreshed. Like conventional television receivers, some raster scan terminals divide the displayed video image into two interlaced fields consisting of alternating scan lines refreshed 30 times per second. More expensive models refresh the entire image 60 times per second. The resulting image is generally free of obvious or subliminal flicker, but the resolution of such noninterlaced displays may be limited. Some raster scan terminals can operate in either the interlaced or noninterlaced mode, depending on application requirements.

Raster scan terminals display bright, high contrast images. Solid objects can be depicted with realistic shadings and textures. Both monochrome and color displays are available. The latter require larger internal memories, but are indispensible in many applications. Depending on the model, the user may be able to select from a palette of several thousand colors, although only a specified number of different colors can be displayed on the screen at one time. While they are not as fast as vector refresh devices, raster scan terminals offer sufficiently rapid drawing capabilities for many interactive graphic applications. Since the displayed image changes each time the screen is refreshed, selective erasure is possible.

Resembling conventional television receivers and video monitors, low resolution color raster scan terminals can display approximately 200 to 600 horizontal scan lines with up to 500 picture elements per line. Such terminals are appropriate for videotext and many educational and consumer applications. For serious technical and business applications, higher resolution color models can display approximately 1,200 horizontal scan lines with up to 1,000 picture elements per line. With continuing improvements in raster scan technology, 2,000-line color displays are expected in the future. Such devices are now available for monochrome applications.

A special class of monochrome raster scan terminals are designed as high resolution video output devices for digitized document images transmitted from the facsimile, microfacsimile, and optical video disk systems described in chapter 6. They typically feature vertically oriented, letter-size screens and can display 2,200 horizontal scan lines containing 1,728 picture elements each—the facsimile resolution equivalent of 200 by 200 picture elements per inch (figure 46). Given the 3.8 million bits used to represent a single letter-size document at such high resolution, these terminals require very large internal memories and are consequently expensive, with current prices ranging upward from $15,000. As noted in chapter 6, some models also support an alphanumeric mode that can be used for data base searching prior to document display. For the same application, some less expensive models utilize image enhancement techniques for high quality display at 1,100 horizontal scan lines of 864 picture elements each. Regardless of resolution, these terminals typically display images in the positive polarity associated with paper documents. In most cases, a white phosphor is used.

FIGURE 46

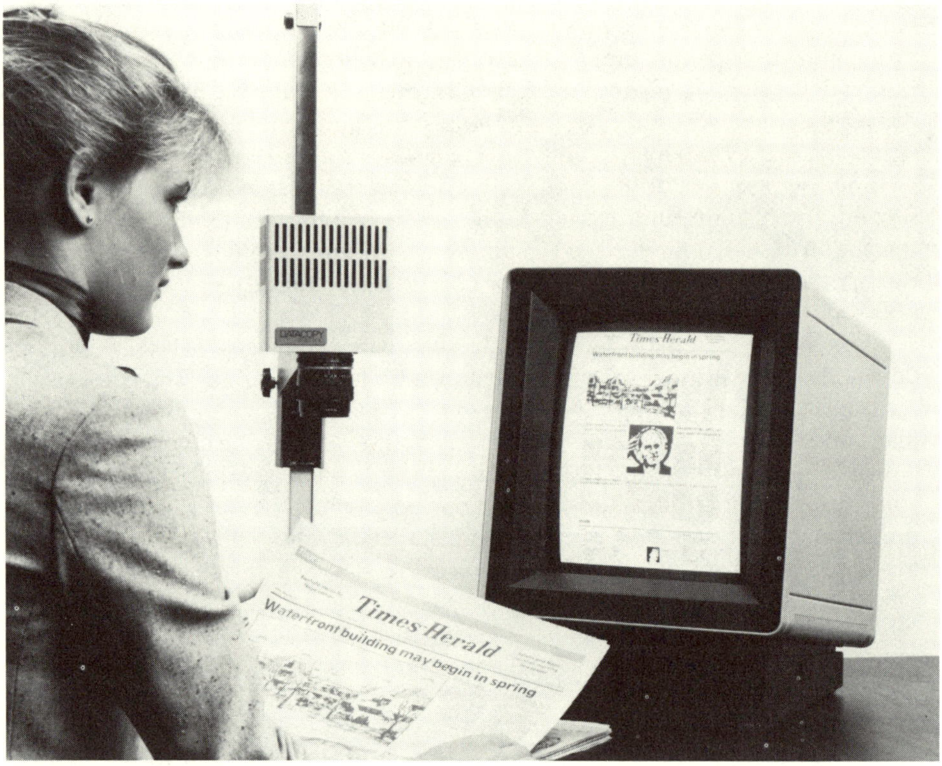

A special class of graphics terminals are specifically designed for the high resolution display of digitized document images in information storage and retrieval systems. (Courtesy: Datacopy)

Health Considerations

Whether designed for alphanumeric or graphic information, CRT displays have been the recent subject of a number of health-related concerns and complaints. The most serious of these deals with potential hazards to video display terminal operators resulting from radiation emissions. Cathode ray tubes emit various types of radiation, including visible, infrared, and ultraviolet rays; microwaves; radio frequency waves; and x-rays. These emissions have been named as suspect agents in several court cases involving health problems of video display terminal operators, but there has been no conclusive evidence establishing any such causative relationship. On the contrary, studies done by the National Institute for Occupational Safety and Health (NIOSH) have concluded that the radiation emitted by CRT display terminals are within levels considered safe by U.S. government standards.

Labor unions and other groups remain concerned about the health implications of prolonged terminal use, however, and critics of the NIOSH studies contend that U.S. government standards tolerate unacceptably high radiation levels. Federal regulations currently allow the emission of .5 millirads of x-ray radiation per hour measured at a distance of 6 centimeters from the video screen. For purposes of comparison, a typical x-ray involves 30 millirads of radiation. The amount of radiation that actually reaches the CRT operator varies inversely with the viewing distance. At 6 feet, for example, little radiation is detectable. But while most operators do not sit within 6 centimeters of a CRT screen, they seldom sit 6 feet away. In addition, some operators may periodically lean forward for close examination of displayed data. Concern has been expressed about the potential for harmful radiation exposure under such circumstances. Other critics cite defects in radiation measurement methods or uncertainties surrounding the effects of radiation even at presumably safe levels.

While the prevailing consensus is that operators of CRT displays are not at risk, some authorities recommend obtaining the terminal manufacturer's certification of conformity to government radiation emission standards, followed by the periodic monitoring of installed units for variations in emission levels over time. Where additional precautions are desired, several companies market protective shields made of leaded acrylic that can be attached to the CRT screen to block potentially harmful x-rays and ultraviolet rays.

Musculo-skeletal discomfort resulting from prolonged terminal use is a second major health concern. Operators of CRT displays have complained widely of eyestrain, blurred vision, and headaches. With some older models, such symptoms of visual fatigue could be attributed to poorly lit screens, poorly defined characters, excessively flickering images, or similar display defects. As described in preceding sections, most newer terminals feature greatly improved display characteristics that can minimize or eliminate these problems. Examples include the use of higher contrast green or amber phosphors on a very dark background, the increased availability of positive appearing displays, larger dot matrix sizes for improved character legibility, and a "smooth scrolling" feature, which maintains the legibility of displayed alphanumeric information as it moves line by line up the video screen.

Much of the visual fatigue experienced by video display terminal operators is attributable to glare that results from light reflections on the terminal screen. To minimize such reflections, an increasing number of new CRT terminals feature etched or matte-finished screens. Some newer models are likewise equipped with swivelling and/or tiltable screens that can be positioned to reduce glare while minimizing musculo-skeletal fatigue resulting from static postures. Like the detached keyboards, such features are considered mandatory in many European installations where human engineering considerations play a decisive role in equipment selection. Since the terminal's keyboard and exterior surfaces can also be a source of disturbing glare, many newer terminals are finished in materials and colors designed to minimize reflectivity.

In many installations, discomfort glare results from gross luminance differences between the terminal's immediate work area and the surrounding room. In the typical office, ambient light levels are too high for the comfortable use of CRT displays. General illumination in the 24 to 40 footcandle range is recommended, with the luminance difference between the terminal's work area and surrounding room environment not exceeding a ratio of 3:1. Both artificial and natural light should be diffused. Display terminals should be located as far away from windows as possible, and operators should never face windows or very bright surfaces.

As an often overlooked point, some of the visual complaints of CRT display operators are the result of uncorrected vision disorders. The importance of such vision disorders will increase as display terminals are routinely used by greater numbers of office workers whose eyes have lost the ability to accommodate close work. Periodic vision screenings for all terminal operators are strongly recommended. Operators who wear corrective lenses may require some modification in their prescriptions. This is often the case, for example, with bifocal lenses that are typically intended for conventional book reading at a distance of about 16 inches. Most display terminal operation involves greater focal distances, especially with the widespread use of detached keyboards, which allow the operator a greater choice of seating postures.

Flat Panel Displays

As described in the preceding subsections, the cathode ray tube is a well-developed display technology that offers high resolution, varied visual attributes, color capabilities, steadily falling prices, and other advantages appropriate to a very wide range of alphanumeric and graphic applications. By way of contrast, flat panel technologies are at an early stage of development. While some flat panel displays have been commercially available for a number of years, others operate only in laboratories. As a group, however, they offer potentially valuable features and capabilities that CRT displays cannot provide. Their collective name indicates their most significant attribute: flat panel displays are thin. Depth is their smallest dimension, and they require much less desk space than bulky CRT terminals. Their compactness and light weight also make them highly portable, while low power consumption allows them to be battery-operated for long periods of time. As an additional advantage, flat panel displays are more rugged than CRT-based terminals. They can withstand vibration and shock, can operate reliably at a wider range of temperatures and relative humidity, and are less susceptible to magnetic or electrical interference. From the visual standpoint, some flat panel technologies can display large, bright characters and are free of the linear and orthogonal distortions inherent in CRT devices. A final advantage is that flat panel technologies emit no radiation.

On the negative side, flat panel displays are significantly more expensive than their CRT counterparts. At the time this chapter was written, their use was restricted to those applications where performance is more important than price. The most interesting and innovative flat panel displays have been developed for military applications where compact, reliable, rugged portable terminals are required for field operations. More conventional models are designed for those business and technical applications where space considerations are paramount.

Regardless of application, all available flat panel displays are matrix devices that use a grid of electrodes to energize sensitive components or chemicals at specific coordinates. With active flat panel displays, the energized components emit light. With passive flat panel technologies, the components' reflectivity characteristics are changed. Light-emitting diode (LED) displays, probably the most familiar example of active flat panel technologies, are widely used in calculators, watches, appliances, scientific instruments, and other consumer and industrial products. They consist of compact, solid-state components that emit a bright red, orange, green, or blue light when voltage is applied. While single-segment light-emitting diodes often serve as simple on/off indicators, more complex multisegment devices can be selectively energized to display numeric or alphabetic characters. LED devices are reliable and durable, but relatively small component sizes, combined with high power consumption, limit their use to single-line displays.

With passive liquid crystal displays (LCDs), selectively applied voltage generates alphanumeric characters by altering the light reflectance properties of liquid chemical compounds. Designed for many of the same consumer and industrial applications as LEDs, their very low power requirements are well suited to battery operation. As described in chapter 1, several manufacturers have recently announced small-screen television receivers using LCD technology. For business and home applications, LCDs are used in an increasing number of portable terminals and microcomputers where they can display several lines of data containing 20 to 40 characters each. Larger LCD data panels have been demonstrated, but are not yet commercially available. As passive devices, liquid crystal displays are suitable for outdoor use, but they do not operate effectively in poorly lit rooms. As a further limitation, display response is noticeably slower than that of other technologies.

Electroluminescent (EL) displays consist of a thin, polycrystalline film that glows when energized at specific points. The resulting orange images feature good resolution, grayscale reproduction, and sufficiently rapid response for conventional video or interactive graphics applications. Developed largely for military applications, the limited number of available electroluminescent data displays are very thin, can be easily carried, and consume little power. Electroluminescent technology offers considerable future potential for both data and television display, especially if color capabilities are developed, brightness and contrast improved, and the display size increased. Because of technical impediments, existing electroluminescent panels rarely exceed 5 by 6.5 inches in size.

Where large displays for alphanumeric or graphic applications are required, alternating current (AC) gas plasma devices are the flat panel technology of choice (figure 47). First demonstrated in the early 1960s, AC gas plasma displays utilize an alternating electrical current to energize gas trapped between gas plates. The glowing gas creates an orange image that features good resolution, brightness, and contrast. Once energized, the display retains its image until erased, thereby eliminating the need for a bit-mapped internal memory as well as screen refreshment with its potential for flicker. Display characteristics are unaffected by size, and AC gas panels measuring up to 3 meters diagonally have been demonstrated. Several companies currently offer commercially available models measuring 1 meter diagonally. With their rapid response, AC gas plasma displays are suitable for interactive graphics; scientific and technical applications are primary markets for available equipment. For maximum flexibility in computer graphics applications, AC gas plasma displays can operate in either the raster or vector modes. As briefly noted in chapter 1, several Japanese companies have demonstrated the future potential of AC gas plasma for large-screen television, although such devices are far from commercial availability.

DC gas plasma displays, as their name implies, utilize direct electrical current to display information by energizing trapped gas. As an alternative to conventional CRT displays, DC gas plasma video terminals have been available since the mid-1960s, the most widely encountered example being the Burroughs Self Scan panels, which are used in a variety of business applications. Compared to AC gas plasma technology, DS gas plasma displays are smaller in size, require refreshing, and lack the random

FIGURE 47

Gas plasma display. (Courtesy: IBM Corporation)

addressability essential to vector generation in graphics applications. They are primarily designed for alphanumeric applications where compactness is an important consideration.

Among other flat panel technologies with possible future implications for video terminal design, electrophoretic displays feature electrically charged pigment particles in a dielectric liquid of contrasting color. Potential advantages include good image quality and low power consumption, but electrophoretic technology is not well developed. Slow response will likely limit applications to alphanumeric data display. Electrochromic technology is likewise at an early stage of development. It displays images by electrically altering the tonality of chemical compounds. Its slow response appears best suited to watches, digital clocks, and other consumer products.

Additional Readings

COMMUNICATIONS CHARACTERISTICS

Edelheit, D. Wide diversity in SNA/3270 compatibility. *Data Communications* 11: 105–13 (October 1982).

Hagelbarger, D. W., Anderson, R. V., and Kubik, P. S. Experiments with teleterminals. *IEEE Journal on Selected Areas of Communications* 1: 310–15 (1983).

Klapman, R. N. Enhanced communications in an executive office. *IEEE Journal on Selected Areas of Communications* 1: 327–32 (1983).

CRT TECHNOLOGY

Bylander, E. G. *Electronic Displays*. New York: McGraw-Hill, 1979.

Cakir, A., Hart, D. J., and Stewart, T. F. M. *Visual Display Terminals*. New York: Wiley, 1980.

Koi, D. Cathode ray tubes: Recent trends for character-graphic display. *Display Technology and Applications* 4: 197–200 (October 1983).

Sherr, S. *Video and Digital Electronic Displays: A User's Guide*. New York: Wiley, 1982.

Usher, D. M. Comparison of a touch sensitive VDU and computer-aided keypad for plant control. *Display Technology and Applications* 4: 157–61 (July 1983).

DISPLAY QUALITY

Bauer, D., Bonacker, M., and Cavonius, C. R. Influence of VDU screen brightness on the visibility of reflected images. *Displays* 2: 242–44 (April 1981).

Beldie, I. P., et al. Fixed versus variable letter width for televised text. *Human Factors* 25: 273–77 (1983).

Bury, K. F., et al. Windowing versus scrolling on a visual display terminal. *Human Factors* 24: 385–94 (1982).

Grandjean, E., et al. VDT workstation design: Preferred settings and their effect. *Human Factors* 25: 161–75 (1983).

Hunt, B. R. Information theory and visual displays. *Reports on Progress in Physics* 46: 515–53 (1983).

Isensee, S. H., and Bennett, C. A. Perception of flicker and glare on computer CRT displays. *Human Factors* 25: 177–84 (1983).

Murch, G. How visible is your display? *Electro-Optical System Design* 14: 43–49 (March 1982).

Netravali, A. N., and Pirsch, P. Character display on a CRT. *IEEE Transactions on Broadcasting* 29: 106–9 (1983).

Pastoor, S., et al. Relative suitability of four dot matrix sizes for text presentation on color television screens. *Human Factors* 25: 265–72 (1983).

Payne, S. A. J. Readability of liquid crystal displays: A response surface. *Human Factors* 25: 185–90 (1983).

Santisteban, A. Perceptual color space of digital image display terminals. *IBM Journal of Research and Development* 27: 127–32 (1983).

Tullis, T. S. Evaluation of alphanumeric, graphic, and color information display. *Human Factors* 23: 541–50 (1981).

Wilkes, A. J., and Wiseman, N. E. Soft-edged character set and its derivation. *Computer Journal* 25: 140–47 (1982).

FLAT PANEL TECHNOLOGY

Aldersey-Williams, H. Flat panel displays. *Data Processing* 25: 36–38 (May 1983).

Amano, Y., et al. New dc plasma display panels and their applications. *Displays* 3: 187–91 (October 1982).

Apperley, N., et al. Large screen plasma display design. *Electronic Imaging* 2: 56–64 (May 1983).

Biancomano, V. Flat panel displays grow larger, focus on full color performance. *Electronic Design* 30: 79–84 (November 11, 1982).

Boardman, C. M., and Deschamps, J. Plasma display panels have come of age. *Displays* 3: 135–46 (July 1982).

Chang, I. F. Electrochromic and electrochemichromic displays. *Displays* 2: 275–78 (July 1981).

Cola, R. Gas discharge panels with internal line sequencing (Self Scan displays). In B. Kazan, ed., *Advances in Image Pickup and Display*, pp. 83–170. New York: Academic Press, 1977.

Engibous, T., and Draper, G. Flat displays—An alternative to CRTs? *Computer Design* 22: 199–207 (September 1983).

Johnson, R. L. Plasma display construction and operation. *Electronic Imaging* 2: 47–53 (July 1983).

Meyer, F. Picture brightens for flat-panel displays. *High Technology* 2: 33–40 (March-April 1982).

Ohkoshi, A., et al. Compact flat cathode ray tube. *IEEE Transactions on Consumer Electronics* 28: 431–36 (August 1982).

Randin, J. P. Electrochromic displays prepare to hoist their colors. *Electronics* 54: 89–91 (December 29, 1981).

Ravich, L. LED displays—Their application and use. *Electronic Imaging* 1: 32–36 (November-December 1982).

Schaeur, A. Plasma lights up 14-inch panel display. *Electronics* 55: 128–30 (December 15, 1982).

Smith, J. Gas discharge displays for compact desk-top word processors. *IEEE Transactions on Electronic Developments* 29: 174–78 (1982).

Teschler, L. New technology for flat displays. *Machine Design* 53: 52–59 (July 17, 1981).

Wedding, D., and Ernsthausen, R. Large area flat panel displays. *Computer Graphics World* 6: 68–70 (April 1983).

Wedding, D., et al. Mammoth displays that measure in meters. *Computer Design* 22: 177–80+ (July 1983).

GRAPHICS DISPLAYS

Bonice, P. E. How to evaluate raster scan CRT monitors. *Computer Graphics World* 6: 29–40 (April 1983).

Cleveland, W. S., Harris, C. S., and McGill, R. Human factors and behavioral science: Experiments on quantitative judgements of graphs and maps. *Bell System Technical Journal* 62: 1659–74 (1983).

Davis, E. G., and Swezey, R. W. Human factors guidelines in computer graphics. *International Journal of Man-Machine Studies* 18: 113–33 (1983).

Doctor, L., and Coit, S. Using raster scan in color graphics. *Mini-Micro Systems* 14: 101–8 (December 1981).

House, W. C., ed. *Interactive Computer Graphics Systems*. New York: Petrocelli Books, 1982.

Kenealy, P. Product profile: Graphics workstations. *Mini-Micro Systems* 16: 165–83 (July 1983).

Okamoto, H. Selecting a high performance color display. *Mini-Micro Systems* 14: 95–98 (December 1981).

Reed, J. Direct view storage tube displays. *Electronics and Power* 28: 319–21 (April 1982).

Scott, J. E. *Introduction to Interactive Computer Graphics*. New York: Wiley, 1982.

HEALTH CONSIDERATIONS

Matula, A. Effects of visual display units on the eyes: A bibliography (1972–1980). *Human Factors* 23: 581–86 (1981).

Miller, R. B. Radiation, ergonomics, ion depletion, and VDTs. *Information Technology and Libraries* 2: 151–58 (1983).

Mourant, R. R., et al. Visual fatigue and cathode ray display terminals. *Human Factors* 23: 529–40 (1981).

Raferty, C., and Keener, J. Providing terminal comfort. *Mini-Micro Systems* 14: 119–26 (August, 1981).

Sauter, S. L., et al. Job and health implications of VDT use: Initial results of the Wisconsin NIOSH study. *Communications of the Association for Computing Machinery* 26: 284–94 (1983).

Stewart, T. Terminal design: A European perspective. *Data Communications* 12: 195–96 (May 1983).

Warren, C. Adapting to human needs, terminals become easy to use and easy on the user. *Electronic Design* 30: 97–100 (December 23, 1982).

LIBRARY APPLICATIONS

Byerly, G., and Lindell, S. Terminals in libraries: Help or hazard? *Library Journal* 107: 2146–49 (1982).

Grosch, A. N. The selection of cathode ray tube (CRT) terminals for library applications. *Library Technology Reports* 18: 273–371 (1982).

ABBREVIATIONS AND ACRONYMS

ABC	American Broadcasting Corporation
AC	alternating current
ACSN	Appalachian Community Service Network
AFT	automatic fine tuning
AHD	audio high density
ANSI	American National Standards Institute
ANTIOPE	Acquisition Numérique et Télévisualisation d'Images Organisées Pages d'Ecriture
AP	Associated Press
ARTS	Alpha Repertory Television Service
ASCII	American Standard Code for Information Interchange
ASR	automatic send-receive
AT&T	American Telephone and Telegraph
BET	Black Entertainment Television
BNR	Beta Noise Reduction
BPO	British Post Office
BRS	Bibliographic Retrieval Services
CAD/CAM	computer-aided design/computer-aided manufacturing
CAPTAIN	Character and Pattern Telephone Access Information Network
CAR	computer-assisted retrieval
CATV	community antenna television
CAV	constant angular velocity
CBS	Columbia Broadcasting System
CCD	charged-coupled device
CCETT	Centre Commun d'Etudes de Télévision et Télécommunication
CCIR	Comité Consultatif International des Radiocommunications
CCIS	Coaxial Cable Information Service
CCITT	Comité Consultatif International Téléphonique et Télégraphique
CED	capacitance electronic disk
CEPT	Conference Européenne des Postes et Télécommunications
CHN	Cable Health Network

CIBS	Character Information Broadcasting Station
CLV	constant linear velocity
CNN	Cable News Network
CTRL	Control
COM	computer-output microfilm
CRT	cathode ray tube
CSA	Canadian Standards Association
C-SPAN	Cable Satellite Public Affairs Network
CTNA	Catholic Telecommunications Network of America
CUG	closed user groups
CVC	compact video cassette
DAVINS	Data and Video Information Network System
DBS	direct broadcast satellite
DC	direct current
DNR	dynamic noise reduction
DRAW	direct read after write
DRCS	dynamically redefinable character sets
DVA	DiscoVision Associates
DVST	direct view storage tube
ECMA	European Computer Manufacturers Association
EBCDIC	Extended Binary Coded Decimal Interchange Code
EIA	Electronics Industries Association
EL	electroluminescent
ELP	extended long play
ESC	escape
ESPN	Entertainment and Sports Programming Network
EUS	European Unified Standard
HBO	Home Box Office
HDTV	high definition television
HTN	Home Television Network
HTN	Home Theater Network
IBA	Independent Broadcasting Authority
IP	information provider
ISO	International Standardization Organization
ITT	International Telephone and Telegraph
ITV	Independent Television
JVC	Japanese Victor Company
KSR	keyboard send-receive
LCD	liquid crystal display
LED	light-emitting diode
LNA	low noise amplifier
LNC	low noise converter
LP	long play
LPTV	low-power television
LV	LaserVision
MCA	Microband Corporation of America
MDS	Multipoint Distribution Service

MDTV	multipoint distribution television
MSN	Modern Satellite Network
MSO	multiple system operator
MTV	Music Television
NABTS	North American Broadcast Teletext Specification
NAPLPS	North American Presentation Level Protocol System
NBC	National Broadcasting Company
NHK	Nippon Hoso Kyokai
NIOSH	National Institute for Occupational Safety and Health
NTSC	National Television Systems Committee
OCLC	Online Computer Library Center
OCR	optical character recognition
OVD	optical video disk
PAL	phase alternation line
PBS	Public Broadcasting System
PDI	picture description instruction
PELS	picture elements that compose frames of a video image; also known as "pixels"
PMS	Picturephone Meeting Service
PPV	pay-per-view
RBG	red-blue-green monitors
PSSC	Public Service Satellite Consortium
RAM	random-access memory
READ	relative element address designate
RCA	Radio Corporation of America
RF	radio frequency
RO	receive-only
ROM	read-only memory
SECAM	Sequential Couleur à Memoire
SIN	Spanish International Network
SLP	super long play
SMATV	satellite master antenna television
SNC	Satellite News Channel
SP	standard play
SPACE	Society for Private and Commercial Earth Stations
SSTV	slow-scan television
STC	Storage Technology Corporation
STC	Satellite Television Corporation
STV	subscription television
TTL	through-the-lens viewfinder
TVRO	television receive-only
UCM	ultra compact machine
UHF	ultra high frequency
VBI	vertical blanking interval
VCR	videocassette recorder
VDT	video display terminal
VDU	video display unit

VHD	video high-density disk
VHF	very high frequency
VIR	vertical interval reference
VRS	video response system
WICAT	World Institute for Computer-Assisted Teaching

INDEX

Prepared by Carol R. Kelm

William Saffady is on the faculty of the Department of Library and Information Science at Vanderbilt University. Among his previous publications are *The Automated Office* (1981) and *Introduction to Automation for Librarians* (ALA, 1983).